Unprecedented?

T0279689

Unprecedented?

How Covid-19 Revealed the Politics of Our Economy

by William Davies, Sahil Jai Dutta, Nick Taylor and Martina Tazzioli

Goldsmiths
Press

Copyright © 2022 Goldsmiths Press
First published in 2022 by Goldsmiths Press
Goldsmiths, University of London, New Cross
London SE14 6NW

Printed and bound by Versa Press, USA
Distribution by the MIT Press
Cambridge, Massachusetts, USA and London, England

Copyright © 2022 William Davies, Martina Tazzioli, Nick Taylor
and Sahil Jai Dutta

A CIP record for this book is available from the British Library

ISBN 978-1-913380-12-0 (pbk)
ISBN 978-1-913380-11-3 (ebk)

www.gold.ac.uk/goldsmiths-press

Goldsmiths
UNIVERSITY OF LONDON

Contents

Notes on Contributors

William Davies is a Professor in Political Economy at Goldsmiths, where he is Director of the Political Economy Research Centre. He is author of *This is Not Normal: The Collapse of Liberal Britain* (Verso, 2020), *Nervous States: How feeling took over the world* (Jonathan Cape, 2018), *The Happiness Industry: How the government and big business sold us wellbeing* (Verso, 2015) and *The Limits of Neoliberalism: Authority, Sovereignty and the Logic of Competition* (Sage, 2014). He writes regularly for *The Guardian* and *London Review of Books*.

Sahil Jai Dutta is Lecturer in Political Economy at Goldsmiths and a member of the Political Economy Research Centre. His research focuses on British political economy, financialisation, sovereign debt and public sector reform. He has published in *Review of International Political Economy*, the IPPR's *Progressive Review*, *Tribune* and *OpenDemocracy*.

Nick Taylor is Lecturer in Political Economy and Deputy Director of the Political Economy Research Centre at Goldsmiths. He researches and publishes on unemployment and welfare as well as on the political economy of green finance. His work has appeared in *Area*, *Journal of Cultural Economy* and *Capital & Class*.

Martina Tazzioli is Lecturer in Politics & Technology at Goldsmiths. She is the author of *The Making of Migration: The biopolitics of mobility at Europe's borders* (Sage, 2020), *Spaces of Governmentality* (Rowman & Littlefield, 2015) and *Tunisia* *as a Revolutionised Space of Migration* (Palgrave, 2016). She is co-editor of *Foucault and the History of our Present* (Palgrave, 2015) and *Foucault and the Making of Subjects* (Rowman & Littlefield, 2016). She sits on the editorial board of *Radical Philosophy* and is an associate editor of *Politics*.

Preface

One of the abiding concerns of political economy, which distinguishes it from mainstream economics, is uncertainty. Ever since the Industrial Revolution, both the critics and advocates of capitalism have recognised it as an unusually dynamic system, which generates periodic upheavals, and is in turn transformed by the cultural, political, ecological and technological disruptions that it has contributed to unleashing. While these disruptions may be foreseeable and predictable in their broad outlines (though the visionaries are not always listened to), they exceed efforts to subject them to precise statistical analysis. Uncertainty, as the critics of neo-classical economics never tire of pointing out, is never entirely reducible to risk. The excitement and the danger of capitalism consists in the guarantee that, sooner or later, the unexpected will arrive.

Part of this dynamism derives from the forward-facing character of the capitalist system itself, the fact that it involves making investments whose return is not guaranteed, and entering contracts with parties (including workers) whose intentions and capabilities cannot be fully ascertained in advance. Under capitalism, investors and entrepreneurs who correctly anticipate the future, or else help shape it, are rewarded handsomely for their foresight, while those who get it wrong can be punished through losses and even bankruptcy. Yet even a system that celebrates constant 'change' and 'innovation' is reliant on secure and predictable institutions. Markets require rules, laws, norms of conduct and trust. Workers must be adequately skilled and turn up in workplaces in a predictable fashion. International agreements allow people, goods and services to cross borders in a peaceful and reliable fashion. Money and other financial instruments must be endorsed by social norms and the state, if their value isn't to be entirely obliterated by uncertainty. Uncertainty might be welcome, but not if it threatens to blow up the very foundations on which the system of investment, credit, employment and trade depends.

During periods of economic stability, it is possible to become preoccupied by the activities going on in markets themselves, like a sporting spectacle: the financial bets being made, the new products being marketed, who's up and who's down. Politics appears absent from the economy during these phases of relative calm. Only during the periods of the deepest uncertainty do the true underpinnings of the system become visible. These moments may be generated from within the economy itself, as occurred with the banking crisis of 2008, which revealed the extent to which states serve as the underwriters of the financial system. Or they may be triggered by forces that are not ordinarily considered part of 'the economy' at all – such as a novel coronavirus. In either case there is something valuable to be observed and learnt in moments of crisis: what persists, what sustains us, when the normal and predictable routines of economic life are suspended? Whose interests come first, and whose come last? Who is protected at all costs and who is left to their fate? The political nature of the economy becomes undeniable when the conventional motions of market societies grind to a halt. This book treats the Covid-19 pandemic as an opportunity to investigate the structures and political assumptions on which our economy rests, which are too often concealed and could become so again, if we allow them to be forgotten.

The economic collapse of 2020 differed from previous crises of capitalism in being, at least at the outset, deliberate: the public health emergency led to the closure (or partial closure) of workplaces, national borders, venues, schools and campuses. The hope was that this would be temporary, and therefore less a crisis than a hiatus. But this itself raises political questions about how interruptions in economic time are to be bridged, whether through state bailouts, debt, furlough, or the sustenance offered by public services, family and mutual aid. The role of social and legal conventions (balance sheets, contracts, risk models and so on) in establishing security *for some* in the face of uncertainty is a major concern of political economists and economic sociologists, but it is cast in a more acutely political light once a society faces a clear set of choices as to who is offered safe passage over a hiatus, and who is left to cope with the contingencies of the present.[1] Emergencies render people more dependent on basic infrastructure or what the political theorist Bonnie Honig terms "public things", such as telecom networks and parks, which potentially offer a "democratic holding environment" capable of withstanding upheaval.[2] They also offers opportunities for the rules of the economy to be reset, often at a speed that defies moral accountability.[3] This hiatus therefore offers potential insights to the implicit hierarchies of value that are attached to different people and institutions, but which are otherwise concealed or repressed.

[1] See Jens Beckert, *Imagined Futures* (Cambridge, MA: Harvard University Press, 2016); Katharina Pistor, *The Code of Capital: How the Law Creates Wealth and Inequality* (Oxford: Princeton University Press, 2019).
[2] Bonnie Honig, *Public Things: Democracy in Disrepair* (New York: Fordham University Press, 2017).
[3] See Naomi Klein, *The Shock Doctrine: The Rise of Disaster Capitalism* (London: Penguin, 2014).

Soon after Covid-19 first struck, its unequal socio-economic consequences were palpable. Mainstream media commentators recognised that this emergency shone a light on existing social divides. "They tell us coronavirus is a great leveller – it's not", ran the opening sequence of an acclaimed BBC *Newsnight* episode in April 2020. Visual metaphors were common, with one headline reporting that "Coronavirus is like an x-ray of society". In asking what Covid-19 reveals about the politics of our economy, this book shares that sense of the pandemic performing an optical function, which helps us see more clearly. Yet Covid-19 hasn't only illuminated underlying conflicts and tendencies; it has simultaneously accelerated and expanded them. In many areas that we will explore, it both illuminates *and* it feeds, as sunlight does to plants. For that reason, we might speak of the pandemic as having a 'photosynthetic' function, simultaneously shining a light on key features of capitalism while also contributing to their growth.

When major crises strike, it is understandably tempting to try and explain them with reference to an established theory or metanarrative. That, after all, is what academic disciplines offer in various ways. While we draw copiously on various critical and theoretical sources in this book, it began from an instinct that historical events such as those unfolding over 2020–21 should not be hastily theorised or crammed into existing conceptual schemes; first and foremost, they needed to be described and mapped, with disciplines serving that goal. Paying respect to the novelty of the upheavals, and to the suffering they've incurred, involves starting from a place of some humility and attempting to get a handle on what has gone on, as far as is reliably known. At the same time, novel events are shaped by the socio-political circumstances that precede them, and it is crucial to locate them in their contexts, and not treat them as entirely *sui generis*.

To do this, we identified four different institutional and policy domains, where the effects of the pandemic have been transformative, and where often dramatic interventions were necessary in order to sustain the economy and society at all. These were: public and private finance (the topic of Chapter 2), work and the labour market (Chapter 3), bordering and surveillance infrastructure (Chapter 4) and education (Chapter 5). We selected these specifically because they are areas where the scale of upheavals and rescue packages was greatest, in the hope that we might therefore be able to note certain patterns in how events transpired, often across quite disparate areas. Where possible we have drawn on our individual expertise and prior research in order to inform these chapters, but they are also attentive to the exceptional qualities of what occurred, drawing on the most recent evidence produced by government agencies, academics, NGOs, statistics offices, trade unions and independent research institutes.

Co-authoring a book as a small team is a messy, difficult and rewarding process, for which there are inspirations but no rulebooks. Its advantage lies in the pooling of resources, allowing for a type of conjunctural analysis to be produced while a crisis is still underway. The example of *Policing the Crisis* (1978) written by five scholars at the Birmingham Centre for Contemporary Cultural Studies is perhaps the iconic case of a book that mobilises a team to respond to a contemporary crisis. We were especially inspired by the work of the CRESC team based at Manchester University, whose multi-authored reports and books on the financial crisis and the failures of British capitalism are a model of how a research team can combine resources and disciplines to critically illuminate the status quo, for a potentially wide readership. Our own approach has been to prioritise the collection and sharing of available evidence, and to then discuss, process and analyse it as a team, in the hope that overlapping narratives and explanatory frameworks would emerge over the course of our meetings. Intellectual dialogue and collegiality have methodological value, though 21st-century academia steadily reduces the spare time and space in which they occur. The synthetic and conceptual results of these conversations have shaped the analysis in Chapter 1, and the concluding arguments in Chapter 6.

Empirically speaking, the book focuses on a particular window of time and a particular national context. The window is the 18 months that began with the spread of Covid-19 around the world in early 2020, and which ended with economies in the Global North cautiously 'reopening' in the summer of 2021 with the aid of vaccines. In the UK, this period was book-ended by the beginning and end of the furlough scheme. Clearly the health crisis is far from over, the virus shows no signs of disappearing, and there will be ongoing debates over how political and economic life should adapt to this new world. The situation remains mired in uncertainty: new coronavirus variants, political events and economic crises may yet overshadow many of the events we analyse here. The signs are that vaccination alone will be insufficient to fight the virus, at least in the near-term, and countries such as the UK which rely almost entirely on vaccinations to do so have encountered sharply rising infection and hospitalization rates all over again. Yet this 18-month window undoubtedly contains moments of especially acute uncertainty and vulnerability, when some of the bones of our political economy were laid bare. Periods of economic crisis (such as the mid-1970s or the post-2008 era) have always received particular attention from historians and political economists, and the fall-out from the pandemic is no different. It does, however, cast a different light on the capitalist system from many previous crises – less on its contradictions, vulnerability and unsustainability, and more on the extraordinary social and political sacrifices and interventions that are made in order to sustain it, against all odds.

While the main focus of the book is on the political and economic fall-out from the virus, it is impossible to understand or explain this without also attending to the pre-Covid-19 world. Indeed, much of what transpired over 2020–21 was an embedding and exacerbation of tendencies that were already apparent. For this reason, in addition to providing an account of the lockdowns, confinements and emergency policies, each chapter begins by identifying salient features of the *pre*-2020 landscape, that (we argue) were decisive in shaping what transpired.

The national context is that of the United Kingdom, not because it is exceptional or because it is especially typical, but because it provides us with a case study, one with which the authors are already familiar. Many of the decision-making powers related to the pandemic are devolved to the four nations of the UK, and we specify these where relevant. This context allows us to scrutinise a number of tendencies in contemporary capitalism – the power of outsourcing rentiers, the acute strains placed on households and social reproduction, our dependence on digital platforms – that should be pertinent to a range of other national contexts. The UK does, however, stand out in the severity of its economic and health outcomes; by the summer of 2020, it had suffered one of the highest mortality rates *and* one of the deepest recessions in the OECD. A political model, which had for decades expected markets and marketisation to mediate as many social relations as possible, was badly exposed on both an economic *and* a social front, once normal transactional activity was suspended.

The crisis is obviously a global one: "the first global event in the history of humankind" according to one prominent economist.[4] And yet, crucially, the institutions and policy levers that have responded to it are largely embedded in nation states. The most radical measures – the lockdowns and the border closures – were at the discretion of the most senior *national* decision-makers. The priority accorded to the nation and to national policy-making is in many ways one of the tragedies of this pandemic, and is reflected in strongly divergent social and economic results. It has also become manifest in escalating tensions surrounding border control, migration and asylum. We explore this heightened nationalism and the border infrastructures in subsequent chapters.

There will be many, many books written about Covid-19, to add to the many that have already appeared. There are plenty of empirical, political and theoretical questions that deserve to be addressed, but which are outside of the scope of our enquiry. To name but a few, this book is *not* about the woeful performance of the Johnson administration in protecting lives or reducing infections; it is not an audit or critique of particular health strategies, medical interventions or the governance of the health service. It does not speculate on what the correct policy choices were at given junctures, or on the proximate causes of key policy decisions. As in every society, the distribution of infections and deaths serves as a troubling reflection of the racial, class and geographic inequalities at large in the UK today. While we draw on the leading work of people such as Michael Marmot on this question, and view it as a profoundly sociological one, we do not pretend to be epidemiologists, social or otherwise. Nor can we adequately interrogate the politics surrounding vaccine supply, 'big pharma'

------

[4] Branko Milanovic, "The First Global Event in the History of Humankind", *Social Europe*, 7 December 2020.

and intellectual property rights, all of which have potentially vast consequences for the Global South. All of these are questions of the greatest importance, which other better qualified authors and research teams are surely addressing.

This, then, is a study of political economy, rather than of public health policy, epidemiology or global governance. The pandemic is an opportunity to remove the veil of 'the market', and to witness how power and inequality shape economic processes. In each of our four empirical domains, policy-making in the UK has deployed certain rhetorical devices and ideas, to conceal underlying politics. Our economy has been shaped by the power of 'leverage', a euphemism that conceals the fact that some economic actors get to defer their payments indefinitely into the future, while others soon find the bailiff at their door. The labour market has been governed around an ideal of 'flexibility', which concealed political questions of *flexibility for whom*. Our border and surveillance infrastructures are governed with appeal to 'protection' of the public from foreign threats and harms, a term that misrepresents how borders are actually woven through everyday life. And the mantra of education is of 'learning', which hides the explosion of audit, testing and behavioural control that now overshadows schools and, with a more financial logic, universities. In a variety of ways, the opportunity provided by Covid-19 is to pull back these rhetorical and ideological veils, and see what lies beneath.

October 2021

1

The Great Interruption

On 17 March 2020, as the economic implications of the Covid-19 pandemic were becoming clear, the Chancellor of the Exchequer, Rishi Sunak, announced an "unprecedented package" of support for businesses, amounting to £330 billion of guarantees. Three days later, he announced a further set of economic interventions "unprecedented in the history of the British state",[1] the most significant one being the 'Job Retention Scheme' (colloquially known as 'furlough') in which the government offered to cover the cost of 80% of employees' wages. Within three months, the UK economy had shrunk by over 20%.[2] The government, Sunak argued in August, was "grappling with something that is unprecedented".[3]

In an obvious sense, Sunak was correct. While there had been pandemics before and there had been economic crises before, never had economies such as the UK's been deliberately closed down to the extent that they were in the first half

---

[1] "The Chancellor Rishi Sunak Provides an Updated Statement on Coronavirus", Gov.UK, 20 March 2020.

[2] Office for National Statistics (ONS), "GDP Monthly Estimate, UK: June 2020", 12 August 2020.

[3] Szu Ping Chan and Robert Plummer. "UK Officially in Recession for First Time in 11 Years", *BBC News*, 12 August 2020.

of 2020, and in many cases continuing into 2021. Almost a quarter of all UK businesses – and more than 80% of the arts, entertainment and recreation sector – were shut down in the first lockdown.[4] Across the world, eight out of every ten workers were at one point under some kind of lockdown restriction[5] and the effect was to push the global economy into its deepest recession since 1945.[6]

The crisis was unusual for economies such as the UK's in that it hit the service sector the hardest.[7] Normally, an economic shock would shake business and consumer confidence, slowing investment and purchases of material goods like cars and dishwashers. But historically, consumer services have proved more recession-proof. Things like haircuts and childcare typically work as a counter-balance to an economic downturn. Yet it was precisely these *reliable* sectors that were hit. The fear was that as these sectors lost out, and workers lost income, the contagion would then spread across the economy as a whole. And in contrast to a 'goods' recession, what was forgone could not be easily deferred for later purchase. Unemployment would have hit equally exceptional

---

[4] ONS, "Coronavirus and the Economic Impacts on the UK – 23 April 2020", 23 April 2020.

[5] International Labour Organization, "ILO Monitor: COVID-19 and the World of Work. 2nd Edition", 7 April 2020.

[6] World Bank, *Global Economic Prospects, January 2021* (Washington, DC: The World Bank, 2021).

[7] Gabriel Mathy, "The First Services Recession", *Phenomenal World*, 25 March 2020; ONS, "The Impact of the Coronavirus So Far: The Industries That Struggled or Recovered", 9 September 2020.

heights, dwarfing the levels of the Great Depression, had governments not intervened in exceptional ways, such as those announced by Sunak on 20 March. Many governments also moved swiftly with emergency measures to close borders and commission new infrastructure, such as test-and-trace facilities and vaccination centres. Schools and campuses were closed to the majority of learners, with teaching shifting online where possible, with all of the limitations and inequalities that go with that. Never before had a public health emergency forced policymakers to intervene so forcefully to suspend economic activity, nor to act so decisively to mitigate the consequences.

And yet in a host of other less eye-catching ways, the events of 2020–21 were not at all unprecedented. Economic inequality, which had been on an upward trend since the late 1970s, shaped the divergent experiences of the pandemic, in terms of which sections of society bore the greatest risks to their health, mental health and economic security. The geography of the disease (which determined where economic sectors such as hospitality were worst hit and where children lost the most school days) mirrored the geography of economic deprivation. The impact of structural racism in the labour market, healthcare and housing meant that racialised minorities were disproportionately exposed to infections and mortality risk. An economic model that had long relied on markets, credit and marketisation to hold society together was especially exposed once the circulation of labour, money, goods and services ground to a halt. Many of those who had benefitted from that model, especially those who owned assets such as housing, continued to prosper, with house prices booming and total household wealth increasing by around £900 billion or 5% of pre-pandemic levels – the first recession in over 70 years in which net household wealth had risen.[8]

The policies that Sunak unveiled in March 2020 were unprecedented, but away from these headline announcements, there was something familiar about the shape of governmental interventions, and the identity of the contractors, resources and instruments that were relied upon to keep the economy and society afloat. Already powerful institutions were granted more power, under conditions of the health emergency; already dominant firms were able to exploit their positions for higher profits, where they were able to serve basic social needs. Already ascendent business models and routines – notably those of platforms – took off, while their traditional rivals languished. The reassertion of national borders was dramatic in its severity and speed, but it occurred in a context of already-rising nationalism and protectionism. The pandemic was photosynthetic: feeding tendencies that already existed, while also illuminating them, with important political implications.

It is this collision between the unprecedented and the precedented that concerns us in this book. Many political economists have understood capitalism as an 'evolutionary' system, whose constantly generated innovations and shocks are always conditioned by what came before them. This is perhaps most famously expressed in Karl Marx's claim that "Men make their own history, but they do not make it as they please; they do not make it under self-selected circumstances, but under circumstances existing already, given and transmitted

---

[8] Jack Leslie and Krishan Shah, *(Wealth) Gap Year: The Impact of the Coronavirus Crisis on UK Household Wealth* (London: Resolution Foundation, 2021).

from the past". Viruses make their own history, but they do not make it as they please either. The experience of the Covid-19 pandemic suggests a further feature of evolutionary political-economic change: that it is precisely where a disruption is gravest and most shocking that the social and political resort to the already-known will be strongest. An event such as a pandemic is revelatory, but much of what it reveals are deep-lying structures and hierarchies, which are denied or obscured during periods of stability.

In this chapter, we discuss some of the central social and political preconditions of the pandemic economy, which ultimately shaped and fuelled the policies and trends that we detail over subsequent chapters. These are all institutions and dynamics that have long been the concern of critical political economy, but which are strategically excluded from orthodox economics and from dominant representations of the 'market economy'. Firstly, we examine what we term the deep 'wells' of debt that are drawn upon to mitigate crises, namely the balance sheet of the sovereign state and the largely unmonetised obligations of care. The UK's model of capitalism *already* relied on these hidden reserves of value (the first misrepresented as a finite quantity, the second misrepresented as an infinite quantity) but the pandemic rendered this dependency acute and impossible to ignore.

In the second half of the chapter, we turn from temporal questions (of how debts bind past, present and future) to spatial ones, of how particular forms of capital, technology and property rights are reconfiguring the rhythms and distribution of everyday economic activity. We argue that Covid-19 has accelerated an existing 'crisis of space', while also rendering it more visible. Any epidemic or pandemic raises novel questions about spatial politics, contextualised by existing forms of political and economic geography. Our account of this 'crisis of space' focuses on three interrelated factors: housing, digital platforms and border technologies. Ultimately, we suggest, it is the politics of debt and of space that will shape what kind of economy emerges over the years following the interruption of 2020–21. The spatial innovations of the pandemic themselves have a temporal dimension, projecting initially 'temporary' measures and solutions into the long-term future. This is the nature of infrastructure, whose material durability often outlives its initial justification and need, and which – in the hands of corporations such as those that operate platforms – allows capital to colonise the future.[9]

Wells of Value: Sovereign Debts, Care Debts

Viewed as a space of exchange, a market economy appears governed by scarcity: the fixed quantity of goods, services, money and time that can be traded. This is the dominant view of liberal economics, which has made a great virtue of efficiency, prudence and value for money. Viewed as a space of debts and obligations, however, and things appear very different. Promises are not a strictly limited resource. If I am viewed as sufficiently trustworthy and capable, there is no clear limit to how many promises I can make. And there is no cap on how many promises I can receive, so long as I am happy to keep accepting them, or else have little choice but to do so. The commitments we make to one another are an elastic resource, because they extend into the future. Debts make time into an economic resource.

---

[9] See Timothy Mitchell, "No Business of Yours: How the Large Corporation Swallowed the Future", Lecture given at Kings College London, 17 January 2019.

Were an economy simply an aggregation of finite resources, the arrival of Covid-19 in early 2020 would have sunk economies such as the UK's, which ordinarily involve a perpetual circulation of payments, goods and services. A society that relies on market mechanisms for its coordination is also especially sensitive to interruptions, seeing as everyone is relying on everyone else to keep making the payments that are due, to enable them to make their own payments. The closure of whole sections of the UK economy could have led the entire system, including its financial and social underpinnings, to collapse. The fact that this did *not* happen is an astonishing thing, which should jolt us out of the naive presumption that markets are, or ever have been, as foundational to capitalist economies as so often assumed. The reality is that our economy was sustained, as it had been in the past, by drawing on resources that are peripheral or external to the terrain of orthodox economics, but on which the entire system routinely depends. We refer to these resources as 'wells', to highlight the fact that they are largely invisible (hidden 'underground') and are – or are assumed to be – inexhaustible.

Here, we draw particular attention to two such 'wells', both of which reside in the making and taking of promises. These have co-existed with market economies since early modern times, but frequently get excluded from dominant economic narratives – indeed that exclusion is arguably fundamental to how 'the economy' is imagined and studied.[10] And yet it was only thanks to the availability of these two resources that, when Covid-19 struck, money continued to circulate, people continued to eat, emergency infrastructure

---

[10] Timothy Mitchell, "Fixing the Economy", *Cultural Studies*, 12:1 (1998): 82–101.

was paid for and children continued to be educated. In the face of a potentially overwhelming natural threat, our capitalist system quietly drew from a combination of *immeasurable* and *unmeasured* sources of value to survive. As we shall see, the precise depth and exhaustibility of these wells is a moot point and a site of political contestation. Our initial point is simply that, when the limits of market exchange and calculation are breached, the politics of debt and mutuality becomes exposed.

Sovereignty

The first is the modern sovereign state. As Max Weber famously defined it, the modern state is distinguished by the fact that it holds a "monopoly over the legitimate use of violence". The power and the authority of the state consists in its capacity to overwhelm any challenges to its sovereignty, within designated borders. This is, in principle, a limitless power, which exceeds efforts to economise or calculate it, and which is ultimately realised in the use of violence. Unlike the idea of 'governmental' power, sovereign power is not something that can be measured or subjected to cost-benefit analysis, but is indefinite in its potential. And yet, in the liberal tradition, it is also this limitless power that enables the state to make promises to its own citizens to keep them safe and to enforce the law.

In what sense does state sovereignty serve as an economic resource? Historically speaking, the answer lies with the origins of modern states, when monarchs began to issue gilts to merchants and financiers, in exchange for the money they could use to fight wars. The emergence of an official 'national debt' in 17th-century England, followed by the establishment of the world's first central bank in 1694 (the Bank of England), formalised a symbiotic relationship between state sovereignty and finance houses, mediated by calculable paper promises between the two.[11] Government bonds became a type of dependable asset that were trusted to hold their value in circulation, given the physical might of the issuer. The growth of further fiscal instruments, namely taxation and public spending administered by Treasury departments, was built upon an already-existing compact between states and financial markets, in which military power reinforced the credibility of paper money. The idea of separate spheres of 'politics' and 'economics', which was so crucial to the development of liberalism from the 18th century onwards, was – and remains – enabled by an already-existing monetised national debt.

The only limit that sovereign states face, when it comes to their debts, is the capacity of the economy to put them to good use. Unlike a household, the UK government is the issuer of the currency it spends. It's not necessary, therefore, for it to raise taxes or make cuts in order to finance public spending.[12] National debts are represented in the lingua franca of money, which produces the misunderstanding that they are a fixed constraint of some kind, or run the risk of bankruptcy (like other financial debts). But the reality is that sovereign debts can grow indefinitely, so long as there is the political will to keep issuing paper denominated in a national currency and a national economy able to absorb it. As Keynes put it, "anything

---

[11] Joseph Vogl, *The Ascendency of Finance* (London: John Wiley & Office for National Statistics, 2017).

[12] For an accessible exploration of the limits of public deficits see Stephanie Kelton, *The Deficit Myth* (London: John Murray, 2020).

we can actually do, we can afford".[13] This is true of efforts to build a more prosperous society in the long run, but as the pandemic revealed, becomes an imperative in moments of crisis.

The national debt is therefore something of a paradox: a quantified expression of the state's unquantifiable power and commitments. As such, it can *in principle* rise without limit, as has occurred in times of war, and as occurred over the course of the coronavirus pandemic. As Covid-19 first appeared in the UK at the end of January 2020, the national debt was approximately £1.8 trillion, just under 80% of GDP; within six months, it had exceeded £2 trillion and 100% of GDP. This was the first time that the national debt had exceeded GDP since 1961.[14] This rise in government debt in no way dampened the willingness to finance it: bond yields remained at a historic low, below the rate of inflation, even as borrowing soared. Investors were *paying* states such as the UK to borrow their money.[15]

However, as we detail further in Chapter 2, this was no ordinary set of sovereign promises, because the principal buyer of all the additional bonds was the Bank of England, raising profound questions as to where precisely financial 'sovereignty' actually lies. The policy of 'quantitative easing', which was relied upon by the Federal Reserve, Bank of England and

---

[13] Adam Tooze makes this point with this quote in Adam Tooze, *Shutdown: How Covid Shook the World's Economy* (London: Allen Lane, 2021), 13.

[14] ONS, "Public Sector Finances, UK: August 2020", 25 September 2020.

[15] Adam Samson and Philip Stafford, "UK Sells Negative-yielding Government Bonds for First Time", *Financial Times*, 20 May 2020.

European Central Bank from 2009 onwards to avert deflation, was quickly adopted once more in order to keep money flowing, to counteract the forced closure of the 'real' economy in 2020. This policy sees central banks release new money into circulation by purchasing assets, such as government bonds, from private financial investors like pension and insurance funds. To do this, the Bank of England creates new money and buys financial assets from the seller. These assets get added to the Bank's own balance sheet, and the seller gets the cash. The result is that the total balance of the central bank's assets and liabilities grows. From a situation where the Bank's balance sheet was worth around 6% of GDP in 2007, it was approaching 50% of GDP by the summer of 2021. The survival of the UK economy over 2020-21 was effectively dependent on a relatively recent symbiosis between two sovereign agencies, in which vast sums of money were added as liabilities to the balance sheet of the Treasury, and as assets to the balance sheet of the Bank of England – money that was brought into being through the force of those two respective balance sheets, neither of which faces any material constraint. Unprecedented interruptions in the flow of goods, services, labour and payments were effectively bridged by the sheer might of sovereign decision. The ultimate promises, on which entire economies (both national and global) depended when Covid-19 struck, were those made between Treasuries and central banks.

An important side-effect of quantitative easing is that, by artificially inflating demand for assets, it drives up their prices (or, in the case of government paper, drives down the rate of interest). As interest rates fall, investors seek returns elsewhere, in equities. This leads to booming stock markets and housing markets, even while the rest of the economy may be stagnating. Those who own assets, either directly such as homeowners or indirectly via their pension funds, benefit from the policy far more than those who don't.[16] An economy of cheap credit and rising asset prices offers copious opportunities to asset owners to use those assets as collateral to take on additional debt, then acquire more assets, leading to further advantages to the already asset-rich. But, since 2009, underlying this spiralling wealth inequality has been the bottomless well of the state balance sheet (or rather central banks') to produce money as if out of thin air, and inject it into the value of financial assets.

Yet it's not only via its balance sheet that the immeasurable force of state sovereignty serves as a potential economic resource. Liberal states make promises to their citizens as well as their creditors. The first of these, as Thomas Hobbes argued, is to keep people safe from one another, that is, to offer security and rule of law. But over the past 150 years, they have been drawn into making ever more promises: of social security, education, unemployment benefit, healthcare, housing, pensions and protection from social harms. While many states have sought to retreat from these commitments since the 1970s, it remains the case that there are various obligations that they cannot easily abandon, and yet lack the political incentive or managerial capacity to deliver themselves. This has enabled the rise of a commercial 'public service industry', which hovers around a 'franchise state', whereby a small cluster of firms bids to deliver a wide range of public services, from waste management to migrant detention, and from government IT to healthcare.[17] The UK has been at the forefront of this industry

---

[16] Bank of England, "The Distributional Effects of Asset Purchases", 12 April 2012.

[17] Andrew Bowman et al., *What a Waste: Outsourcing and How It Goes Wrong* (Manchester: Manchester University Press, 2015).

since the 1980s. Prior to the pandemic, the UK government was spending £292 billion a year on procurement, more than a third of all public spending and most of the global public services corporations are headquartered in the UK.[18]

The companies that make up this industry, such as Serco, G4S, Capita, Amey, Kier and Interserve, do not specialise in delivering any particular branch of public service; they specialise in winning contracts to deliver public services. In that sense, they are what the political economist Brett Christophers terms 'contract capitalists' and, more specifically, 'contract rentiers', inasmuch as their business model depends on trapping the state into contractual obligations, which the contractor can then use to shield itself from competition or the consequences of failure.[19] Contracts are effectively assets, to be won, controlled and drawn on as sources of revenue. As contracts have grown longer, so have the guaranteed streams of income from state to contractor. Profits are effectively guaranteed, regardless of whether any risk or capital investment is involved – a kind of 'sham capitalism' that depends wholly on the state cooperating with this private financial agenda.[20] The state becomes trapped between its political obligations to its citizens and its financial obligations to outsourcing contractors, while the employees in outsourced sectors (which are typically labour-intensive) tend to be squeezed in search of higher profits. Meanwhile, the UK government has grown

---

[18] Tom Sasse et al., *Government Outsourcing: When and How to Bring Public Services Back into Government Hands* (London: Institute for Government, June 2020).

[19] Brett Christophers, *Rentier Capitalism: Who Owns the Economy, and Who Pays for It?* (London: Verso, 2020).

[20] Bowman et al., *What a Waste*.

increasingly reliant on large consultancy and business service providers for the design and implementation of public services. The 'Big Four' consultants, KPMG, PwC, Deloitte and Ernst & Young, and global IT firms, such as Microsoft, IBM, Atos, Palantir and AWS, occupy pivotal positions, not just as contractors but as decision-makers and strategists.

The dependence of 'contract rentiers' on the state also runs the other way. The most basic functions of government and its most fundamental claims to sovereignty are regularly parcelled out and undertaken by the private sector. Most controversially, Weber's 'monopoly on the legitimate use of violence' and the oversight of national borders has been handed over to a few giant corporations – as we explore further in Chapter 4. The vast public sector outsourcing industry has a carceral role, restricting where people can move and on what terms. Moreover, the lines of accountability are frayed, as subcontracting is key to the outsourcing business model, giving central government and large contractors ample opportunities for 'blame avoidance'.[21] The companies that win contracts from government to deliver public services are rarely the ones who actually deliver the frontline service. Instead, responsibilities are subcontracted, and subcontracted again. The tangle of bureaucracy means continual audit for many workers but little direct accountability for the companies that employed them.

The Covid-19 pandemic demonstrated quite how close the relationship between the state and these para-state industries had grown, often outside of the public eye. Consultants and 'contract rentiers' quickly adopted a pivotal role in the

---

[21] Christopher Hood, *The Blame Game: Spin, Bureaucracy, and Self-Preservation in Government* (Oxford: Princeton University Press, 2011).

delivery of infrastructure, data analysis, school meals and much else, as the pandemic unfolded. Just as government bonds offer a safe harbour for investors in times of uncertainty (because the state is the most secure borrower around), so contracts for essential public services – border control, criminal justice, life-saving infrastructure – will continue to be issued no matter what, because they are the very basis of the state's legitimacy. Meanwhile smaller businesses with links to the Conservative Party were awarded procurement contracts, often with limited transparency or competition, such that by April 2021, Transparency International had flagged 20% of Covid-related procurement contracts as potentially 'corrupt'.[22] The discovery of a 'VIP lane' for procurement contracts, in which certain firms were awarded them without the need for competitive tendering, deepened the sense that the public finances were now being diverted directly into businesses, without the mediation of any kinds of market. Analysis by Byline Times showed that £1 billion-worth of contracts were awarded to firms linked to Conservative donors, and £2 billion to firms linked to Conservative associates, leading the published profits of these firms to leap by 57.1%.[23] What these discoveries suggested was that mere *proximity* to the state (or the Conservative Party) now represented a business model, a source of revenue whose security grew commensurately with that proximity. Conversely, as universities and certain cultural

---

[22] Transparency International, "Concern Over Corruption Red Flags in 20% of UK's PPE Procurement", Press Release (21 April 2021).

[23] Byline Times and The Citizens, "£121.7 Million Increase in Profits for Covid Contract Winners with Conservative Links", 12 October 2021.

sectors would discover, cultural and political *distance* from the state and governing party became a source of financial risk. Sovereignty may be a bottomless well of economic potential, but that does not mean that everyone has an equal right to draw from it. The pandemic exposed a hierarchy of claims upon the national balance sheet that owed little to the logic of markets, and much to that of political strategy.

Care

The second 'well' of economic promises is one that rarely gets quantified or monetised at all, and has therefore also been eliminated from the sphere of orthodox economics: the sphere of care and social reproduction.[24] This well is not bottomless in the way that sovereign balance sheets are; pushed beyond a

---

[24] Dowling defines care as "all the supporting activities that take place to make, remake, maintain, contain and repair the world we live in and the physical, emotional and intellectual capacities required to do so". Care is often a significant part of 'social reproduction' which describes the "whole sphere of unpaid human activity", often highly gendered, that fundamentally underpins and enables the production of economic value in a capitalist economy. But as Dowling notes, care is "not reducible to the labour of social reproduction" because it concerns "the maintenance of life *for* itself" and not simply the reproduction of a workforce and its capacity to labour. Care is also not only limited to the unpaid sphere, but may be provided as a commercial service, in the voluntary or community sector, or as part of welfare state provision. See Emma Dowling, *The Care Crisis: What Caused It and How Can We End It?* (London: Verso, 2021), 21, 33–38.

certain point, carers, parents, frontline workers working unpaid overtime, will collapse with stress or exhaustion. Time is a finite quantity. And yet it is treated as a well that can be drawn on indefinitely, and without any calculable cost, to make up for the withdrawal of government – that is, it is treated *as if* it were limitless. The necessity of care stems from the basic interdependence of human beings, whether in families, local communities or society, and the obligation to offer it (often a highly burdensome one) is rooted partly in the emotional force of another's need. The needs that care seeks to satisfy and the impulses that drive us to promise it are not always easy to measure, and the work of care is never entirely complete. This work, which the market economy depends upon but refuses to recognise fully through remuneration, has historically been rendered invisible through gendered norms: work is unpaid or underpaid on the basis that it is done by women. Where it is paid, it is often done by migrant workers and racialised minorities, who are expected to perform this work cheaply and with minimal job security. Feminist authors, scholars and activists have offered the richest critical insights into this crucial sphere of value.[25]

As the critical theorist Nancy Fraser has argued, different eras of capitalism deal with the problems of care and social reproduction in different ways, though all have demanded

---

[25] For example, Marilyn Waring, *If Women Counted: A New Feminist Economics* (London: Macmillan, 1989); Diane Elson, "The Economic, the Political and the Domestic: Businesses, States and Households in the Organisation of Production", *New Political Economy*, 3:2 (1998): 189–208; Nancy Folbre, *The Invisible Heart: Economics and Family Values* (New York: The New Press, 2002); Catherine Hoskyns and Shirin Rai, "Recasting the Global Political Economy: Counting Women's Unpaid Work", *New Political Economy*, 12:3 (2007): 297–317; Susan

more emotional labour and unpaid time from women than from men.[26] The work of child-rearing, care for the elderly, the household economy, provision of clothes and food has been organised in various ways, with fluctuating roles for the state, market and civil society at different points. There are many varieties of what sociologist Emma Dowling terms a 'care fix'.[27] The post-War expansion of the welfare state socialised *some* of these responsibilities, but wage stagnation and fiscal retrenchment since the 1970s has left many women in the situation of having to do more hours of paid work *and* more unpaid care work every week. The austerity that followed the global financial crisis, cutting the budget for benefits, schools, public sector pay and local government (which in turn funds social care and children's services), disproportionately harmed women both in financial terms and in the amount of unpaid labour that was required of them.[28] As of 2016, women were doing 60% more unpaid work than men.[29]

Himmelweit, "The Prospects for Caring: Economic Theory and Policy Analysis", *Cambridge Journal of Economics*, 31:4 (2007): 581–599; Tithi Bhattacharya (Ed.), *Social Reproduction Theory: Remapping Class, Recentering Oppression* (London: Pluto Press, 2017); Madeleine Bunting, *Labours of Love: The Crisis of Care* (London: Granta Books, 2020).

[26] Nancy Fraser, "Contradictions of Capital and Care", *New Left Review*, 100 (July–August 2016): 99–117.

[27] Dowling, *The Care Crisis*.

[28] Ruth Pearson and Diane Elson, "Transcending the Impact of the Financial Crisis in the United Kingdom: Towards Plan F—A Feminist Economic Strategy", *Feminist Review*, 109:1 (2015): 8–30.

[29] ONS, "Women Shoulder the Responsibility of 'Unpaid' Work", 10 November 2016.

The market devaluation of care works in tandem with the cultural and political devaluation of those who provide it. Implicitly gendered and racialised hierarchies have an economic function of enabling certain forms of essential labour to be provided on the cheap and with minimal employment rights (see Chapter 3). Being both socially necessary but also characterised by heightened exploitation of workers, the social care sector is ripe for the kinds of 'rentier' activities touched on above. Residential care has become increasingly dominated by for-profit care home chains owned by private equity firms and underwritten by complex financial engineering, as well as an increasingly precarious and underpaid workforce.[30] Highly risky forms of debt-leveraged buyouts are employed to buy and sell these chains, and high returns are drawn out, including through cash extraction and often into offshore tax havens.[31] To secure these returns, labour costs are minimised as far as possible, squeezing a workforce that is disproportionately female and of racialised minorities (a fifth of the social care workforce in England are from 'BAME' backgrounds), and compromising the quality of care delivered.

In the face of social crises, many public service workers (such as teachers) end up providing care for which they are not

---

[30] Amy Horton, "Financialization and Non-Disposable Women: Real Estate, Debt and Labour in UK Care Homes", *Environment and Planning A: Economy and Space*, July 2019.

[31] Diane Burns et al., *Where Does the Money Go? Financialised Chains and the Crisis in Residential Care* (Manchester: CRESC, 2016); Christine Corlet Walker, Angela Druckman and Tim Jackson, *Careless Finance: Operational and Economic Fragility in Adult Social Care* (Guildford: Centre for the Understanding of Sustainable Prosperity, 23 March 2021).

publicly recognised or rewarded. As the political economist Matthew Watson has observed, "large parts of the postwar British welfare state have remained functional only through enhanced reliance on the good-will of the service providers".[32] The rise of food banks in the UK since 2008 is evidence of how fiscal policy implicitly assumes a bottomless well of empathy, in the drive to balance state finances. Rather than accept the indefinite elasticity of sovereign debt, states such as the UK's insisted on the indefinite elasticity of informal social debts. The immeasurable moral obligation to meet social needs is there-fore the invisible, presumed resource that fills the gaps left by public sector cuts and wage stagnation. This is the moral-economic terrain of what the anthropologist David Graeber named 'baseline communism', which we take for granted in our everyday lives to the point of devaluing it.[33]

During the pandemic, workers in the health and social care sectors were responsible for trying to protect a population who were exceptionally vulnerable to the virus. They contin-ued to work under often unbearable circumstances, still trying to attend to the emotional and physical needs of those relying on them while limiting the extent to which they themselves

---

[32] Matthew Watson, "The Contradictory Political Economy of Higher Education in the United Kingdom", *The Political Quarterly*, 82:1 (2011): 24.

[33] "I will call this 'baseline communism': the understanding that, unless people consider themselves enemies, if the need is considered great enough, or the cost considered reasonable enough, the principle of 'from each according to their abilities, to each according to their needs' will be assumed to apply", David Graeber, *Debt: the First 5,000 Years* (New York: Melville House, 2011), 13.

might pose a danger. They were also much more exposed to the virus as a consequence. As is explored further in Chapter 3, the pandemic most affected those areas of work that required close physical proximity, above all health and care work. There are multiple causes behind Covid-19 morbidity and mortality. But it has emerged that those in sectors rife with insecure work are twice as likely to have died from the virus than those working in more secure jobs, and that deprivation was likely to have driven racial disparities in death rates.[34] In health and care, this will have contributed to extraordinary death rates among NHS staff recorded in March–April 2020, nearly two-thirds (63%) of which were from a 'BAME' background despite representing only 21% of NHS workers overall.[35] More generally, it speaks to an economy that has fostered poverty and precarity, leaving particular populations vulnerable in all kinds of ways.

Lockdowns also placed tremendous new demands upon households and neighbourhoods. School closures placed obligations on parents to balance childcare, education and work, which fell predictably heavily on women. These closures led to a whole new set of risks to vulnerable children, who were no longer within the purview of professional services. Many teachers were thrust into the role of social workers, checking up on the emotional and physical wellbeing of disadvantaged

---

[34] Trades Union Congress (TUC), *Covid-19 and Insecure Work* (London: TUC, April 2021); Cameron Razieh et al., "Ethnic Minorities and COVID-19: Examining Whether Excess Risk Is Mediated through Deprivation", *European Journal of Public Health*, 31:3 (2021): 630–634.

[35] Tim Cook, Emira Kursumovic and Simon Lennane, "Exclusive: Deaths of NHS Staff from Covid-19 Analysed", *Health Service Journal* (22 April 2020).

children (see Chapter 5). Mutual aid groups sprang up – an estimated 4,300 by May 2020 – to help get food parcels and social contact to shielding and elderly neighbours.[36]

The national debt is a set of obligations between financial markets and the state, represented as a number. The cost and value of care also resides in mutual obligations – parents to children, care workers to those they care for, adults to elderly parents – but ones that society abstains from putting numbers on, leading to an under-valuation of these bonds. This has costs that also rarely show up in financial terms, both to those struggling with care responsibilities who pay with their stress and mental health, and to those whose care needs are inadequately met by society. Care workers take on the burden of society's debts to the young, vulnerable and elderly, but society refuses to honour its full debts to those workers. These accumulating losses are comparable to the 'depletion' suffered by the environment, also as a result of non-monetised extraction.[37] The full scale of the depletion to carers over 2020–21 may take many years to be adequately recognised.

Entering a New Crisis – Or Exiting an Old One?

Looked at side by side, sovereign debt and care obligations are inverses of one another. The former is an ultimately limitless resource, which *appears* like it is limited in quantity because

---

[36] Anne Power and Ellie Benton, "Where Next for Britain's 4,300 Mutual Aid Groups?", *LSE COVID-19 blog*, 6 May 2021.

[37] Shirin Rai, Catherine Hoskyns and Dania Thomas, "Depletion: The Cost of Social Reproduction", *International Feminist Journal of Politics*, 16:1 (2014): 86–105.

it is represented in monetary terms. The latter is an exhaustible resource, which *appears* like it is unlimited because it is represented in terms of 'love', 'charity' and gendered visions of emotional labour. Covid-19 has cast new light on these two sources of value, but the growing reliance of the British economy and others in the Global North on these 'wells' is not new. Awareness of our dependence on national balance sheets and on un(der)paid care has increased markedly since March 2020 – but the dependence was already there.

In numerous ways, the economic fall-out of the Covid-19 crisis resembles that following the 2008 banking crisis. We have already mentioned some of them. As in the 'great recession' that followed 2008, states resorted to 'unconventional' monetary policies (quantitative easing) in order to provide financial liquidity, and in the process drove up asset prices and inequality. The immediate fall-out from 2008 did at least involve an initial fall in house prices, though they then climbed steadily from January 2009 onwards, coinciding with a historically unprecedented period of wage stagnation. The Covid-19 crisis witnessed a boom in house and other asset prices, *at the same time* as GDP (unsurprisingly, indeed, deliberately) collapsed. By 2021, UK house prices were 50% higher than they were in 2009.[38] In the US, the median price of existing homes rose by an astonishing 23% in the year from June 2020–21, a trend that was evident all over Europe.[39] Underlying this, in both cases, was the overwhelming force of a sovereign balance sheet that ended up inflating demand for assets.

---

[38] ONS, "UK House Price Index: June 2021", 18 August 2021.

[39] Martin Arnold, Colby Smith and Matthew Rocco, "House Prices Climb to Record Levels in US and Europe", *Financial Times*, 22 June 2021.

And as in the 'great recession', informal, emotional and unpaid labour, done disproportionately by women and racialised minorities, plugged the gaps in the failure of the state and the market to meet basic human needs. An unspoken industrial policy, which relies on a mixture of precarity, powerlessness and human sympathy to incentivise care work, propped up society through both austerity and latterly through the pandemic. Cuts to benefits and public services post-2010, combined with wage stagnation, were 'paid for' in the additional toil and obligations of mothers, teachers, care workers, social workers and extended family networks. The retrenchment of the welfare state presumes that there is always more that can be squeezed out of people's time and altruism.

The institutional foundations and policy responses to the crisis of 2020–21 were not, then, unprecedented. Central banks knew immediately what to do when the virus threatened to sink the financial system, because they had already mastered these policy innovations a decade earlier.[40] There was, however, one way in which the politics of the pandemic economy differed from that of the austerity economy: it was recognised as politics. The politics of the economy was, however briefly, revealed. This was visible with respect to both of the 'wells' we describe above.

First of all, take the politics of the national debt. The chief way in which politics was ostensibly eliminated from macroeconomics following the stagflation crisis of the 1970s was in focusing all attention on inflation control as a technocratic goal, best pursued by independent central banks.[41] Central

[40] Tooze, *Shutdown.*

[41] Greta Krippner, *Capitalizing on Crisis: The Political Origins of the Rise of Finance* (Cambridge, MA: Harvard University Press, 2012).

banks have maintained the pretence ever since that they are not 'political' institutions, but are responding to and anticipating market signals. Yet the scale of the Bank's lending to the UK Treasury over 2020–21, necessitated by the pandemic, meant that this pretence has been destroyed. A survey of the largest 18 purchasers of UK government bonds in early 2021 revealed that they viewed the Bank's asset-purchasing programme as a deliberate strategy to finance the Treasury deficit and keep bond yields low.[42] The heterodox economic school known as 'modern monetary theory' (MMT), which argues that governments can (and should) use their money-producing powers to finance as much social spending as they wish, regardless of revenue, has moved from the fringes to the mainstream of debate.[43] The fiscal largesse of the Johnson administration suggests that the politics of fiscal policy was very different in 2021 from how it was in 2011, at the very least on a rhetorical level. The Biden administration's $1.9 trillion stimulus package that passed Congress in March 2021, then subsequent $1 trillion infrastructure bill, was evidence that a new fiscal era may have dawned.[44] The declaration by Jerome Powell, Chairman of the US Federal Reserve, in August 2020 that he would accept higher inflation in the short term, was another decisive international shift.

Then take the politics of care. In a host of ways, at least for a while, the pandemic brought the value and burden of care into the public eye. Rituals such as 'clap for carers' (in

---

[42] Tommy Stubbington and Chris Giles, "Investors Sceptical Over Bank of England's QE Programme", *The Financial Times*, 5 January 2021.

[43] Kelton, *The Deficit Myth*.

[44] Cedric Durand "1979 in Reverse", *Sidecar*, 1 June 2021.

which the public stood on their doorsteps at a certain time each week to applaud) were a mixture of moving sincerity and political opportunism, but at least recognised that society had *some* kind of debt that it had not been adequately paying. New designations were invented to determine who should continue going to work during lockdowns, and therefore whose children could take up school places: 'essential workers' and 'key workers' included those in the health service, but also those in retail and public services, without which society would become entirely unviable. And the partial closure of schools and workplaces led to a harsh encounter for many with the challenges of childcare, housework, teaching and eldercare, on top of paid work, which brought gender inequalities into stark relief. The care crisis was very far from resolved, but it was more visible. The question (to which we return in Chapter 6) is what legacies this politicisation of the economy might have, and how it might be beneficially exploited.

A Crisis of Space

Any infectious disease requires its carriers to come into proximity with one another. Pandemics have always had distinctive spatial conditions and consequences, and often arise from disruptions in economic and political geography. The cholera epidemics of the 19th century were linked to imperialism and the trade routes connecting Europe to South Asia; the 'Spanish flu' was linked to the intense proximity, and subsequent dispersal, of troops in the trenches of World War One.[45] Covid-19

---

[45] Alex De Waal, *New Pandemics, Old Politics: Two Hundred Years of War on Disease and Its Alternatives* (London: Wiley, 2021).

was first identified in Wuhan, but was traversing the globe within a few weeks thanks to international travel routes of business and tourism: the first airborne pandemic in the age of jet travel.[46] The cities that were most likely to suffer an outbreak during the first wave of Covid-19 in early 2020, and the ones that suffered the highest mortality rates, were the most internationally connected ones, regardless of other spatial factors such as density.[47] This was first and foremost a pandemic facilitated and shaped by the economic 'globalisation' of previous decades, which has now thrown that spatial regime (further) into question.

Epidemics and pandemics also elicit innovations in the design and control of space. Michel Foucault wrote of how a new political logic of 'hygiene' emerged in Europe in the 18th century, which – with the advice of emerging public health experts – sought to reconfigure housing and the built environment, together with nutrition and education, in order to safeguard public health in cities.[48] The spread of Covid-19 witnessed an emergency measure that had never been attempted in peacetime: nationwide lockdowns, causing unprecedented upheavals in patterns of work, education, social life and the

---

[46] Richard Florida, Andrés Rodriguez-Pose and Michael Storper, "Cities in a Post-COVID World", *Urban Studies* (June 2021).

[47] Tiberiu Pana et al., "Country-Level Determinants of the Severity of the First Global Wave of the COVID-19 Pandemic: An Ecological Study", *BMJ Open*, 11:2 (2021): 1–10. Yair Daon, Robin Thompson and Uri Obolski, "Estimating COVID-19 Outbreak Risk Through Air Travel", *Journal of Travel Medicine*, 27:5 (July 2020): 1–8.

[48] Michel Foucault, "The Politics of Health in the Eighteenth Century", *Foucault Studies*, 18 (October 2014): 113–127.

arts. Subsequent forms of spatial regulation, such as quarantining, social distancing policies, mobility tracing and tightening of borders, outlasted the lockdowns themselves, and will
leave significant legacies. New surveillance infrastructures,
centred around apps and data analytics, have been created at
speed in the hope of rendering such regulations enforceable.
Micro-governmental interventions, such as one-way routes in
buildings, mandatory facemasks, and new norms of physical
distancing in shared spaces, altered everyday conviviality, and
some will not be fully reversed.

The spatial politics of the pandemic are impossible to
ignore, but so are the economic dimensions of those spatial
changes. The question we wish to raise here is how political,
technological and medical innovations in the organisation
of space will intersect with existing tendencies in economic
geography. Critical geographers in the tradition of Henri
Lefebvre stress that space is never simply a given. It is not, as
we assume when we look at traditional maps and architec-
tural plans, a neutral 'container' of human activity without
any politics of its own. On the contrary, how space is produced, governed, visualised and ritualised are all intensely
political issues. Capitalism simultaneously exploits existing
forms of space (for instance, trade routes or urban agglom-
erations) while also disrupting them and generating new
ones (via offshoring, downsizing, privatising, gentrifying and
so on).[49] This is another evolutionary process through which
existing spatial orders provide the conditions for unprecedented disturbances, undermining and remaking spaces.
Equally, states do not simply exist in territorially defined

---

[49] Henri Lefebvre, *The Production of Space*, trans. Donald
Nicholson-Smith (Oxford: Blackwell, 1991), 85.

'containers' or seek to impose themselves upon already-existing national spaces, but are integrally involved in producing, delineating, representing and transforming spaces.[50] Ideas of national sovereignty and technologies of border control are mutually reinforcing.

The pandemic has both challenged (in some cases terminated) previous spatial patterns and norms, and provoked new ones. How this happened was not determined simply by the nature of the virus, though its material qualities were obviously significant, in particular the specific risks it posed in crowded indoor spaces. It was mediated via institutions and technologies that were already available and were *already* at the heart of geographic transformations of capitalism prior to 2020. As with debts, the effect of the pandemic was photosynthetic, both accelerating and rendering visible political forces that were already present. These can be observed in three particular spheres.

Hyper-domestication

The first concerns an entity that was already a source of financial mania and social distress, only now came under entirely new pressures: housing. We have already noted the house price boom that coincided with the first 18 months of the pandemic, helped by ultra-low interest rates and the asset-purchasing programmes of central banks. It was further encouraged by a stamp duty holiday announced by Sunak in July 2020, which wasn't fully reversed for over a year. Such are the demands on housing in many cities that banks and asset managers such

---

[50] See Neil Brenner et al. (Eds.). *State/Space: A Reader* (London: Wiley, 2003).

as Blackstone have increasingly moved into the private rental market, buying up and building homes for let, including the student accommodation market.[51] However, the material nature of the coronavirus led to a new appreciation of outdoor space, fresh air and ventilation, which became a new expression of class inequalities. Meanwhile, the partial closure of schools and workplaces meant that additional value became placed on spare bedrooms, home offices and larger homes in general. The bleak political order to 'Stay home' inevitably led to a reappreciation of domestic space. Estate agents observed a 'race for space' over 2020–21, with price increases most pronounced among large, detached houses with outdoor space, especially those in areas of outstanding natural beauty such as the Yorkshire Dales and the Cotswolds. Wealth elites tended to spend lockdowns in second homes, outside of the major cities. Others have departed cities for good, as signalled by divergent trends in the rental market. The inflated London housing market has meant that a property-owner in the city can potentially acquire a much larger home elsewhere, and many have used the pandemic to reassess priorities and exploit the surge in home-working. The status of the office, as a default place of work, and of the high street, as a default place of retail, have both been diminished as the economic importance of the home has risen.

The broadband-connected home had been taking on more and more social and economic functions in the decades

---

[51] See Christophers, Brett, "Mind the Rent Gap: Blackstone, Housing Investment and the Reordering of Urban Rent Surfaces", *Urban Studies* (August 2021). The 'build to rent' financial sector barely existed in the UK in 2011, but boomed throughout the pandemic, with investment of £3.5 billion in 2020.

prior to the pandemic: work, entertainment, social communication, shopping, education. The introduction of e-commerce
and digital assistants (such as Amazon Echo) makes it a space
where desires, emotions and needs can be monitored. The
writer Paul Preciado has observed that Covid-19 was managed
very differently from previous pandemics due to the connec-
tivity of the domestic sphere:

> The home is no longer only the place where the body is confined, as
> was the case under plague management. The private residence has
> now become the center of the economy of tele-consumption and
> tele-production, but also the surveillance pod.[52]

These technological conditions have only added to the importance of the *residence* as the pivotal space in our economy
and our culture. 'Home entertainment', 'homeworking', 'home
deliveries' and 'home school' were all familiar expressions
prior to 2020, but the pandemic has frequently rendered them
default options. Covid-19 therefore offered a glimpse of a viable future for the spatial organisation of the economy, in which
middle-class homes were economically integrated via broadband cables and delivery workers.

Covid-19 also shone an unforgiving light on longstanding
social pathologies of the UK's housing towards the lower end
of the income scale. As the UK struggled to comprehend why
its mortality rate was so much worse than comparable nations
over the first year of the pandemic, work by the social epidemi-
ologist Michael Marmot pinpointed underlying economic and
geographic conditions, which had been years in the making,

---

[52] Paul Preciado, "Learning from the Virus", *Artforum* (May/
June 2020).

that correlated strongly with above-average mortality and lower life expectancy, both before and during the pandemic.[53] Cuts to health and social spending were key among these, but so were overcrowded housing, access to outside space, and ability to isolate adequately within the home – a particular problem for large and multigenerational households, and housing shared by multiple families.

Poverty makes people more likely to share spaces with more people (for instance, lifts and stairwells) and to share space within the home with vulnerable people. Around the world, deaths were especially clustered in the poorer suburbs of major cities, where housing is cheap enough for precarious workers to afford, and close enough to the urban centres where low-wage service work was available. These are the neighbourhoods where over-crowding is most acute. Those in the private rental sector have less space, less outdoor space, more respiratory-related problems such as damp, and were found to suffer more stress during lockdowns.[54] Private rental tenants are on average younger than the rest of the population, but older racialised minorities are also more likely than average to live in privately rented homes – the same demographic that has been most harmed by Covid-19. In all these ways, an already dysfunctional housing system became critical to the nature and depth of the UK's health crisis, which in turn provoked a further quest by asset owners to deploy their balance sheets in search of more space for themselves and their families.

---

[53] Michael Marmot et al., *Build Back Fairer: The Covid-19 Marmot Review* (London: The Health Foundation/Institute of Health Equity, 2020).

[54] Adam Tinson and Amy Clair, "Better Housing Is Crucial for Our Health and the COVID-19 Recovery", *The Health Foundation* (blog), 28 December 2020.

Platformisation

The ratcheting up of the pressure upon housing, whose proximate cause was the need to reduce the rate of infections, was in turn facilitated by a second spatial innovation of contemporary capitalism: the growth of digital platforms. For the most part, these are provided by giant US technology firms, whose business strategies are as focused on the extraction of data as much as of profit.[55] Were it not for the near-universality of broadband internet, and the availability of platforms such as Zoom, Amazon, Google Classroom, Deliveroo and Microsoft Office, the social and economic geography of the pandemic would have been unrecognisably different. Had Covid-19 arrived a mere 15 years earlier, lockdowns would either have been impossible at the same scale, or else have generated even greater social and economic damage. Instead, lockdowns and restraints on travel forced organisations to revive many of the earlier promises of the internet – that it would herald the 'end of the office', the 'death of distance', 'massive open online courses' – with commensurate damage to the status of spatial conglomerations, such as high streets, university campuses and civic spaces. Covid-19 has raised deep questions over the long-term future of urban centres and office blocks, which extend well beyond the timespan of lockdowns themselves, but only because platforms have demonstrated their capacity to mediate and sustain far more of our working, commercial and cultural lives than had previously been attempted.

The power of platforms consists in their ability to connect up any assembly of 'users' and service suppliers, for virtually any purpose, so long it allows data to be extracted. As numerous analysts and critics of platform capitalism have noted, the

---

[55] Nick Srnicek, *Platform Capitalism* (London: Wiley, 2016).

very amorphous and multi-purpose nature of the platform business model is what grants it such extraordinary capacity to intrude into new markets, evade regulation and remake the norms of social and urban life.[56] Because such businesses have been backed by patient venture capital, which emphasises long-term growth over short-term profitability, they are able to focus on expanding their reach and data extraction to the point where they become like social utilities, but which exploit their data for commercial advantages and further expansion. The result is that a wider and wider range of interactions, interfaces and thresholds are now opportunities to accumulate data. Covid-19 plus platformisation has led to a remaking of what Lefebvre termed 'spatial practices', the rhythms and patterns of everyday life.

Our rising dependence on platforms, accelerated by the pandemic, has led to huge financial gains for the companies concerned, making them another genre of 'rentier capitalist', whose revenue is extracted from monopolistic control over valuable utilities rather than from production.[57] But this dependence has also unleashed a new political economy of

---

[56] See Jamie Peck and Rachel Phillips, "The Platform Conjuncture", *Sociologica*, 14:3 (2020): 73–99; Paul Langley and Andrew Leyshon, "Platform Capitalism: The Intermediation and Capitalisation of Digital Economic Circulation", *Finance and Society*, 3:1 (2017): 11–31; Jose van Dijck, Thomas Poell and Martijn de Waal, *The Platform Society: Public Values in a Connective World* (Oxford: Oxford University Press, 2018); K. Sabeel Rahman and Kathleen Thelen, "The Rise of the Platform Business Model and the Transformation of Twenty-First-Century Capitalism", *Politics & Society*, 47:2 (2019): 177–204.

[57] See Christophers, *Rentier Capitalism*, Chapter 4.

space, in which homes, local labour markets, municipal transport, hospitality venues, classrooms and campuses, and public space all become spaces of capitalistic surveillance, that is,
opportunities for the extraction of data, which is then treated
as a private asset.[58] The 'disruptive' logic of platforms is to first
liberate individuals from their dependence on analogue services, face-to-face relations and bureaucracy, and then lock
them into reliance on the platform alternative, partly through
seeking to eliminate competition. One of the consequences is
to reconfigure cities, public services and households as laboratories for the acquisition of behavioural data, and the identification of new opportunities for profit.[59]

That platforms have benefitted in terms of growth and
profitability from Covid-19 is scarcely any surprise. The heightened dependence of consumers on Amazon, restaurants and
pubs on Deliveroo, pupils on Google Classroom and white-
collar workers on Zoom was immediately clear in March
2020, and reflected in the share prices of such companies.[60]

---

[58] See Kean Birch and D. T. Cochrane "Big Tech: Four Emerging
Forms of Digital Rentiership", *Science as Culture* (2021).

[59] Jathan Sadowski, "The Internet of Landlords: Digital
Platforms and New Mechanisms of Rentier Capitalism,"
Antipode, 52:2 (2020): 562–580; Jathan Sadowski, "Cyberspace
and Cityscapes: On the Emergence of Platform Urbanism",
Urban Geography, 41:3 (2020): 448–452.

[60] In May 2020, Zoom's market capitalisation was greater than
that of the world's biggest seven airlines. Half of the gains in
the US stock market in 2020 went to 'tech giants', whose stocks
were up an average of 44% over the year. Amy Borrett, "Why
Big Tech Stocks Boomed in the Pandemic", *Tech Monitor*, 16
December 2020.

But public–private platformisation was also at work in the governmental interventions during the pandemic, such as the NHS Covid-19 app, which was designed to play a role in contact tracing and venue 'check-ins'. The use of the resulting data, the involvement of data analytics firms such as Palantir in the vaccination programme, and the potential commercial uses of NHS data more broadly were all matters of political concern that arose over 2020–21. The health emergency meant that populations became resources to be mined for data, in the service of both profit and biosecurity, and access to those resources provided the basis for another type of symbiotic relationship between the state and 'rentier capitalists'. The role of platforms in the remaking of space over this crisis was therefore multi-pronged. They softened the economic and social impact of confinements and closures, and in the process extended their reach into urban, domestic, cultural and community life, while also increasing their intimacy with the state and public services.

Re-bordering

Despite being a global pandemic, whose emergence and transmission routes are owed to the geography of global capitalism, Covid-19 has hastened the reassertion of the nation as the primary unit of what the geographer Neil Brenner has termed 'state space'.[61] If the era of globalisation saw power and decision-making being reallocated to a multiplicity of different spatial tiers, from the global down to the very local, numerous political counter-movements (often labelled 'populist') have challenged this on grounds that veer between the nationalist

---

[61] See Brenner et al., *State/Space.*

and the democratic, or mixtures of the two. In the UK, this became most clearly expressed in the popular vote for Brexit in 2016, which led to the departure from the EU in 2020. Existing devolution of powers to Scotland, Wales and Northern Ireland, rising national independence movements, and the stresses that Brexit placed on the Union were additional factors that shaped the contingent spatial context of Covid-19 in the UK. Thus, the emergency of 2020 arose under political and spatial conditions that were already leading to rising national insularity, re-bordering, and a re-nationalisation of many governmental and economic institutions.

Borders, which were already represented and governed as sources of risk and security threats, became significantly less permeable, seeing as each nation state adopted its own distinctive political and technical approach to the pandemic, while international cooperation and strategy was secondary. The permeability that remained was dictated by financial and political considerations. Each nation state adopted its own combination of lockdowns, restrictions on public gatherings, test and trace, border control, vaccination programmes, and policing of social distancing and quarantine. Meanwhile, statistical charts displaying how each nation was 'performing' in terms of infections and mortality, as if in a league, constructed a new visualisation and imaginary of international rivalry. Policy, which was largely confined to and anchored at the spatial tier of the national (which in the UK has meant the four nations of England, Wales, Scotland and Northern Ireland), also occurred against a backdrop of comparison, in terms of which nations had selected which policies, and how they were faring in those macabre statistical rankings. If, as Lefebvre argued, the production of space is always partly about new 'representations of space', the world in 2020 became displayed and spoken of as an international contest to combat, save, contain, vaccinate at the fastest pace. As historian Adam Tooze puts it, "the pandemic became an Olympics of national governance".[62] The UK experience of this 'Olympics' witnessed growing schisms between England and the other three nations of the Union, which could yet contribute to its break-up.

In the absence of a global public health policy, and a global vaccination programme in particular, one of the most significant political consequences of the pandemic has been significant constraints upon travel, migration and asylum, often fuelled by logics of 'protection' and 'hygiene' aimed at excluding foreign populations (the topic of Chapter 4). The first quarter of 2021 saw an astonishing 96% drop in visits to the UK by non-residents compared to a year earlier, and a 94% drop of UK residents leaving the country.[63] In the summer of 2021, the Johnson administration was widely criticised across the political spectrum for allowing travel from India (the allegation being that this was done to sustain goodwill for a post-Brexit trade deal), thereby admitting the 'Delta' variant into the country that went on to cause a large third wave of infections. The wisdom of closing or tightening borders, as many nations in Asia and Australasia had done, became a new political orthodoxy, as a matter of technocratic reason as much as of nationalist protectionism. But the permeability of these stricter borders has been unequally distributed, depending on class stratification and perceptions of risk attached to different nations and racialised groups. Special dispensations were made available to business elites to allow them to cross borders without quarantining.

The new territorial order that came into being in 2020, and which will undoubtedly leave a mark on international

---

[62] Tooze, *Shutdown*, 73.

[63] ONS, "Overseas Travel and Tourism, Provisional: January to March 2021", 23 July 2021.

geopolitics for many years into the future, was therefore – as with the other spatial reconfigurations we detail here – a combination of the precedented and the unprecedented. The precedents were derived from the existing ascendency of economic protectionism, ethno-nationalism and anti-migrant politics, which sought to re-establish the nation as the fundamental unit of 'state space', as a form of resistance to what nationalists referred to as 'globalism', and an effort to re-naturalise the nation as the container of 'true' sovereignty. Yet this often ran into the obstacle of countervailing economic forces, deriving from the global logic of capitalism. This contradiction became publicly manifest over the summer of 2021, as shortage of foreign workers in areas such as hospitality and haulage saw restaurants closing and supermarket shelves emptying. What Covid-19 has done is to generate the emergency that allows the state to overwhelm and suppress those extra-national economic forces, and dramatically re-localise and re-nationalise. If pandemics have historically always involved new techniques and spaces of confinement, the perceived need to reassert the nation in the face of the global has yielded the expansion of new confinement technologies at the border, for purposes of quarantining and detention. Again, policies such as the use of hotel chains for purposes of detention at airports were already available, but they have now become normalised and rendered more visible. What remains largely invisible (and could become more so) are the populations excluded, now on grounds of public health, in addition to longstanding official justifications.

A New Spatial Fix?

These spatial forces – of hyper-domestication, platformisation and national re-bordering – had been in the ascendency for many years before the appearance of Covid-19. But, again, they were both illuminated and accelerated by the pandemic. Governments seized these forces in pursuit of a drastic immobilisation of people: to stay, work, shop and socialise at 'home', in both the domestic and the national sense of 'home'. The public health emergency demanded a radical suspension of public space and the informal norms of conviviality that distinguish it, but this suspension was facilitated by economic and technological trends that were already acting to de-value and reconfigure public space, and to delimit its political potential.

Added to both the gradual remaking of space and to the emergency of multiple lockdowns, the British government passed the hugely controversial Police, Crime, Sentencing and Courts Bill in July 2021, which granted the Home Office the right to decide whether a peaceful protest is lawful or not. This authoritarian measure, described by one barrister as "the biggest widening of police powers to impose restrictions on public protest that we've seen in our lifetimes", was particularly motivated by the desire to tackle Extinction Rebellion protests.[64] However, coming a year after vast Black Lives Matter protests had filled otherwise deserted city streets at the end of the first national lockdown, it signalled a new war of attrition over the political character and potential of shared urban space. Whether the public street could provide, in Honig's terms, a basic 'holding environment' for democracy, or whether this would become colonised by private infrastructure and platforms, was thus in question throughout 2020 and 2021. We return to this conflict in the final chapter.

---

[64] Hannah Westwater, "How Priti Patel's New Policing Bill Threatens Your Right to Protest", *The Big Issue*, 13 September 2021.

How housing, platforms and borders co-evolve and intersect is an important question for geographers to address. The pandemic has seen relations between the three tightening, including some surreal innovations such as the so-called 'Stanley Johnson clause' in British borders policy, which for a while permitted people to travel to check on overseas properties but not to visit overseas relatives. Financially speaking, the asset appreciation and rent extraction that characterise the housing market and platform economy suggest the entrenchment of a distinctive spatial fix, oriented around the privatisation and surveillance of space, which then works in concert with sovereign efforts to control public space and mobility.

Conclusion: What Makes 'Society'?

A few days into the UK's first national lockdowns in March 2020, Boris Johnson made a statement including a line that was clearly selected to reinforce his personal brand, and the rebranding of his party: "there really is such a thing as society". The implicit contrast was with Margaret Thatcher's famous remark to the contrary. But what is the substance of this 'society'? The Johnson administration tended to treat it as interchangeable with 'nation', demanding national togetherness and a blitz spirit, as embodied by the World War Two veteran Captain Tom Moore, who hit the headlines in the summer of 2020 for walking one hundred lengths of his garden as a fundraiser for the NHS.[65] Following his discharge from hospital after his own bout of Covid-19, Johnson released a video claiming

---

[65] Malcolm James and Sivamohan Valluvan, "Coronavirus Conjuncture: Nationalism and Pandemic States", *Sociology*, 54:6 (2020): 1238–1250.

that "we are making progress in this national battle because the British public formed a human shield around this country's greatest national asset – the National Health Service". The appeal was clearly to the insular British nation that emerged out of World War Two.[66]

Challenging a nationalistic understanding of 'society' requires an empirical and critical perspective on what holds people together (and what separates them), when markets fail or are suspended. This chapter has emphasised two questions in particular that need to be confronted if we are to grasp what kind of 'society' was sustained over the course of 2020–21. Firstly, who owes what to whom? Without interrogating the role of sovereign debt and of informal, unpaid and underpaid care in our economy, we can't begin to understand how it was possible for a model of capitalism – habitually dependent on constant market transactions – to make it through the enforced hiatus of lockdowns and partial closures of so many institutions. The ability of certain commitments to endure, despite deep uncertainty elsewhere, signals that if 'society' means anything at all, debts are integral to its constitution and persistence. Secondly, who is granted access to which spaces, and who is constrained? Covid-19 accelerated the rise of a 'platform-enabled household', further heightening the demands placed upon housing, and further widening the inequalities of space and tenure. It has also accelerated the raising of national borders, most of all with regard to those populations deemed 'risky' or economically low value. Inequalities of class, gender and race have long had their spatial manifestations, in patterns of deindustrialisation, gentrification, domestication

---

[66] David Edgerton, *The Rise and Fall of the British Nation: A Twentieth-Century History* (London: Penguin, 2018).

and migration policies. Thanks especially to new digital infrastructures, the handling of the pandemic allows for more acute forms of political and cultural discrimination, in how access to spaces is allowed and denied.

Over the next four chapters, we will encounter these political questions – concerning both time and space – recurring in different fields of economic activity and policy. We will also see them combine in different ways, with the remaking of economic space creating new strains upon care obligations (for instance with respect to childcare during school closures), while the state and its 'rentier contractors' conspire to construct new tools of surveillance and confinement, financed thanks to the endless 'well' of sovereign debt. The most potent political technologies of our age are the balance sheet and the digital platform, and it is these as much as anything that have enabled societies to persist in some form (with considerable exclusions and caveats) over the course of an unprecedented interruption in the market economy. What neither of these tools does is to grasp the social and human costs of seeking to govern society on the basis of assets, liabilities and data, or to see the various values that evade quantification.

2

Endless Temporary Measures: The Politics of 'Leverage'

Announcing his February 2020 budget, Rishi Sunak reported that the imminent pandemic would cause a 'temporary disruption' to the British economy. Even as the first lockdown prompted an extraordinary 25% contraction in economic output, there was optimism that this would soon be recovered once the virus had somehow been dealt with. Speaking in the July of that year, Andy Haldane, then Chief Economist of the Bank of England, was confident that the UK was experiencing a 'v-shaped' recession, in which a sudden stoppage of economic activity would be swiftly compensated for, once the hiatus of lockdown was out of the way. A year later, GDP had still not recovered to pre-pandemic levels, largely because of the failure to adequately tackle infections. Over time, questions arose as to whether spatial patterns of work and consumption might in fact be permanently altered, becoming more centred around homes and digital platforms, and less around high streets and offices.

The idea that the pandemic was a brief, manageable interruption in economic time dominated policy thinking at the outset, and prompted extraordinary public interventions in financial and labour markets. From this view, the job of government was to build a bridge over the hiatus that would allow businesses, investors, households and employees a safe passage to a future moment, whereupon the economy could be happily switched back on again. Echoing Mario Draghi's famous statement that pulled the Eurozone back from the precipice, Sunak promised to "do whatever it takes".[1] The mechanism that would enable this bridge to be built was already the UK's most reliable and persistent economic resource: debt. The deep 'well' of the sovereign balance sheet, discussed in the previous chapter, would be drawn on to an extent unprecedented in peacetime, in the hope that the economy could be suspended in time, and then quickly revived when a better future had arrived. Mobilising the overwhelming power of state borrowing and money creation would allow other creditors and debtors to traverse the hiatus.

The result was a tangle of nearly 400 different government and Bank of England programmes and schemes, expected to cost £370 billion, through which the state jumped in to make payments for some, delay the payments of others, and ensure the system as a whole was kept afloat.[2] Some actions, like the furlough scheme, were unprecedented. Others, like taxpayer guarantees for risky mortgages, well worn.[3] The effect was to pile debt upon debt, public and private, in a series of paper promises about a rosier future on the horizon.

But to focus only on these novel interventions, through which the 'temporary disruption' might be navigated, would be to miss a key feature of the economy that the Treasury and Bank of England were attempting to sustain. The UK economy

---

[1] Rishi Sunak, "Budget Speech 2020", GOV.UK, 11 March 2020.
[2] NAO, "Covid-19 Cost Data", COVID-19 Cost Tracker (accessed 25 September 2021).
[3] HM Treasury, *The Mortgage Guarantee Scheme*, Policy Paper, 3 March 2021.

was *already* constituted as a web of debt relations, under-pinned by a state that was *already* deploying exceptional measures in order to keep a pyramid of promises from collapsing. The British model of capitalism, as it had evolved over the preceding decades, and been sustained *in extremis* post-2008, was such that the economic priority of government was to ensure the credibility of its financial system at all costs. It's not that the UK had a functioning system of production, which occasionally needed helping through a crisis via the financial deferment of certain costs; financial deferment *was* the UK's economic system. Novel and 'unconventional' measures, designed to plug interruptions in time, had become permanent. This model produced starkly divergent fortunes across the population – 'k-shaped' growth – in which asset owners grew exponentially wealthier, while those without stagnated. The financial system reinforced the dynamic, offering cheap credit to asset owners looking to leverage up and acquire more wealth, and punishing higher-interest loans to those forced to borrow for basic needs.

This chapter looks more closely at the financial and policy measures that were taken in order to sustain the UK's economic and financial system in the face of extraordinary material obstacles, namely the closure of many of the institutions and infrastructures on which capitalism fundamentally depends. Our argument is that, while the trigger and the scale of public financial interventions were unprecedented, the resulting costs and benefits were horribly familiar in their distribution. Central to our analysis is the politics of time and of leverage: the way balance sheets are deployed in order to extract income out of the future, and to either defer costs or push them onto less powerful parties. This financial manipulation of time is how sovereign authorities conjured a solution to the extreme economic threat of Covid-19. However, it is also at the heart of the economic system that those authorities were seeking to protect, and had been keeping on life support over the previous 12 years. In doing so, they were also protecting and sustaining a model of capitalism that generated fierce inequalities. It is an economic model that has long *appeared* unsustainable, except that nothing – not even a 25% hit to GDP – yet seems able to derail it.[4]

We start by exploring the crucial role played by balance sheets in the UK economy, which become tools of enrichment under broader conditions of stagnation. We then narrate the events of the lockdown of 2020, and the policies that were rolled out in response. In the third section, we show how these events and policies exacerbated an existing 'k-shaped' growth model, in which asset-holders gained, and everyone else limped along. Finally, we reflect on some of the political implications of this, and pose the question: who is benefitting when others are paying?

Paper Promises: Rising Indebtedness Pre-pandemic

A simple fact of economic life is that we rarely pay for the things we buy. Or at least, we don't pay *when* we first buy them, nor when we've received them, and often still not even after we've consumed them. Instead, we make *promises* to pay eventually in the future. A designer might win a contract to re-brand a company website, but she is rarely paid upfront. Instead, she will do the work, invoice, and wait. Ideally, she would be paid soon

---

[4] Daniel Harari, Matthew Keep and Phillip Brien, "Coronavirus: Economic Impact", Research Briefing (House of Commons Library, 2020). Accessed 25 September 2021.

after, though smaller suppliers are often left waiting longer. On a bigger scale, a professional services corporation like Balfour Beatty or the now-collapsed Carillion might win a lucrative government contract to build and manage a hospital over a five-year time scale, and will receive partial payment throughout and often long after completion. These promised projects and promised revenues, however credible, are still uncertain. In the lag between promises made and payments and services actually delivered, a lot can happen. Time and the uncertainty it introduces becomes a stubborn fact of the politics of economic life.

It is why the heterodox economist Hyman Minsky thought it useful to model all economic units, be they underpaid key workers or giant corporations and nation states, as 'balance sheet entities' that could be analysed in similar terms to a bank.[5] They have assets – what they own – and liabilities – what they owe. Assets see future cash flow coming in and liabilities mean future cash flowing out. At the heart of economic life, everyone shares the same fundamental problem: How to make sure you can access money on the day the cash flow out is due. Every day a bank will have customers demand their deposits back and the bank must be ready to pay out, just as every day the designer will have payments she cannot avoid – her rent, her grocery bills. The necessity to 'make payment' is what Minsky described as the 'survival constraint'. Even a failing company can limp along if they can find ways to make their payments, but an otherwise flourishing firm would quickly collapse if they can't access cash on the day their payments are due.[6] As Perry Mehrling put it, "liquidity kills you quick".[7]

---

[5] Daniel H. Neilson, *Minsky* (Cambridge: Polity, 2019), 21.

[6] Ibid., 48.

[7] Perry G. Mehrling, "First Liquidity, Then Solvency", *Institute for New Economic Thinking*, 6 October 2011.

In the scramble to make payment, economic units rely on three sources: draw on savings, access credit, or – if all else fails – liquidate your assets. All of these are routes to accessing the cash needed to make payment. The financial sector's crucial purpose is to offer the credit needed to bridge the chasm in time between the payments due today and the notional incomes due to arrive at some point in the future. It provides the liquidity that ensures nobody need liquidate their assets in order to survive. Money gets lent, so payments can be made, on the promise that down the line these debts will be repaid. That way, one debt connects to another in a long chain of promises. Along the way, it becomes harder to decipher where the 'real' economy ends and the 'notional' world of financial promises begins. A mortgage is a loan made to a real economy borrower on the basis of a solid material collateral asset, a home. But when a set of mortgage repayments gets bundled up and sold off as a new financial asset for investors to buy, the links to the underlying real-economy asset loosen. All kinds of bespoke financial products derived from an initial loan can then be developed. As the notional world of financial values supersedes the real, the income these financial assets are expected to deliver becomes the collateral to borrow more again to finance further speculation. This capacity for leverage is what makes finance so potent. One asset becomes the basis for a chain of multiple debts. What happens 'on the ground' gradually becomes less important than conditions in financial markets.

While credit keeps flowing, this arrangement is perfectly stable. Each repayment can be funded by another loan, which can be repaid with another loan, and so on. The final settlement is forever deferred by yet more borrowing. Indeed, as economists Massimo Amato and Luca Fantacci describe, if everyone were to deleverage and *settle* their debts, the result would pull the whole system down.[8] A loan that is fully repaid is no longer the basis of multiple new financial assets derived from it. The leveraged economy rests on sustaining the value of the financial assets upon which further borrowing is secured. If firms made payment by selling off these assets rather than borrowing, it would imply a rapid and chaotic deleveraging, and asset prices would collapse and the system of liquidity freeze. Though it feels counter-intuitive, it is the *suspension* of debt rather than its continual creation that unleashes financial instability.

These conditions of systemic leverage structure how households and businesses organise their political economic lives. As the UK economy has stagnated over the Long Downturn of the last few decades, economic power has concentrated among those best able to acquire assets and leverage their balance sheets.[9]

---

[8] Massimo Amato and Luca Fantacci, *The End of Finance* (Cambridge: Polity, 2013).

[9] OECD country GDP growth rates slowed from 5.7% in the 1960s to 3.6% in the 1970s, 3.0% in the 1980s, 2.6% in the 1990s, and 1.9% between 2000 and 2019. In the UK GDP growth in the 1970s (2.64%) and 1980s (2.66%) was more than the 16 consecutive years of growth between 1992–2008 (2.2%). Since 2008 real growth is near zero and wage growth has declined. See Robert Brenner, *The Economics of Global Turbulence: The Advanced Capitalist Economies from Long Boom to Long Downturn, 1945–2005* (London: Verso, 2006); Aaron Benanav, "Service Work in the Pandemic Economy", *International Labor and Working-Class History* (12 October 2020); ONS, "Gross Domestic Product: Year on Year Growth", 12 August 2021; ONS, "Trends in the UK Economy", 27 February 2015.

As the leveraged economy took hold, the home was transformed from a matter of security and domesticity into a speculative financial asset that determined material wellbeing across generations. In 1971 the average house in the UK cost around £5,500, but by the start of 2021, it was around £250,000.[10] As the housing charity Shelter noted, if food prices followed the same trajectory a basic battery-farm whole chicken would now cost more than £50.[11] The wild escalation in house prices has greatly outpaced growth in incomes (especially since 1998).[12] This has helped forge the k-shape separation in economic fortunes between those who could get assets and those who could not, and fundamentally changed the character of political economic life in the UK.[13] It compelled those who could to borrow greatly to acquire expensive housing assets, and rely on rising house prices to make their debts sustainable. The key economic unit, as Lisa Adkins, Melinda Cooper and Martin Konings have argued, has become the 'Minskyian household': families who come to manage assets and liabilities across multiple generations, financing the acquisition of housing and higher education through careful manipulation of their 'balance sheet' over several years.[14] Parents use the security of

---

[10] ONS, "UK House Price Index: February 2021", 21 April 2021.

[11] Tristan Carlyon, "Food for Thought: Applying House Price Inflation to Grocery Prices", *Shelter*, February 2013.

[12] Amy Borrett, "How UK House Prices Have Soared Ahead of Average Wages", *New Statesman*, 20 May 2021.

[13] Johnna Montgomerie and Mirjam Büdenbender, "Round the Houses: Home Ownership and Failures of Asset-Based Welfare in the United Kingdom", *New Political Economy*, 20:3 (2015): 386–405.

[14] Lisa Adkins, Melinda Cooper and Martijn Konings, *The Asset Economy* (London: Wiley, 2020).

housing assets to help their children borrow more and keep the cycle of leverage, asset acquisition and more leverage within the family. This was seen in the year before the pandemic, with the 'Bank of Mum and Dad' gifting £6.3 billion to help their children onto the housing ladder, amounting to the UK's tenth biggest mortgage lender.[15] High-street banks developed new mortgage products predicated on parental guarantee, and building societies offered new family savings accounts to formalise this familial wealth transfer. Despite the promises made by Third Way governments in the 1990s to revive economic fortunes through 'modernisation' and meritocratic human capital investment, this very traditional form of familial capital has become the surest route to material wellbeing. As Cooper argued, the moral order of contemporary capitalism is less a championing of individualistic entrepreneurialism than it is a conservative re-centring of the traditional family.[16]

Housing is the most visceral example of the dynamic between debt and wealth acquisition. But corporations have also followed this path. The companies that can organise their balance sheets to make their assets look strong (even if this is misleading) are able to pull great flows of liquidity in their direction and that way make their payments and secure their survival.[17] The promises of future income are enough to deliver

---

[15] Financial Times Money Reporters, "Bank of Mum and Dad 'Tenth Biggest Mortgage Lender'", *Financial Times*, 31 August 2019.

[16] Melinda Cooper, *Family Values: Between Neoliberalism and the New Social Conservatism* (New York: Zone Books, 2017).

[17] Andrew Baker et al., *Against Hollow Firms: Repurposing the Corporation for a More Resilient Economy* (Sheffield: Centre for Research on Accounting and Finance in Context, 2020); Christophers, *Rentier Capitalism*.

riches today. This liquidity is then used to acquire more assets and concentrate gains among top executives and already-wealthy shareholders. The insistence that shareholder value must be maximised is because high share prices are a basis for leveraging corporate balance sheets and rewarding company insiders. Again, the post-crisis period is instructive. The UK's 100 biggest non-financial firms paid out £400 billion in dividends to manager-shareholders between 2011 and 2018, 68% of their profits over that period.[18] Another £61 billion was spent on share buybacks, concentrating control among the managerial elite and lifting the prices of the shares in which they were enumerated. Along the way, companies borrowed greatly, with UK-listed company borrowing reaching a record £443 billion by 2018, to ensure the cash flow needed to make all these payouts.[19] Since 2008 FTSE 100 returns to manager-shareholders rose by 56%, while the median wage for UK workers increased by just 8.8%, the k-shape reproducing.[20]

The result of this leveraged model is that debt of all kinds has grown since 2008. The public debt jumped to pay for the bank bailout and has increased ever since to reach £1.89 trillion (85% of GDP) by the eve of the pandemic. At the same time household debt was £1.8 trillion (84% of GDP), 91% of which was property debt,[21] and UK households were borrowing 130%

---

[18] Mathew Lawrence et al., *Commoning the Company* (London: Common Wealth, April 2020).

[19] By 2018, UK-listed company borrowing had reached a record £443.2 billion. Data from Link Asset Services, *UK plc Debt Monitor*. No. 2. (August 2019).

[20] Lawrence et al., *Commoning*.

[21] ONS, "Household Debt in Great Britain: April 2016 to March 2018", 5 December 2019.

of their incomes. Non-financial company debt was £1.6 trillion (72% of GDP)[22] and most tellingly financial corporations had liabilities worth £5.13 trillion (185% of GDP).[23] In all, the UK's total liabilities by the end of 2019 was 447% of GDP.[24] A tower of debt piled unsteadily (or so it seemed) on a clapped-out economy.

This is what makes the central bank such a potent force in contemporary capitalism. Its vast balance sheets can help breathe credibility into the debts of others and keep systemic leverage propped up. At any time it looks like an asset may stop trading and deleveraging begin, it can step in, promise to buy and sustain the asset prices that allow debts to keep flowing and payments to keep being made. This is what happened haphazardly in 2008 and decisively again in 2020. Central banks were less a 'lender of last resort' than the ultimate dealers of last resort, promising to buy when nobody else would.

This backdrop is vital to understanding the economic impact of the pandemic and the policymaker response. What stopped the economy as a whole from keeling over in the last 40 years – and what also sharpened the k-shape inequality between the wealthy and the rest – was the promise

---

[22] BIS, "BIS Statistics Explorer: United Kingdom Debt Securities Issues and Amounts Outstanding: Table C3", 14 September 2021; ONS, "UK National Accounts, The Blue Book Time Series", 30 October 2020.

[23] Ibid.

[24] BIS, "BIS Statistics Explorer: United Kingdom Debt Securities Issues and Amounts Outstanding: Table C3"; ONS, "UK National Accounts, The Blue Book Time Series." Calculations by Jack Cregan, Nuffield Department of Medicine, University of Oxford, United Kingdom.

that tomorrow things will improve, and debt could make do until then. Sunak's claim of a 'temporary disruption' was how political and financial elites had been responding to disappointing economic indicators ever since the 1970s. The pandemic was the ultimate stress test for this economy of uneven promises and despite the disruption and immiseration, it held on.

The Lockdown Economy: Building the Bridge

The last global recession exploded out from the deep recesses of financial markets. On 9 August 2007, French bank BNP Paribas issued a press release announcing that it would suspend three of its funds that had invested in US mortgage-related securities. It was, they wrote, "impossible to value certain assets fairly, regardless of their quality or credit rating".[25] That is, they were suddenly unsure about whether their assets were actually worth anything, making their promises to investors suddenly worthless. It triggered a crisis in interbank short-term lending, a run on the banks' banking system. For all the upheaval it unleashed in the 'real' economy, 2008 was a *financial* crisis. The acronyms – CDOs, Repos, MBSs – spoke to how technical and faraway the crisis and its protagonists seemed from the 'real' economy. The Covid-19 shock was the very opposite: an overnight shutdown of shared physical workspaces. The very *concreteness* of economic action was the problem. And while in 2008 authorities had to act decisively to protect the real economy from financial market infection, 2020 saw the opposite.

---

[25] BNP Paribas, "BNP Paribas Investment Partners Temporally Suspends the Calculation of the Net Asset Value of the Following Funds", BNP Paribas Press Release, 9 August 2007.

Financial markets needed immediate protection from the consequences of the pandemic.

The lesson gleaned from 2008 was the systemic dangers of banks doubting each other. Financial relations are upheld on promises to pay being re-made with more promises and re-made again. This dense network of IOUs will hold only insofar as a bank can be convinced any IOU it buys can be sold again without trouble. In 2008 mortgage-backed securities, and financial products derived from them, like those that BNP Paribas felt unable to price, gradually became harder and harder to sell. At that moment their capacity to serve as a collateral that grounded the network of promises vanished.[26] Suddenly, a promise to pay was no longer enough. The time had come to actually do so, and at once financial market participants all moved in step to sell off their assets and acquire the safety of cash. It was the moment of *de*leveraging that the economic system could not abide.

The City

In the teeth of the Covid-19 shock a similar dynamic developed. By February 2020, with the first lockdowns in China and East Asia unfolding, investors made a 'flight to safety', pulling their money out of riskier investments and into safer assets like American and British government debt.[27] In the leveraged economy, even big investors are big borrowers. When uncertainty takes hold, they prefer to have assets on hand that can be readily exchanged into cash, in case repayment is required

---

[26] Neilson, *Minsky.*

[27] Bank of England, *Interim Financial Stability Report (May 2020)*, 5 May 2020.

and deleveraging begins. Accordingly, an estimated $103 billion was withdrawn from emerging markets assets between January and May 2020, most in the single month of March.[28] In doing so it exposed again how volatile and fickle investment into Global South economies can be. The promise that attracting free-flowing capital from investors in the North is the key to jump-starting international development proved empty.[29]

While emerging markets may have expected this, what followed was more of a shock. The February 'flight to safety' morphed rapidly into a March 'dash for cash' and even the financial system's safest assets were suddenly in doubt. The $20 trillion market in US federal government debt – Treasury Bills – was threatened as investors looked to sell their Treasury holdings and acquire cash. Though smaller than the US, the same happened to British government debt, the 'gilt' market. Investors that had bought UK gilts tried on mass to sell their holdings and get hold of cash instead. Yet they could find few buyers. The result was gilt prices dropped, the 'spread' between buy and sell prices widened, and the yield on UK government debt climbed rapidly. As this system-wide demand for liquidity grew, £25 billion was withdrawn from money market funds in eight days between 12 and 20 March.[30] With investors desperate for cash to make payments but nobody ready to supply it,

---

[28] OECD, *COVID-19 and Global Capital Flows* (Paris: OECD, 3 July 2020).

[29] IMF Blog, "Toward an Integrated Policy Framework for Open Economies", *IMF Blog*, 13 July 2020.

[30] Bank of England, "Seven Moments in Spring: Covid-19, Financial Markets and the Bank of England's Operations – Speech by Andrew Hauser", 4 June 2020.

interest rates on short-term money market lending jumped 30 basis points above Bank Rate.[31] For those leveraged investors dependent on short-term borrowing to finance their assets, this increase forced them to instead sell off their assets, putting yet more downward pressure on the price of government debt.[32] Collectively, if what happened to mortgage-derived bonds in 2008 happened to these government debt securities, the fall-out would have been uncontainable. The governor of the Bank of England, Andrew Bailey, later described it as "a situation where, in the worst element, the government would have struggled to fund itself in the short run".[33] It was an extraordinary admission.

With the very basis of government action under threat from panicked financial markets, central banks around the world took immediate, coordinated and bold interventionary action to undergird the promises of the state, and with that the leveraged economy as a whole. On 15 March 2020, the Federal Reserve announced a $500 billion fund to directly support the Treasury Bill market, and finding even this was not enough, a week later announced that $500 billion was to become '*unlimited*'. In effect, the central bank had promised to create near infinite amounts of new money to buy up state debt if nobody else would. Immediately this forged a floor under their price. Anyone holding US Treasury Bills knew they would always have a buyer if needed, and that promise was enough to reassure them against the need to fire-sale today. This was combined with a $200 billion fund to support government-backed

[31] Bank of England, *Interim Financial Stability Report (May 2020)*.

[32] Ibid.

[33] Chris Giles, "UK Government Almost Ran out of Funds, Says BoE Governor", *Financial Times*, 22 June 2020.

mortgage securities and \$300 billion to support credit to households and businesses.[34] On top of this came a phalanx of other monetary actions that made state liquidity available at just the moment when indebted actors feared they may need cash to pay up. The result was that by December 2020, the Fed's portfolio of financial securities had grown from \$3.9 trillion in March to \$6.6 trillion.[35] All to ensure asset prices sustained and the leveraged economy did not collapse.

The Bank of England followed the same path. On 19 March a special meeting of the Bank's monetary policy committee agreed to push base interest rates down 65 basis points to 0.1%. At the same time it announced a £200 billion asset purchase programme, which was followed a week later with a further £250 billion programme, all with money it had simply typed into existence. As a Bank economist later noted, "this was by far the largest and fastest single programme ever launched", equivalent to around a tenth of UK GDP and worth half of the Bank's entire existing QE portfolio.[36] The effect of this measure was that any gilt investor in need of cash could find a willing buyer at the Bank of England, and with that the market for government bonds was instantly calmed.[37] At the same time,

---

[34] Federal Reserve, "Federal Reserve Announces Extensive New Measures to Support the Economy", Board of Governors of the Federal Reserve System, 23 March 2020.

[35] Jeffrey Cheng, Tyler Powell, Dave Skidmore and David Wessel, "What's the Fed Doing in Response to the COVID-19 Crisis? What More Could It Do?", *Brookings* (blog), 30 March 2021.

[36] Bank of England, "Seven Moments in Spring", 7.

[37] Bank of England, *Interim Financial Stability Report (May 2020)*.

the Bank reactivated a scheme first launched in 2012 to lend 'unlimited amounts' at near zero percent interest to financial institutions in need.

These monetary schemes were acts of near alchemy. QE was first used in its modern form in the UK in 2009 as an 'unconventional' policy to buy £200 billion of government debt. Since then it has been used lots more, and in 2016 was deployed to buy even corporate debt, taking *private* financial assets onto the central bank's balance sheet. By the eve of the pandemic, the Bank had amassed £435 billion worth of assets through QE.[38] In the space of a few weeks in 2020 this was more than doubled again, making the Bank of England the single biggest investor in UK government debt, holding a third of the entire portfolio.[39] In simple terms, this meant the Bank was creating money to lend to the government. It was – and remains – the ultimate taboo of public finance but had become thoroughly conventional.

Through these programmes of monetary intervention, central banks worked as the ultimate guarantors of the leveraged economy. They made the ultimate promise to uphold the promises of all others, allowing debts to multiply and cash to keep flowing. On the narrow terms of financial stability they were an unquestionable success, bridging the chasms in payments created by the pandemic, and buying time through the interruption. It was a remote, devolved form of governance that deferred questions about distributional impacts and normative purposes

[38] Bank of England, *IEO Evaluation of the Bank of England's Approach to Quantitative Easing* (Independent Evaluation Office, 13 January 2021).

[39] UK Debt Management Office, "Quarterly Review for Apr–Jun 2021" (UK DMO, 17 August 2021).

to another time. This was to become the template of the broader economic response to Covid-19.

The High Street

The shock to financial markets was dramatic and the government and central bank took drastic action to rescue it. It was, nonetheless, a drama played out largely behind closed doors and with limited immediate consequence to the everyday lives of the vast majority of the population. To stabilise financial markets, the Bank of England opened access to its vast balance sheets and promised the availability of liquidity without limits. It was a macro, systemic intervention into abstracted financial asset values that was easily made, and easily absorbed, by a financial system that, more than any other sector, was used to dealing in promises. What worked in the City, though, was not as smooth on the high street, where the spatial politics we described in Chapter 1 was viscerally felt.

Policymakers wanted to build a financial bridge over the interruption and ensure 'otherwise viable companies' would not 'lose access to finance' and be forced into liquidation.[40] There was a need to stop a crisis of liquidity becoming a crisis of solvency. By casting the economic problem as a temporary crisis of cash flow – one to which all shutdown firms were equally subjected – the more endemic problems and inequities were ignored. These were hard to grasp from a distance. 'The economy' can easily look like a coherent system of interlocking balance sheets or statistical aggregates like 'GDP' and 'unemployment' but, on the ground, the differences between sectors, firms and geographies are vast.

------

[40] Bank of England, "Seven Moments in Spring", 9.

The fortunes made by financiers in the City of London did not clearly boost the wellbeing of millions of health and care workers around the country, nor did the Amazon shopping revolution hit prime retail in city centres in the same way it did shopping centres in post-industrial towns. Similarly, the optimistic assumption of a 'v-shaped' recovery, which no doubt contributed to governmental complacency over the summer of 2020, failed to grapple with the fact that a virus – spread in confined spaces – threatened certain sectors of the economy far more gravely than others. When the lockdowns were belatedly announced these differences were quickly exposed, because this was a crisis emanating from the material and spatial reality of a pandemic, and not from the abstract calculations of the financial system. Debt bridges could work for some, but many lost out.

The shutdown of all but 'essential' retail unleashed the power of apps, websites and deliveries to fill the commercial vacuum. The street gave way to the platform. By the end of the first year of the pandemic, more than 50 companies and 11,000 stores around the country had closed down, including many of the marquee names of UK retail.[41] Oasis, Warehouse, Laura Ashley, Peacocks and Jaeger all fell into administration in 2020, as did the Arcadia group, which owned Topshop, Dorothy Perkins and Miss Selfridge. John Lewis made its first year-on-year loss and closed a third of its stores while Marks & Spencer suffered heavy losses too.[42] Alongside this, the move to homeworking meant urban centres that relied on

---

[41] Chris Rhodes and Georgina Hutton, "Retail Sector in the UK", Research Briefing (House of Commons Library, 21 June 2021).

[42] Sarah Butler, "John Lewis to Close Eight More Stores, Putting 1,500 Jobs at Risk", *The Guardian*, 24 March 2021.

office-worker commuters and tourists were hit hard. This so-called 'Pret Economy' of food outlets in high-rent office areas was increasingly unviable. The size and resilience of the big café and restaurant chains was enough to see many survive, but the high-street hospitality sector as a whole took a batter-ing. Nearly 10,000 bars, pubs, restaurants and clubs had gone under by the spring of 2021, taking 180,000 retail and hospital-ity jobs with them.[43]

More and more consumers preferred online delivery to an in-shop experience and the pandemic accelerated the trend. Food-delivery platforms like UberEats and Deliveroo gained millions of customers in the first few months of the lockdown, which furthered the growth of delivery-only 'dark kitchens.'[44] More broadly, the proportion of internet sales, which had grown from under 5% of all retail in 2008 to around 20% before the pandemic, almost doubled by the end of 2021.[45] Online entertainment followed the same trend. Stuck indoors, peo-ple depended on Netflix, Amazon Prime and other platform sites for entertainment. Though a demonstration of the basic necessity of arts and culture, the sector as whole was badly hit and barely supported. Bigger venues successfully tapped the government's Cultural Recovery Fund distributed by the Arts Council, and places like the National Theatre streamed live shows through Google-owned YouTube, but community and

---

[43] USDAW, "How Many Retail Job Losses Does It Take for the Government to Act?", 11 February 2021.

[44] Alice Hancock and Tim Bradshaw, "Can Food Delivery Services Save UK Restaurants?" *Financial Times*, 28 November 2020.

[45] ONS, "Internet Sales as a Percentage of Total Retail Sales (Ratio) (%)", 17 September 2021.

independent arts suffered. 70% of theatres and production companies, and 93% of grassroots music venues were expected to close permanently by the end of 2021.[46] Meanwhile, Nevill Holt Opera, established on his own country estate by the founder of Carphone Warehouse, Tory donor and close friend of Boris Johnson, David Ross (worth £650 million), received an emergency £100,000.

Inevitably, these cuts to high-street income worked their way up the chain of payments to hit real estate landlords and investors too. With income stopped overnight, full rental payment was impossible. So in an instructive move, the government banned evictions on commercial property when it announced the first lockdown, and tenants instead amassed large rental debts. From the first lockdown to the summer of 2021, £6.4 billion of commercial rent arrears had built up,[47] mostly in the hospitality (£2.5 billion) and retail (£3 billion) sectors.[48] These delayed payments were debts that ensured more high-street companies did not go bust. But without a moratorium and renegotiation of terms, or yet more borrowing, many more firms could go under. The creeping extinction of both familiar shops and independent arts are a likely a fundamental shift to character of the high street and, coupled with

---

[46] Digital, Culture, Media and Sport Select Committee, "Culture, Tourism and Sport Bring Us Together in a Shared Experience", House of Commons, 23 July 2021.

[47] George Hammond and Alice Hancock, "Unpaid Rent: The £6.4bn Dispute That Will Shape the UK High Street", *Financial Times*, 12 August 2021.

[48] Treasury Committee, "Oral Evidence: Economic Impact of Coronavirus", House of Commons, HC 306, 7 June 2021, https://committees.parliament.uk/oralevidence/2319/html/.

the impacts on work that we discuss in the next chapter, the nature of urban space.

The Response

The hit to the high street was profound but the political technology that forestalled more outright economic collapse was debt. The government and Bank of England together committed to support which by the autumn of 2021 was expected to be worth £370 billion.[49] Across the economy, from big businesses to small, and from high-income earners to low, liquidity was provided on mass. This money, some in the form of grants and tax holidays, and lots in the form of debt, replaced flows of income payments suspended by the shutdown with flows of credit payments instead. This way, they ensured most companies and citizens would not be forced to make asset sales to survive. For some big businesses this was a bonanza of free liquidity. Corporate giants got conditionality-free public support they did not need. But for others, public support was insufficient, with hospitality and retail companies in particular given small grants worth far less than the incomes lost and costs they still faced. Instead, it was private debt – backed by the public balance sheet – that became the crucial 'bridge' to safety politicians had promised.

This came in the form of state-sponsored loan programmes established during the first lockdown which worked by government entering into costly partnerships with high-street banks.[50] Companies took out emergency loans from the banks at 2.5% interest, and the government committed to

---

[49] NAO, "Covid-19 Cost Data" (accessed 25 September 2021).
[50] The CLBILS, CBILS, BBLS and Future Fund.

guarantee the loan, pay the interest and pay the arrangement fees the banks charged. Given the Bank of England had set base interest rates to 0.1%, this was another significant subsidy to the big banks.[51] By the autumn of 2021, £129 billion had been lent to almost two million companies, mostly the SMEs that make up the vast majority of UK business.[52] These Treasury-supported schemes were also complemented by a raft of measures taken by the Bank of England to provide direct support to the largest corporations. During the first lockdown, the Bank established a special facility which provided condition-free loans to companies like British Airways, G4S, chemicals giant BASF and car manufacturer Nissan. Overall, £37 billion was lent to 107 companies through the scheme.[53]

The idea in all of this was for debt to substitute for actual income that businesses were not receiving. It was predicated on the belief that the pandemic delayed economic activity rather than terminating it altogether. Alongside these substitutes for private income, government interventions suspended many of the typical payments businesses would expect to make. VAT was deferred, business rates were suspended, and of course wages and sick pay were covered by the furlough system.

---

[51] British Business Bank, "Our Programmes", www.british-business-bank.co.uk/ (accessed 25 September 2021).

[52] NAO, "Covid-19 Cost Data". COVID-19 cost tracker, https://nao-mesh.shinyapps.io/Covid_cost_tracker/ (accessed 25 September 2021); James Hurley et al., *Impacts of the Covid-19 Crisis: Evidence from 2 Million UK SMEs*, Bank of England Working Papers (11 June 2021).

[53] Bank of England, "Covid Corporate Financing Facility (CCFF)", 20 August 2021.

Simply, the government was helping businesses make their payments in emergency conditions and thereby keeping them alive. The problem remained, though, of what would happen when the schemes ended. From the moment the grant, loan and furlough schemes opened in March 2020, there was a lingering threat of a 'cliff-edge' moment when the schemes came to their scheduled end a year later. Indeed, 15% of UK companies warned they could go bankrupt within three months after the loan schemes stopped.[54] The smallest businesses felt most exposed, and expert reports warned almost 400,000 companies could fail.[55]

Yet, as has become a quirk of the UK's endlessly patched-up debt-based model, the cliff-edge never seemed to arrive. The initial 'business interruption' and 'bounceback' loan schemes were replaced in April 2021 with a Recovery Loan Scheme, furlough was extended again, and the success of the vaccine roll-out buoyed confidence. Of course, all the debt was still there – and indeed was growing – but the idea that it must be repaid was pushed forward to another time. Government liquidity came from a seemingly bottomless well, and could again be used to kick the crisis of private sector solvency down the road. This fiscal and monetary flexibility became a defining feature of how governments called in support from the private sector to deliver their Covid-19 response.

---

[54] ONS, "Business Insights and Impact on the UK Economy", 7 January 2021.

[55] Peter Lambert and John Van Reenen, "A Major Wave of UK Business Closures by April 2021? The Scale of the Problem and What Can Be Done", Covid-19 Analysis Series (London: Centre for Economic Performance, January 2021).

Public Money, Public Services, Private Gain

Underwriting the mountain of private and local authority debt was the effectively inexhaustible well of value that is the central bank's balance sheet. In a moment that threatened to unravel the webs of debt, the central bank emerged as what the cultural theorist Joseph Vogl described as the 'government of last resort'.[56] As we detailed in Chapter 1, public debt, whether issued explicitly through publicly acknowledged fiscal commitments or technocratically through the independent central bank money creation, radically increased through the pandemic response. This should, perhaps, have been difficult for the governing Conservative Party that had for years styled itself as the guardians of fiscal probity. While the reality has never matched this rhetoric, it remains a deeply held assumption of British politics. But under the pandemic conditions, that was laid to waste. The government borrowed a peacetime record £303 billion in the first full financial year of the crisis and showered spending on the friends, well-wishers and 'contract rentiers' that surrounded Johnson's administration.[57] The largesse revealed just how reliant the UK's public infrastructure was on the private sector to complete basic functions of government like security and wellbeing (we return to this in Chapter 4), and just how lucrative a business model this could be for some companies. The outsourcing industry sits at the interface of financial leverage and elite legal expertise, a highly lucrative combination that has become – for a handful of companies – a seemingly risk-free way of sucking money out of the

---

[56] Vogl, *The Ascendancy of Finance*, 121.
[57] ONS, "Public Sector Finances Tables 1 to 10: Appendix A", 23 April 2021.

state balance sheet, and passing it into private hands. Legal and social intimacy with the government became an economic resource to be mined, without limit.

Prior to Covid-19, the UK was often lauded as a model of how to 'partner' public and private services. In 2019, the World Economic Forum ranked the UK (and the US) as one of the best prepared countries in the world for tackling a pandemic, and the UK had itself undertaken eight separate pandemic preparation measures from 1997 to 2017.[58] But outsourcing had left the state lacking the capacity to act in a way that could secure the nation's health. Whitehall was dependent on private companies for public services, who in turn were themselves dependent on government contracts for their private profit.

The NHS Test and Trace system was the case that best captured this failing arrangement. The system cost £37 billion over two years, was designed to be wholly centralised, and a year into the pandemic had been found by the National Audit Office (NAO) to have had no effect in combating Covid-19 in England. Though run notionally in the public sector it had been designed and implemented in large part by private companies. Deloitte helped design the programme, design the app, assist and expand the tracing infrastructure, and provide tracing services. These were short-term contracts worth £1 million a day at one point, and nearly £279 million overall.[59] (The pandemic more broadly was a boon for consultants who by May

---

[58] Lee Jones and Shahar Hameiri, "COVID-19 and the Failure of the Neoliberal Regulatory State", *Review of International Political Economy* (1 March 2021), doi:10.1080/09692290.2021.1892798, 2.

[59] Michael O'Dwyer, "Consultants Awarded over £600m of UK Covid Contracts", *Financial Times*, 4 May 2021.

2021 had been handed £600 million of government Covid-19 contracts – though in reality this is an underestimate since many contractual details went unreported.) The outsourcing firm G4S – paid £57 million – were tasked with logistical support; Sodexo were paid £223 million to manage the Covid-19 testing facilities; sourcing and developing the testing equipment was done by private providers; Sitel (paid £84 million), and Serco (paid up to £400 million) then managed the contract tracing, which it then subcontracted to dozens of other firms, who then hired unspecialised workers on wages as low as £8.71 an hour to undertake contract tracing.[60] The definitive final costs are yet to be established but as the Public Accounts Committee reported, it was an "unimaginable" amount to spend on system that failed to make a "measurable difference" to the spread of the pandemic.[61]

Test and Trace was emblematic, but by June 2021 £31 billion of Covid-19 contracts had been awarded,[62] most without any kind of competitive tender.[63] Much of this went to suppliers of personal protective equipment (PPE) and test kits, but private healthcare providers were also paid handsomely to support an

---

[60] Josh Halliday, "England's Covid Test and Trace Relying on Inexperienced and Poorly Trained Staff", *The Guardian*, 14 December 2020.

[61] House of Commons Public Accounts Committee, "Covid-19: Test, Track and Trace (Part 1)", Forty-Seventh Report of Session 2019–21, House of Commons, 10 March 2021.

[62] Tussell Database, "Latest Updates on UK Government COVID-19 Contracts and Spending", www.tussell.com/insights/covid (accessed 2 June 2021).

[63] O'Dwyer, "Consultants Awarded over £600m of UK Covid Contracts".

NHS whose capacity had been shredded by a decade of real-terms funding cuts. Even before the pandemic, private hospitals in the UK earned 25% of their income from government deals, and care homes – the key site for so many Covid-19-related deaths – earned 40% of their income from government.[64] In the early part of the pandemic, private providers were paid almost £400 million a month to support NHS capacity, and in March 2021 almost the entire private healthcare market signed up to a further four-year deal worth up to £10 billion, cementing their presence in a notionally nationalised health service.[65]

The webs of collaboration between the companies winning contracts and Conservative Party MPs, Lords and organisations was variously described as a 'chumocracy', 'cronyism', 'sleaze' and more plainly 'corruption'. While true, the Covid-19 contracts were also an exaggeration on the normal functioning of the British state. For decades now, private sector companies have looked to embed themselves into the delivery and increasingly the design of the public sector. When Serco CEO Rupert Soames emailed his staff to describe how Covid-19 contracts could "go a long way in cementing the position of the private sector companies in the public-sector supply chain", he was speaking about a business model that was already well established. Sure enough, by June 2021 Serco were expecting a 50% increase in profits on the back of its vast Covid-19 contracts.[66]

---

[64] Gavin Poynter, *The Political Economy of State Intervention: Conserving Capital over the West's Long Depression* (London: Routledge, 2020), 106, 110.

[65] Sarah Neville and Gill Plimmer, "NHS and Private Sector Forge New Partnerships to Clear Patient Backlog", *Financial Times*, 25 April 2021.

[66] Joanna Partridge, "Serco Expects 50% Jump in Profits on Back of Covid Contracts", *The Guardian*, 30 June 2021.

As we noted in Chapter 1, firms like Serco, Greensill, G4S and before its collapse Carillion, are specialists not just in the delivery of 'professional services', but more emphatically in the winning of government contracts. The health of many such private sector firms is predicated on their capacity to wring cash out of the public sector. Just as private financial markets relied on the Bank of England's balance sheet, blurring any clear notion of separate public and private sectors, here the state's reliance on the private sector to deliver public services did the same thing. Political economists have for years urged against the depiction of political life in the binaries of markets and states, and private and public. It underpins a wholly mistaken notion that the political Right favours markets and the political Left favours the state. The reality is that class cuts through, across and reproduces these boundaries.

Conclusion: Who Gains When Others Pay?

The economic counter to Covid-19 was gargantuan. The vast fiscal commitment, £450 billion asset purchase programme, rock-bottom base interest rate, and multitude of state-backed bank loans combined as a tidal wave of liquidity. Its effect was to forestall a more profound crisis and uphold the status quo. It was a daring, innovative and expensive way to change as little as possible. No conditions were attached, no difficult choices were made and, crucially, to the already financially advantaged, more was given. With the crisis understood – from the very start – as a singular problem of cash flow, the state and central bank combined to provide a bottomless well of liquidity. Though politicians spoke about levelling up, in practice the Covid-19 response only reinforced the inequity that defined the UK economy before the pandemic.

Analysis of the first lockdown support showed that nearly *half* of the furlough payments were spent, ultimately, on rent and debt repayments.[67] This was money borrowed by the state that flowed straight to landlords and banks. For cash-rich companies, state support allowed them to avoid drawing down their savings or selling their assets, and instead meant they could leverage up to pay out to executives and investors through share buybacks and dividend payments. Though some FTSE 100 firms suspended shareholder pay-outs, most did not. The monetary stimulus ensured the stock market continued on the skywards trajectory it has been on since 2008.

The already-rich spent the pandemic working from nice homes, but were unable to spend on travel to work, foreign holidays, office lunches, and restaurant dinners. Instead, they saved. The top quartile of earners found they were saving close to £400 a month more than normal in the six months from the March lockdown, and many were saving much more. The aggregate savings rate jumped to 29%, the highest since records began in the 1970s.[68] The poorest fifth, however, found themselves needing expensive unsecured debt to make basic payments. In the fiscal free-for-all that saw Conservative Party donors showered with government spending, those left on Universal Credit and Statutory Sick Pay were punished. The public sector workers whose importance was revealed throughout the pandemic saw their real pay continue to fall. Nurses were given a 3% pay rise (largely cancelled out by

---

[67] Christine Berry, Laurie Macfarlane and Shreya Nanda, *Who Wins and Who Pays? Rentier Power and the Covid Crisis* (London: IPPR, 13 May 2020).

[68] Brigid Francis-Devine, "Coronavirus: Impact on Household Savings and Debt", Briefing Paper (House of Commons Library, 13 January 2021).

inflation), which itself was 3% more than most of the other key workers on who society depended.

Many of the central characteristics of the UK economy, as they had emerged over previous decades, were not fundamentally endangered by the pandemic, but further embedded. The poorest families took on more debts to pay essential costs, while a record 24 new billionaires were created in the UK in 2021.[69] Their combined wealth grew by more than a fifth, while the incomes of the average household stagnated. The public debt was used to finance an £850 million subsidy to restaurant goers, but care workers working in unsafe conditions were paid near minimum wages.[70] House prices reached record highs,[71] while foodbanks delivered 2.5 million emergency parcels, more than a third more than the previous year.[72] As we have argued, Covid-19's effect has been photosynthetic: to both illuminate tendencies in our political economy, and to nurture their ongoing growth.

An orthodox view of economics and economic policy suggests that 'state' and 'market' exist in parallel to each other, with the former intervening periodically when markets fail. Our account is entirely different, namely that the UK's political economy melds state and market together, generating a deeply resourceful and resilient set of interlocking financial and legal relationships. Promises can be made, a brighter future (for

---

[69] Jasper Jolly, "Number of Billionaires in UK Reached New Record during Covid Crisis", *The Guardian*, 21 May 2021.

[70] NAO, "Covid-19 Cost Data".

[71] Kalyeena Makortoff, "UK House Prices 'Likely to Keep Rising Despite Hitting Record High'", *The Guardian*, 7 June 2021.

[72] Trussell Trust, "The Trussell Trust – End of Year Stats", The Trussell Trust (blog), 2020.

some) can be typed into existence today, and the cliff-edge can always wait for another day.

Certain types of assets that were already pivotal to the UK's over-leveraged economy became even more important, where they enabled the spatial reconfigurations and emergency measures that Covid-19 demanded. The most lucrative position to acquire in an economy such as the UK's is not that of a certain competitor in a certain sector, but to occupy a quasi-infrastructural status, as the necessary condition of basic social and economic activity. Digital platforms and outsourcing contractors were able to exploit the contingent nature of the pandemic to insert themselves into such a role. But above all, the economy and its pathologies have revolved around the asset that became, thanks to Covid-19, yet more fundamental to social and psychological wellbeing, and yet more divisive in its financial effects: housing. The confinements of lockdown were unequally experienced, depending on domestic space, while the monetary response to lockdown paid highly unequal dividends, depending on one's personal or family balance sheet. This social settlement did not simply survive the upheavals of 2020–21, but was publicly affirmed by them.

3

New Divisions of Labour: The Politics of 'Flexibility'

No area of economic activity was disrupted as directly or as significantly by Covid-19 as work. The health imperative during successive waves of the virus was to stop people from moving about, making their commutes and mixing in workplaces. As a result, the nature of work was highlighted, and in many cases fundamentally changed. New focus was brought to where we do it, how we do it and what social function it fulfils, both for our wellbeing and needs as individuals and what counts or is valued by society as valuable work. It also intensified existing inequalities, and revealed new ones, in terms of who could continue to work safely and who was exposed to the virus, who had the resources to weather the pandemic and lockdowns better and who retained their job.

When the first lockdown occurred in March 2020, there was a sudden popular realisation of whose work was essential to the everyday functioning of society. The conception of who is a frontline or 'key' worker expanded to include not only the health workers risking their lives to care for others, but also those jobs usually considered 'unskilled' such as delivery drivers, cleaners and supermarket workers. That many of these jobs are performed under conditions of low pay, high insecurity and lack of autonomy clashed with the recognition that was now being attributed to them in the media. This is not, either, just the case for those working in the 'gig economy' or sectors more readily associated with insecurity. The proliferation of 'flexibility' across the labour market in recent decades means that such working conditions and rewards might be found as much among care home staff as they are among logistics workers or retail assistants.

For many others, the pandemic meant that their homes became their workplaces, and the office faded from view as social distancing and lockdown measures were strengthened. These workers were relatively privileged in that they were less exposed to the virus during their commutes or at work. But they experienced work very differently depending on the availability of space at home and the care responsibilities placed on them alongside their work. Though homeworking was not a new phenomenon, the greater numbers forced into it during the pandemic provoked concerns about the spaces and conditions under which it takes place and debates about the future of the office. Where the space of the home was previously treated as a private realm separate from 'the economy' – despite it being the key site for the essential and typically unpaid 'social reproductive' labour of domestic work and child-rearing – it took centre stage during the periods of lockdown. As it did so, more and more people struggled to match the promise of flexible homeworking to the realities it presented. This holds the potential to politicise the terms of remote work, and open up possibilities for new ones.

At the heart of the UK's labour market model, as it had become entrenched over the four decades prior to 2020, lie contradictory and often elusive promises of flexibility. Champions of the flexible labour market model point to the fact that it has delivered record employment rates, even through a decade of austerity and post-recessionary conditions.[1] Yet it shaped a pre-pandemic labour market that left many groups fundamentally insecure and poorly paid. It may be true that the distinct characteristics of the UK's approach to labour regulation and social security have contributed to raising the employment rate in the past. But the combination of the UK's flexible labour market and a decade of government cuts to benefits and services have contributed to the extreme inequalities that were exacerbated by the pandemic, primarily hitting women, working-class, young and racialised minority populations.

Where some experienced an intensification of work during the pandemic – either as key workers and/or working from home – others were thrown into unemployment or inactivity. Rates of redundancy rose at a faster speed than during the 2008/9 financial crisis, and mostly fell on young and racialised minority populations.[2] Before the pandemic, the UK unemployment protection system supported labour market flexibility by treating work as the best form of welfare – variously known as a 'work-first', 'welfare-to-work' or 'workfare' model – and shifting the responsibility of being

---

[1] Theresa May boasted of a record high 76.1% employment rate in March 2019, the highest since records began in 1971 and 3 million more workers than in 2008. Yet, as economists noted at the time, the greater number in work was mostly the result of households compensating for a historic decline in their incomes. Nicholas Mairs, "Boost for Theresa May as Number of People in Work Hits New All-Time High", *Politics Home*, 19 March 2019; Torsten Bell, "Feel Poor, Work More – The Real Reason Behind Britain's Record Employment", Resolution Foundation, 13 November 2019.

[2] ONS, "Coronavirus and Redundancies in the UK Labour Market", 19 February 2021.

out of work onto individuals, compelling benefit claimants back into what was often poor-quality, low-paid work.[3] But during the Covid-19 crisis, this 'work-first' approach became untenable, instantly demolishing the central ideological tenet of the post-Thatcher welfare state. It was both impossible to suggest that the climbing levels of unemployment were voluntary, and not an option to suggest that people look harder for jobs in sectors that were largely if not completely shut down. Allowing a flexible labour market to adjust to the crisis without substantial government intervention would have been disastrous and self-destructive on health grounds.

The scale and nature of the unemployment crisis provoked the government to freeze huge swathes of the labour market for periods of time by placing millions of workers on 'furlough.' A temporary stay (until July 2020) was also put on sanctions and conditionality related to claiming benefits, such as mandatory work search and work availability requirements for Universal Credit and deductions for overpayments. For some, then, the system of unemployment protection shifted from one in which they were compelled *into* work to one in which they were compelled *not* to work. The furlough scheme no doubt protected millions of jobs and was seen as one of the most successful (not to mention popular) policy responses to

---

[3] Nick Taylor, "A Job, Any Job: The UK Benefits System and Employment Services in an Age of Austerity", *Observatoire de La Société Britannique*, 19 (1 October 2017): 267–285; Katy Jones, "Active Labour Market Policy in a Post-Covid UK: Moving Beyond a 'Work First' Approach". In Philip McCann and Tim Vorley (Eds.), *Productivity and the Pandemic: Challenges and Insights from Covid-19* (Cheltenham: Edward Elgar, 2021).

the economic crisis induced by the pandemic. Yet the manner of its implementation – last-minute extensions to the scheme, insufficient coverage for the self-employed – meant that many still lost their jobs.

The theme at the centre of this chapter is the role of flexibility in the UK's labour market, and the relationship that different groups have to this ideal. As critics of capitalism have always stressed, the labour market is a uniquely political sphere of economic activity, in which different actors are able to mobilise varying degrees of power to assert their interests, or not as the case may be. Some get to dictate the terms of work; others have them dictated for them. Inequalities in power determine inequalities in income, dignity and wellbeing. This underlying truth, which is concealed by optimistic appeals to 'flexibility', has rarely been made more visible than over the course of 2020–21. This chapter focuses especially on the unequal bargain and often false promises built into the message of flexibility, arguing that in the UK labour market flexibility is often for employers and not employees. How you are positioned in this bargain – because of your occupation, age, gender, race or class – determined the conditions under which you continued to work during the pandemic and whether you held onto a job at all. And even though interventions like furlough intentionally disrupted the flexible adjustment of the labour market to the shock of Covid-19, many were still left at the mercy of flexibility.

The photosynthetic effect of Covid-19 has been writ large in the case of work and labour markets. Rarely have the long-standing, gendered contradictions between paid and unpaid work been as visible or as painful as during lockdowns, when informal caring responsibilities co-existed in the same time and space as formal employment obligations. Rarely has the social contribution of certain workers been so publicly recognised, and the failure of labour markets to adequately reflect that value so stark. Where the labour market legacy of the pandemic will likely be greatest concerns the accelerating crisis of space that we identified in Chapter 1. The continued ascendency of the household as the pivotal node in our economic system not only concerns the exalted financial status of housing, but also now its growing role as a space of paid (as well as unpaid) work, with all of the additional stressors and forms of managerial intrusion that go with that. The associated spatial effects of platformisation both embed the home into networks of production, and decentralise work in the form of the 'gig economy'. The home–platform combination thus generates the spatial logic of work whose reach was greatly expanded with the aid of Covid-19.

The rest of the chapter is structured as follows. In the next section, we explore the background labour market conditions to the pandemic, focusing on the development of a flexible labour market in favour of 'employer discretion'. It surveys the rise of new and established forms of contingent work and their distribution among particular groups in society. Finally, it suggests that the welfare system that operated in sync with labour market flexibility, and which was further stripped back through a decade of austerity, left these groups all the more vulnerable to the pandemic's economic and public health crisis. The second section charts a narrative of the crisis, concentrating on key workers, homeworking, and unemployment and the furlough scheme. It points to the intersecting inequalities that have shaped who continues to work and who doesn't, and under what conditions. The chapter then steps back to ask what has been revealed in the UK's economic model – what structural issues or pathologies have been exposed and how has flexible and insecure work shaped the crisis? It concludes by suggesting that the way we understand some forms of 'key' work may have changed the popular imagination of socially useful work, and considering whether the prominent shift to homeworking may have opened up the politics of flexible working in new ways.

Failing to Work: Labour Markets Before the Pandemic

A landmark ruling by the UK Supreme Court in 2021, which judged that Uber drivers are indeed 'workers' and not merely 'independent contractors', is striking for the unusual direction of travel it signalled regarding employment relations.[4] Worker status grants drivers the minimum wage, paid annual leave, and a range of other employment protections that have so far been denied to those in the 'gig economy'. It was a remarkable outcome, given that the trend in employment law and regulation in the UK had been for employers to progressively relinquish such responsibilities and protections, while simultaneously increasing control and flexibility over other aspects of employment contracts and conditions.[5] The background conditions to the pandemic set the scene for how the crisis impacted the labour market and deepened entrenched inequalities. This section charts some of the recent history to the UK labour market in pandemic times, identifying the divisions that have been actively encouraged through a deepening and broadening of flexibility for some, and flexible insecurity for others.

---

[4] Charlie Rae, "What Does the Supreme Court Decision in the Uber Case Mean for Employers?", *Shoosmiths*, 3 March 2021.

[5] Fair Work, *The Gig Economy and COVID-19: Looking Ahead* (Oxford: The Fair Work Project, September 2020), 3.

While there has been a general trend towards liberalisation across advanced economies since the 1970s, the UK is considered an extreme case for the speed and scale at which it dismantled collective forms of regulating its labour market and industrial relations under a series of Conservative governments. The coming to power of the political Right and the Thatcherite project in the 1980s transformed the UK's system of industrial relations. The state took the lead in demolishing the trade union movement's influence and the systems of collective bargaining that covered a large part of the labour market, while opening up the economy to international competition, public enterprises to privatisation and launching an attack on 'welfare dependency'. This process ultimately strengthened 'employer discretion' in the labour market – over wage determination, personnel management, work organisation and hiring and firing practices – which is the defining characteristic of a liberalised system of industrial relations.[6]

This was a trend that was only partially tempered by New Labour governments between 1997–2010 which advocated for a deregulated, 'flexible' labour market to boost employment and deliver economic prosperity. They did so while increasing social spending, introducing some new employment protections and redistributing – sometimes by stealth, such as through tax credits – to low and middle-income households. This drove a convergence of tax, social security and employment law, with the goal of maximising the employment rate.[7]

---

[6] Lucio Baccaro and Chris Howell, *Trajectories of Neoliberal Transformation* (Cambridge: Cambridge University Press, 2017), 20.

[7] Paul Davies and Mark Freedland, *Towards a Flexible Labour Market: Labour Legislation and Regulation since the 1990s* (Oxford: Oxford University Press, 2007), 163.

The Conservative-Liberal Democrat Coalition Government (2010-15) continued to champion the liberalisation process while overseeing a historic period of austerity and erosion of securities in the labour market and welfare system. It attempted to legitimate radical and widespread spending cuts through a 'two nations' project, which pitted 'hardworking people' against benefit claimants, and private sector employees against public sector employees.[8] The post-2010 response to the financial crisis was shaped by this vision, and as a result the UK saw an extraordinary stagnation in real wages compared to previous post-recessionary periods (of a duration unknown since the Industrial Revolution) and a building back of the economy through a form of 'regressive redistribution'.[9] With the ongoing protection of house prices and attacks on the welfare state and employment protections, this entrenched a model of British capitalism that privileges asset owners at the expense of labour, producing the 'k-shaped' growth we discussed in the previous chapter. These circumstances have contributed to the intense inequalities illuminated by the pandemic.

Flexibility and Contingent Work

It is important to understand some of the precise ways in which the labour market and welfare policy rendered certain

---

[8] Scott Lavery, *British Capitalism After the Crisis* (Basingstoke: Palgrave Macmillan, 2019), 157-161.

[9] Jeremy Green and Scott Lavery, "The Regressive Recovery: Distribution, Inequality and State Power in Britain's Post-Crisis Political Economy", *New Political Economy*, 20:6 (2015): 894-923.

sections of the population more vulnerable to the pandemic. Since the early 1990s, labour market flexibility has been advocated by a range of international actors such as the OECD and European Commission as a strategy to improve employment rates, competitiveness, earnings, productivity and job satisfaction. The UK was a particularly strong adopter of flexibility and took it up at the heart of its light touch approach to regulating the labour market.[10] The arguments for labour market flexibility have their corollary in a belief that enforcing stronger employment protections and labour market regulation will be burdensome for employers, reduce economic dynamism and drive up unemployment.

Such views were evident under the Coalition Government's efforts to cut 'red tape' as part of a wide-ranging parliamentary review of employment-related legislation, which recommended repealing or amending employment protections so that employers had the freedom to shed workers and remain competitive.[11] It was also an argument that pro-Brexit politicians and commentators made in seeking to divorce the country from European employment law such as the EU Working Time Directive. Indeed, in relation to European economic integration, the UK was historically subjected to a double dose of 'market fundamentalism' in so far as it both led the charge of labour market deregulation at home and resisted even mild

[10] Davies and Freedland, *Towards a Flexible Labour Market*, 239.

[11] Hannah Jameson, "The Beecroft Report: Pandering to Popular Perceptions of Over-Regulation", *The Political Quarterly*, 83:4 (2012): 838–843; Peter Scott and Steve Williams, "The Coalition Government and Employment Relations: Accelerated Neo-Liberalism and the Rise of Employer-Dominated Voluntarism", *Observatoire de La Société Britannique*, 15 (2014): 145–164.

efforts coming from the EU to protect workers from competitive international pressures.[12]

Flexibility in the UK labour market has therefore often been 'one-sided': flexibility for employers to hire and fire with greater discretion, set wages and manage their employees as they wish.[13] Some have pointed to the authoritarian or 'despotic' control this has given employers in workplaces of the 21st century, arguing that it constitutes a workplace regime of "private government ... [defined by] arbitrary, unaccountable power".[14] This is especially the case for those working in the expanding gig economy, who are managed digitally or work 'on demand' in forms of app-work (e.g. Uber, Deliveroo), crowdwork (e.g. Amazon Mechanical Turk, Fiverr) and capital platform work (e.g. Airbnb, Etsy).[15] Many of these workers became essential to the home delivery economy that serviced

---

[12] Jonathan Hopkin, "When Polanyi Met Farage: Market Fundamentalism, Economic Nationalism, and Britain's Exit from the European Union", *The British Journal of Politics and International Relations*, 19:3 (2017), 4.

[13] Matthew Taylor, *Good Work: The Taylor Review of Modern Working Practices* (London: Department for Business, Energy & Industrial Strategy, 2017), 116.

[14] Alex J. Wood, *Despotism on Demand: How Power Operates in the Flexible Workplace*, Illustrated edition (Ithaca: Cornell University Press, 2020); Elizabeth Anderson, *Private Government: How Employers Rule Our Lives* (Princeton; Oxford: Princeton University Press, 2017), 45.

[15] James Duggan et al., "Algorithmic Management and App-Work in the Gig Economy: A Research Agenda for Employment Relations and HRM", *Human Resource Management Journal*, 30:1 (2020): 114–132.

households in lockdown or working from home. They also represent one example of the evaporation of the so-called standard model of employment, which had greater limits on employer discretion. Though it was never universal, this model provided many people (mostly men) with a full-time, permanent job, a pension and a salary predicated as a 'family wage'.[16]

Forms of non-standard work such as those proliferating in the gig economy have contributed to blurring the lines between 'formal' and 'informal' parts of the UK labour market. A study in 2017 established that 4.4% of the population in Great Britain (2.8 million people) were working in the gig economy: the highest prevalence of such work in Europe.[17] By 2019, the gig economy workforce had doubled to an estimated 9.6% of the adult population (5.8 million people), the vast majority of whom were turning to this work not for their main job but as a 'top up' to their income from other work.[18] This sector has contributed to the proliferation of low productivity, low skill, insecure and poorly paid segments of the UK labour market.[19] But its impact has not been confined to these segments, in that elements of work organisation that characterise the gig economy – such as logging work hours or location

---

[16] Ursula Huws, *Reinventing the Welfare State: Digital Platforms and Public Policies* (London: Pluto Press, 2020), 30–32.

[17] Katriina Lepanjuuri, Robert Wishart and Peter Cornick, *The Characteristics of Those in the Gig Economy* (London: Department for Business, Energy & Industrial Strategy, February 2018).

[18] Huws, *Reinventing the Welfare State*, 35.

[19] Jill Rubery, Arjan Keizer and Damian Grimshaw, "Flexibility Bites Back: The Multiple and Hidden Costs of Flexible Employment Policies", *Human Resource Management Journal*, 26:3 (2016): 235–251.

through an app or website – have bled into 'standard' forms of employment.[20] Digital forms of management are increasingly widespread and workers are more likely than ever to be organised by, to communicate via or be monitored through digital interfaces. This suggests a general trend towards the 'platformisation' of work in the UK and elsewhere, which the pandemic has accelerated.[21]

Zero-hours contracts (ZHCs) have been a particularly egregious example of where flexibility has allowed insecurity to proliferate. Under these types of contract, workers have been offered no guaranteed hours while being prohibited from taking up work elsewhere (through so-called exclusivity clauses), been left in the dark about the terms of their contract, had their hours changed at short notice and been punished for not accepting extra hours.[22] Employee surveys show numbers of people on ZHCs climbing from 585,000 in 2013 to 974,000 in October–December 2019, or 3% of the workforce just before the pandemic.[23] Notably, areas of the labour market that have been badly affected by the pandemic have a high proportion of people on ZHCs, both in terms of industries hit by job losses (9% of workers in wholesale and retail and 23%

---

[20] Ursula Huws, Neil H. Spencer and Dag S. Syrdal, "Online, on Call: The Spread of Digitally Organised Just-in-Time Working and Its Implications for Standard Employment Models", *New Technology, Work and Employment*, 33:2 (2018): 113–129.

[21] Huws, *Reinventing the Welfare State*, 92–99.

[22] Vidhya Alakeson and Conor D'Arcy, *Zeroing In: Balancing Protection and Flexibility in the Reform of Zero-Hours Contracts* (London: Resolution Foundation, 2014).

[23] ONS, "EMP17: People in Employment on Zero Hours Contracts", 17 August 2021.

in accommodation and food were on ZHCs in late 2019) and those relied on for mitigating and responding to the health and care impacts of the pandemic (20% in health and social work).[24] This is especially the case for the social care sector where, for example, almost half (42%) of the domiciliary care workforce in 2020 were employed on ZHCs.[25]

Young people have been overrepresented in these rising forms of insecure, flexible work, for which they are often over-qualified, and have increasingly found themselves locked out of more permanent and secure jobs.[26] In 2019, for example, 9% of the UK workforce aged 16–24 were on a ZHC, three times the workforce average. This speaks to wider concerns around those born after 1980 being affected by 'systematic genera-tional inequality' in education, work, housing and welfare. Some authors have pointed to the need for a 'political econ-omy of generations' that addresses the unequal economic, cultural and political power relations between young and old, and explains the historically unprecedented decline in the living standards of the former.[27] A generational perspective

---

[24] Ibid.

[25] Skills for Care, *The State of the Adult Social Care Sector and Workforce 2020* (Leeds: Skills for Care, 2020).

[26] Craig Thorley and Will Cook, *Flexibility For Who? Millennials and Mental Health in the Modern Labour Market* (London: IPPR, 27 July 2017).

[27] Andy Green, *The Crisis for Young People: Generational Inequalities in Education, Work, Housing and Welfare* (Basingstoke: Palgrave Macmillan, 2017); Judith Bessant, *The Precarious Generation: A Political Economy of Young People* (Abingdon: Routledge, 2017).

that considers the political economic context of the last decade or so also goes a long way to revealing the reasons behind recently emergent political divides based on age.[28] It intersects, most obviously, with the divisions in the asset economy, especially around housing tenure, which in turn generate significant divisions as reflected in everything from voting behaviour to mental health. Young people are overwhelmingly priced out of home ownership today – four in ten millennials rent privately at aged 30, and 16% are likely to do so for their whole lives[29] – and high rents erode their already low income received from work.

The full scale of contingent work – broadly defined by conditional, on-demand and transitory employment – is difficult to estimate. But it is thought to comprise about a quarter of the workforce and has broadly been responsible for the UK's mythical 'record' employment rates.[30] Contingency across the UK labour market has been driven by rising self-employment, which climbed rapidly after the global financial crisis and accounted for just under half of employment growth between 2008 and 2020.[31] While self-employment might provide autonomy and other benefits and signal positive entrepreneurial

---

[28] Keir Milburn, *Generation Left*, 1st edition (Cambridge: Polity, 2019).

[29] Lindsay Judge and Daniel Tomlinson, *Home Improvements: Action to Address the Housing Challenges Faced by Young People* (London: Resolution Foundation, April 2018), 4.

[30] Abi Adams-Prassl, Jeremias Adams-Prassl and Diane Coyle, *Uber and Beyond: Policy Implications for the UK* (Cambridge: Bennett Institute for Public Policy, 2021).

[31] Adams-Prassl, Adams-Prassl and Coyle, *Uber and Beyond*, 6.

ambitions, there is evidence that its rise has been driven by falling job quality in organisational employment.[32] Unfortunately, once dissatisfied workers have escaped their previous jobs, self-employment itself does not always offer adequate security or wages. It has grown in relatively privileged areas such as IT, legal, accounting and other finance-related sectors. But sectors such as cleaning, retail, construction, taxi driving and hairdressing are said to be characterised by high levels of 'bogus self-employment', where, as per the case of Uber above, employers seek to categorise workers as autonomous despite exercising significant control over them.

The political strategy of intensifying labour market flexibility, at first glance, would seem to have delivered some of the benefits that were sought, principally in terms of numbers in employment. The UK's flexible labour market was declared the reason why it weathered the post-financial crisis recessionary period well after the unemployment rate peaked in late-2011 at 8.5% and dropped to around 5% at the end of 2015.[33] Flexibility, in this regard, has acted as something of an unspoken industrial strategy: give employers greater discretion to hire and fire and set the terms of engagement and they will create the right jobs in the right places. Yet stark regional inequalities, flatlining productivity, stagnation of incomes and the rise of contingent forms of work outlined above speak to a fundamentally different narrative.

Focusing on the quality and conditions of work, rather than the quantity of people in employment, gives us a different

---

[32] Andrew Henley, "The Rise of Self-Employment in the UK: Entrepreneurial Transmission or Declining Job Quality?", *Cambridge Journal of Economics*, 45:3 (2021): 457–486.
[33] OECD, *OECD Economic Surveys: United Kingdom 2015* (Paris: OECD, 2015), 8.

picture of the UK's labour market and its vulnerabilities going into the pandemic.[34] This prompts questioning of the numbers too. It is increasingly understood that the headline 'record' levels of employment obscure the absence of well-paying, decent jobs. The fact that wage growth has been historically low amid a recovering unemployment rate and rising *underemployment* (workers seeking more hours) suggests that the UK has in fact been far from full employment.[35] Governments will understandably seek to focus on unemployment figures when they cast policymakers in a positive light, but the record of the UK labour market in the decade prior to Covid-19 weakened the authority of 'unemployment' as a useful social and economic indicator.

Welfare, Austerity and 'Work First' Policy

A decade of austerity policies, which have eviscerated local government budgets and pared down the scale of an already strict benefit system, also formed the backdrop to the pandemic. The austerity measures had disproportionate effects based on class, race, gender and disability. Feminist economists have detailed how in the UK, women, and especially the most vulnerable women (lone mothers, single women pensioners and single women without children), bore the brunt of spending cuts and welfare changes.[36] Tax and welfare

---

[34] Pascale Bourquin and Tom Waters, *Jobs and Job Quality between the Eve of the Great Recession and the Eve of COVID-19* (London: Institute for Fiscal Studies, 25 June 2020).

[35] David G. Blanchflower, *Not Working: Where Have All the Good Jobs Gone?* (Oxford: Princeton University Press, 2019).

[36] Pearson and Elson, "Transcending the Impact of the Financial Crisis in the United Kingdom".

reforms had strong negative impacts on families with at least one disabled person, especially low-income households with a disabled child.[37] Racialised minority households who deal with "persistent structural inequalities in education, employment, health and housing" have also been disproportionately affected, and racialised minority women have faced intersecting gender and racial inequalities.[38]

The years of austerity and welfare state reform leading into the pandemic left these groups socially and economically vulnerable, but also more exposed to infection and death. When compared to other major economies in Europe, such as France and Germany, households in the UK were less financially resilient going into the pandemic, due to a combination of lower incomes and savings, and a less generous social security system.[39] A range of benefits, especially those for working-aged people, experienced a cut in real terms (adjusting for inflation) of 6% after Chancellor George Osborne's 2015 benefit freeze, which only ended in 2020. After a decade of cuts in total, this left the real value of basic unemployment support at a lower

---

[37] Howard Reed and Jonathan Portes, *Cumulative Impact Assessment: A Research Report by Landman Economics and the National Institute of Economic and Social Research for the Equality and Human Rights Commission* (Manchester: EHRC, 2014).

[38] Women's Budget Group and Runnymede Trust, *Intersecting Inequalities: The Impact of Austerity on Black and Minority Ethnic Women in the UK* (London: Women's Budget Group, 2017).

[39] Maja Gustafsson et al., *After Shocks: Financial Resilience Before and During the Covid-19 Crisis* (London: Resolution Foundation, April 2021), 13.

level in 2019–20 than it was 30 years earlier.[40] In the years leading up to the pandemic, this vulnerability was reflected in
stalling or even rising mortality rates across the poorest parts
of the country, an 'unprecedented' trend outside of pandemics, epidemics and war.[41] Public health studies suggested that,
because of the timeframe, geographies and socio-economic
groups affected by these changes in mortality, austerity was
likely to have been a primary cause.[42]

As well as the eroded wage and benefit security, the austerity measures that followed the aftermath of the financial
crisis in the UK had the effect of entrenching the privatisation
of financial and social risk within the household. Feminist
political economists have long focused on the household as a
primary site of 'social reproduction', where unpaid work that is
overwhelmingly performed by women supports the "daily and
inter-generational reproduction of people as human beings,
especially through their care, socialisation and education".[43]
In periods of economic crisis and austerity, this reproductive work acts to absorb the fall-out from contracting labour
markets and the retrenchment of welfare services. It is also

---

[40] Adam Corlett, "The Benefit Freeze Has Ended, but Erosion
of the Social Security Safety Net Continues", *Resolution
Foundation* (blog), 16 October 2019.

[41] Danny Dorling, "The Unprecedented Rise of Mortality
Across Poorer Parts of the UK", *Glasgow Centre for Population
Health* (blog), 11 November 2020.

[42] David Walsh et al., "Changing Mortality Trends in Countries
and Cities of the UK: A Population-Based Trend Analysis", *BMJ
Open*, 10:11 (1 November 2020), 7.

[43] Pearson and Elson, "Transcending the Impact of the
Financial Crisis in the United Kingdom", 10.

reflected in the gendered management and 'care' for household budgets, which have become increasingly strained by rising private indebtedness.[44] During the pandemic, social reproductive work has been depended on more than ever to weather the crisis, and, as explored below, gender inequalities have widened as a result. As we argued in Chapter1, the fact that so much care work is unpaid allows policymakers and employers to treat it as a well that can be drawn on without limit or cost. In reality, it suffers steady depletion through the slow violence of stress, exhaustion and insecurity.

Since the mid-2000s, support for benefit claimants in the UK's social security system has increasingly focused on moving them back into any kind of work as quickly as possible through reduced generosity, restricted eligibility and increased conditionality.[45] During the pandemic, this 'work-first' welfare strategy could not be pursued and has exposed it as a system that is ill-equipped to deal with, and support, people through crisis. It had been evident for some time that a focus on securing employment was not enough to support people's standard of living. Since 2004, the data on rising in-work poverty contradict the idea that any kind of waged work is the best route out of poverty.[46] The whole system of conditionality that drives claimants towards employment, embodied in the set of benefits known as Universal Credit,

---

[44] Johnna Montgomerie and Daniela Tepe-Belfrage, "Caring for Debts: How the Household Economy Exposes the Limits of Financialisation", *Critical Sociology*, 43:4–5 (2017).

[45] Taylor, "A Job, Any Job".

[46] Clare McNeil et al., *No Longer "Managing": The Rise of Working Poverty and Fixing Britain's Broken Social Settlement* (London: IPPR, 26 May 2021).

would inevitably become absurd in a situation where waged work was overwhelmingly impossible to obtain on public health grounds. Where unemployment was conceived as a largely voluntary condition within this work-first approach – you lack employment because you need to look harder and work on your employability – the pandemic forced the idea of involuntary unemployment aggressively back into the frame. An entire paradigm of labour market policy-making, which had underpinned the moral and economic vision of successive governments dating back to the 1970s, had to be shelved overnight.

Work in the Pandemic

The pandemic, and the government lockdowns introduced to deal with it, brought many areas of the labour market to a standstill. This had unprecedented effects on who was still able to 'go to work' or how they were able to do so. Across the periods of national and local lockdown, those who were able to 'work from home' were encouraged to do so, and many offices closed or reduced capacity. The spatial organisation of work was radically transformed in a matter of days, for reasons of the public health emergency. And yet Boris Johnson and several other government ministers repeatedly issued calls for a physical return to the office and other workplaces. Already in early May 2020, when the government's health slogan changed from 'stay at home' to 'stay alert', there was widespread confusion about whether people should be returning to their workplaces, not least when over 3,000 new cases were being reported every day and daily deaths were in the hundreds.

The 'back to the office' call lingered over summer and returned more forthrightly in early September 2020. In March 2021, the Prime Minister suggested people had had enough 'days off' and, later, Rishi Sunak urged workers to return to their physical workplaces as all government restrictions eased in July 2021. The repeated appeals to get back to work betrayed an understanding among some politicians of a zero-sum trade-off between public health and the economy. The UK, though, suffered some of the worst rates of Covid-19 infection and death globally, and at the same time endured "one of the deepest recessions among advanced economies, with UK GDP falling by 10 per cent in 2020 as a whole, twice the advanced economy average".[47] In seeking to trade getting people back to work to kickstart the economy against the impacts of the virus, it would seem that the government failed on both accounts.

This false opposition between economy and health also masked the important epidemiological inequalities of work that the pandemic has manifested, linked to questions of space. Workplaces for many became deadly vectors for the virus, especially in public-facing services. London bus drivers, who were more likely to be from racialised minorities, died in their dozens in the first months of the pandemic.[48] In May 2020, the news that a ticket office clerk at Victoria Station, Belly Mujinga, had been spat at by a passenger in a suspected racist attack, contracted Covid-19 and died highlighted the intersecting gender, race and class inequalities of workplaces during the crisis.[49] Throughout the pandemic, it was becoming

---

[47] OBR, *Fiscal Risks Report* (London: Office for Budget Responsibility, July 2021), 5.

[48] BBC News, "Covid: Bus Drivers 'Three Times More Likely to Die' Than Other Workers", *BBC News*, 19 March 2021.

[49] Sirin Kale, "'I Feel She Was Abandoned': The Life and Terrible Death of Belly Mujinga", *The Guardian*, 25 August 2020.

clear that regulatory oversight or employer responsibility for workplace safety was sorely lacking. By the time of the third lockdown, the government agency responsible, the Health and Safety Executive (HSE), had failed to shut down *any* workplaces that put employees at risk of the virus, despite there having been more than 3,500 outbreaks at work since the start of the pandemic.[50]

Those who were designated 'key workers' and expected to travel into their workplaces experienced work and getting to and from it as a daily, deadly risk. Those who worked from home throughout the pandemic most, or all of the time, were not threatened in the same way. Although the latter were relatively privileged both insofar as they were less exposed to the virus and tended to be in more secure and better paid occupations, important inequalities were revealed for workers in both scenarios. These next two sections review who found themselves in these different circumstances, and how the pandemic exposed existing inequalities in the labour market and society more broadly.

Key workers

The pandemic presented us with a new language and moral validation of 'key work' – those workers who were essential to the provision of critical services and infrastructure. This cast new and provocative light on the social utility of different occupations, which implicitly challenged the authority of the market and wage system to reflect the true value of work. While some key workers could work from home *and* avail

---

[50] Tom Wall, "HSE Refuses to Classify Covid as a 'Serious' Workplace Risk", *The Observer*, 14 February 2021.

themselves of key worker status – including those in essential financial services provision – many key workers continued to travel to their places of work. If we look at who could have been defined as a key worker in 2019 based on the definition used in the pandemic, we find that 10.6 million people, or a third of the workforce, were in key worker occupations or industries.[51] Of these key workers, a third were employed in health and social care and a fifth in education and childcare. A strong majority of key workers were women (58%) rather than men (42%), the mirror image of the male/female division in non-key worker occupations and industries. And the proportion of women key workers in education and childcare was much higher, at 81%, and in health and social care, at 79%.

During the pandemic, key workers were officially defined by occupation and industry and by the benefits that their status granted them. They were given access to school and other educational settings for their children throughout lockdowns and had greater access to and eligibility for the Covid-19 testing regime. The list of 'critical workers', as the government also defined them, extended from education and childcare workers and those needed for essential public service delivery to those involved in producing, processing and distributing food and other necessary goods, public safety and security staff, transport and border workers, and those working in utilities, communication and financial services.[52] Social workers, public

---

[51] ONS, "Coronavirus and Key Workers in the UK", 15 May 2020.
[52] Cabinet Office and Department for Education, "Children of Critical Workers and Vulnerable Children Who Can Access Schools or Educational Settings", GOV.UK, 9 March 2021.

broadcasters and managers in the financial services sector all found themselves in a shared category. Critical workers demonstrated the expansive and interdependent nature of the 'foundational economy', which provides the goods and services on which we rely to guarantee a more civilised and safe life for all.[53]

Although key work came with a new form of validation and value, as well as the more concrete benefits it granted, it was key work specific to the pandemic. While utilities and providential services were designated as key work, a range of provision, most obviously in the creative sectors and recreational services, was not. Those working in film and TV, museums, galleries and libraries, and music and performing arts all saw sharp declines in their hours as well as severe job losses during the pandemic.[54] These industries, which most people would identify as playing an important part in social and cultural life, are nevertheless not 'key' to a pandemic economy.

The category of 'key worker' disrupted the authority of the labour market as the measure of value, but still posed a question of valuation: key to whom? For businesses scaling up their online operations, tech workers who could digitise their operations, cyber security experts who could advise on protecting networks and 'demand planners' who manage supply chain systems were all in high demand, in addition to

---

[53] Justin Bentham et al., *Manifesto for the Foundational Economy* (Manchester: CRESC, November 2013).

[54] Haksan Bakshi et al., "How Differently Has the Creative Workforce Fared under COVID-19?", *ESCoE* (blog), 10 May 2021.

delivery drivers and warehouse workers.[55] Some sectors of the UK economy also appeared to retain more political salience. The property development and construction sector, which has become a significant funding source for the Conservative Party, was encouraged to remain as open as possible through successive lockdowns.[56] Tory politicians and the conservative press exerted great energies in exhorting their long-term scapegoats, teachers and lecturers (in truth facing far larger workloads due to constraints of online education), to 'get back to work'. For owners of retail and hospitality businesses, and major office landlords, the return of city workers as customers and sources of rent were of concern.[57] The hollowing out of city centre life and the service economy that supported professional and financial sectors in London presented a different picture of who and how 'key' applied.

Certain areas of key work reflect acutely gendered and racialised inequalities in the labour market, confirming the critical role played by power and culture in determining how work is rewarded. Much of what we now understand as 'essential' or 'key' work in childcare, education, health and social care, transport, refuse, cleaning and supermarket work

---

[55] Pilita Clark, "The New In-Demand Jobs: Delivery Drivers and Tax Specialists", *Financial Times*, 13 December 2020.

[56] Tom Lowe, "Construction Sites to Stay Open as PM Orders England into Strictest Lockdown since March", *Building*, 4 January 2021; Kadhim Shubber, Jim Pickard and Max Harlow, "Property Donors Provide One-Quarter of Funds Given to Tory Party", *Financial Times*, 29 July 2021.

[57] Daniel Thomas, Delphine Strauss and Jim Pickard, "UK Businesses Push for Return of Office Workers", *Financial Times*, 6 July 2020.

is performed by women, working-class and racialised minority populations.[58] For some working-class women, including domestic cleaners and non-essential shop workers, the pandemic has seen the threat of job loss or hours being cut. But many others are disproportionately more likely to be working in 'frontline' or customer- and patient-facing sectors such as care work, where the physical and mental burden of work has intensified.[59] Migrant labour has historically played an important role in many of these sectors – around 14% of NHS workers, 37% of registered nurses and 16% of the adult social care workforce have non-British nationality – and often in lower-paid and more physically demanding roles.[60] This represents another instance of wells of cheap labour being relied on, and gradually depleted, through the pandemic. The idea of the English or British *nation* performs a tacitly economic function, in serving to cheapen and disempower labour that is in fact indispensable to the everyday running of society.

---

[58] Katie Bales, "A Labour Market Divided: COVID-19 and Employment Regulation", *Futures of Work* (blog), 1 October 2020.

[59] Tracey Warren and Clare Lyonette, "Carrying the Work Burden of the Covid-19 Pandemic: Working Class Women in the UK, Briefing Note 1: Employment and Mental Health", Version 6-11-20 (Nottingham: Nottingham University Business School, November 2020).

[60] Carl Baker, "NHS Staff from Overseas: Statistics", Briefing Paper (House of Commons Library, 4 June 2020); Skills for Care, "Workforce Nationality Figures" (Leeds: Skills for Care, 2020), accessed 7 August 2021; Anna Johnston, *Lessons Learned: Where Women Stand at the Start of 2021* (London: Women's Budget Group, 2021), 10.

Deeper into the pandemic, it was obvious that some of these sources of overseas labour were becoming less available in other essential areas. Reported workforce shortages across food production and processing highlighted the fact that, post-Brexit and under Covid-19 travel restrictions, seasonal workers from the EU were not as readily accessible (we discuss this re-bordering in Chapter 4). A month into the first lockdown, agricultural companies even chartered flights to bring in Romanian and Bulgarian workers – who ordinarily form the majority of this workforce – to perform these jobs. In December 2020, the government tweaked a visa scheme to triple the number of workers (up to 30,000) permitted to travel to the UK to pick and package fruit and vegetables.[61] And later in summer 2021, food manufacturers facing thousands of unfilled jobs pleaded with the government to expand a scheme that gave them access to prison labour.[62] These shortages highlight the breakdown of a system that required cheap, mobile labour to be available to serve provisional and just-in-time systems of production.

Lower-paid key worker occupations have also been characterised by significantly higher rates of death involving Covid-19, visualised here in Figure 3.1.[63] As noted in the previous section, some key worker sectors are defined by higher

---

[61] OSSS et al., "Up to 30,000 Workers to Help Reap 2021 Harvest", GOV.UK, 22 December 2020.

[62] Zoe Wood, "UK Food Firms Beg Ministers to Let Them Use Prisoners to Ease Labour Shortages", *The Guardian*, 23 August 2021.

[63] ONS, "Coronavirus (COVID-19) Related Deaths by Occupation, England and Wales", 25 January 2021.

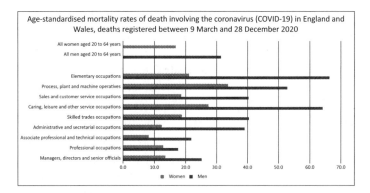

Figure 3.1 Age-standardised mortality rates of death involving Covid-19 in England and Wales, 9 March to 28 December 2020

rates of insecure work as well as forms of work that were vulnerable to infection. Overall, this has led to Covid-19 mortality rates that are *twice as high* in sectors that are synonymous with insecure work than in those that are associated with less insecure work.[64] The Trades Union Congress (TUC) has pointed out that though there are likely many intersecting factors that affect Covid-19 mortality, insecurity has undoubtedly played a role in how the pandemic affected the workforce. The fact that many of those in insecure work had to work outside the home, that their job insecurity meant they were reluctant to take sick leave because they feared being let go, and that they were unable to survive on the inadequate levels of Statutory Sick Pay (SSP) or did not qualify for it because of their extremely low

---

[64] TUC, *Covid-19 and Insecure Work* (London: Trades Union Congress, 2021), 16. 51 deaths per 100,000 people aged 20–64 compared with 24 per 100,000 people.

income (8% of workers), will have all contributed to workers' risk of infection and death.[65]

Before the pandemic, the UK's sick pay system was meagre in its coverage and generosity. Employers only provided occupational sick pay at their own discretion, and a quarter of workers received SSP, which at £95 a week is the lowest mandatory paid sick leave of any OECD country.[66] A survey in May 2021 found that half of insecure workers receive no sick pay at all when off work, and just under a third receive only SSP. A fifth of low-paid workers receive no sick pay at all. A scheme set up as a temporary fix during the pandemic – the self-isolation support payment scheme – failed to provide reliable support to low-paid workers because no one had heard of it and of those who did apply, two-thirds were rejected.[67] This broken system meant that during the pandemic, workers faced an impossible choice between self-isolating and protecting their livelihood. Where rates of insecure and essential work were high, and multigenerational households more prevalent, such as in the East London 'Covid Triangle' of Barking and Dagenham, Redbridge and Newham, Covid-19 ripped through communities and saw some of the highest rates of infection nationally.[68]

The UK's main welfare benefit – Universal Credit – was also tested to the extreme during the pandemic and found wanting.

---

[65] TUC, *Covid-19 and Insecure Work.*

[66] Alex Collinson, "Self-Isolation Support Payments: The Failing Scheme Barely Anyone's Heard of", *TUC* (blog), 21 June 2021.

[67] Ibid.

[68] Anjli Raval, "Inside the 'Covid Triangle': A Catastrophe Years in the Making", *Financial Times*, 5 March 2021.

Despite a record number of new starts – 2.4 million in the first two months of the lockdown alone – and measures to speed up claims, people experiencing Universal Credit for the first time discovered its many inadequacies.[69] The farce of having to wait for five weeks for the first payment and the entrenched stigma surrounding benefits generally meant that many people delayed, and were delayed, in receiving support.[70] The fact that the government uses Universal Credit to recover debt by deducting benefits meant that nearly one million people, or two-thirds of claimants early in the pandemic, were living on less than they were assessed to.[71] Judged on the number of claims processed, it was a muted success story; judged on the adequacy of support people actually received, it highlighted the fundamental problem of a social security system designed to deter its claimants.

'Working from Home': Paid and Unpaid

In Chapter 1, we argued that a combination of the UK's asset-driven, leveraged economy with the platform-enabled constraints of lockdown was unleashing a new wave of 'hyper-domestication', in which housing's already pivotal

---

[69] House of Lords EAC, *Universal Credit Isn't Working: Proposals for Reform* (London: House of Lords Economic Affairs Committee, July 2020).

[70] WASD, *Work and Pensions Select Committee Inquiry: The DWP's Response to the Coronavirus Outbreak* (Salford: Welfare at a Social Distance, December 2020).

[71] Ruth Patrick and Tom Lee, *Advance to Debt: Paying Back Benefit Debt – What Happens When Deductions Are Made to Benefit Payments?* (York: Covid Realities, January 2021).

position in the collective imagination and economy of the UK was becoming yet more entrenched. Homeworking is a major contributor to this. In April 2020, during the first national lockdown, roughly 47% of those in employment did some work from home, and 86% did so because of the pandemic.[72] While homeworking itself is not unprecedented, the greater shift to what has in effect been *enforced* homeworking certainly is a new phenomenon. It has changed the representative traits of homeworkers. Prior to the pandemic, those who worked from home were typically female, part-time workers and working fewer hours.[73] They were generally paid less on average than those who never worked from home, were less likely to be promoted and less likely to receive education or training opportunities.

The turn to mass homeworking transformed these typical characteristics, and it was broadly those in the 'top' occupation groups with higher levels of educational attainment who were working from home. Indeed, there were strong industry- and occupational-based divisions in homeworking through the pandemic. The industries with the highest proportion of homeworking in 2020 were: information and communication (62%); professional, scientific and technical activities (56%); and financial services (54%). Those industries with the lowest proportion were: accommodation and food services (12%); transport and storage (19%); and retail (20%). Half of managers, directors and senior officials did some homeworking in 2020 as compared with just 4.7% of those working in so-called

---

[72] ONS, "Coronavirus and Homeworking in the UK – April 2020", July 2020.

[73] ONS, "Homeworking Hours, Rewards and Opportunities in the UK: 2011 to 2020", 19 April 2021.

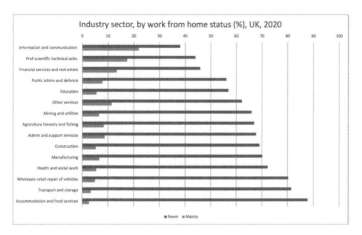

Figure 3.2 Industry sector, by work from home status (%), UK, 2020

'elementary' and manual occupations such as routine work in construction, agriculture and process, plant and machine operation. Figure 3.2 visualises these disparities using responses to an Office for National Statistics (ONS) survey of workers asked about their working from home status across 2020. Of course, this speaks to the kinds of work that *can* be done from home, but it signals a stark division between those who were at risk of infection in the workplace against those who could do at least some of their work from home. If we compare these sectors to the occupational data in Figure 3.1, though the categories are different, we get a sense of how working in an occupation or sector characterised by higher-paid and higher-qualified work meant a higher propensity (and ability) to work from home and a reduced risk of death.

Homeworking across 2020 was also much more prevalent in certain parts of the country than others. In good part, this followed the uneven geographical distribution of industries and occupations across the UK. In London, where finance and other professional services dominate, there was a working from home rate of 43%. By contrast, Northern Ireland saw the lowest rate of homeworking across the UK at 26%, and the North of England and Scotland had much lower rates too. Even after controlling for the distribution of industries, though, regional variations existed: the South of England had much a much higher proportion of people doing work from home than the North.[74]

There were also divisions in homeworking based on housing tenure. Surveys conducted in the summer of 2020 indicated that those who never worked from home were most likely living in social housing, and homeowners were more likely than private or social renters to be working exclusively from home.[75] This again points to the relatively privileged nature of homeworking and its relationship to asset ownership, in which a virtuous circle of hyper-domestication developed – for the privileged – of work, autonomy and capital appreciation, all anchored in the household. We should remember that while the shift to homeworking has been significant, two-thirds of the workforce were not doing *any* work from home across 2020, and even in those industries where figures were higher, a significant minority were also not working from home.

For those who could engage in homeworking there were significant challenges presented by the combination of lockdowns, social distancing measures, closing of schools and nurseries, and inadequate space at home to work. Surveys in the very early stages of the pandemic suggested that there were significant adverse impacts to physical and mental health from homeworking during the crisis. These included

---

[74] Ibid.

[75] Darja Reuschke, "The Surge in Homeworking and New Key Issues for Regional Studies", *Regions* (2020), doi: 10.1080/13673882.2021.00001081.

declines in musculoskeletal health, poor sleep and increased fatigue, reports of waning exercise and less healthy diets, emotional concerns over finance, feelings of isolation, poor work–life balance, and anxieties over job security and family health.[76] However, these initial findings might be set against the reports that, amid widespread homeworking, exercise outdoors boomed in the spring of 2020 and many across the country discovered an appreciation for parks and other green spaces and its positive effects on their wellbeing, as they were not bound by office locations or the commute to them.[77]

By all indications, the experience of homeworking was felt in radically different ways. For some, there were benefits of having more time with family, away from the office and greater control over working hours. The archetype would have been the professional, male worker able to avail themselves of a home office, with relatively few distractions from caring responsibilities. Yet the reality for many others wasn't this, and the impacts on women in particular point to a rather different picture. There has been a surge in the use of flexi-time among mothers during the pandemic, and more than any other demographic they increased their hours worked during evenings and nights in the early stages of the pandemic.[78] This reflects the increased burden of caring or social reproductive

---

[76] Stephen Bevan, Beth Mason and Zofia Bajorek, *IES Working at Home Wellbeing Survey: Interim Findings* (Brighton: Institute for Employment Studies), 7 April 2021.

[77] ONS, "How Has Lockdown Changed Our Relationship with Nature?", 26 April 2021.

[78] Heejung Chung et al., *Working From Home During the Covid-19 Lockdown: Changing Preferences and the Future of Work* (University of Kent and University of Birmingham, 2020), 12.

work borne by women and families, with potentially devastatingly regressive impacts on gender equality.

Indeed, reports indicated that parents' time spent on housework, childcare and home schooling in the pandemic has been unequally divided. In April 2020, mothers on average spent six more hours than fathers doing housework and nine more hours doing childcare and home schooling per week.[79] Women were much more likely than men to be reducing their hours or changing their work schedules because of the time being spent doing childcare or home schooling.[80] As schools and nurseries closed their doors during the pandemic, many households opted for one parent to give up hours of paid work, or give up paid work altogether, to take up full-time childcare. Often, because mothers earn less than fathers, it fell to the former to cut down or leave paid employment.[81]

The pandemic has had particularly destructive impacts on women in terms of health, employment and unpaid work, contributing to increasing poverty and debt and declining mental health.[82] While mental health deteriorated across the UK population, young women experienced significantly higher levels of stress, anxiety and depression.[83] Unpaid care

---

[79] Understanding Society, "Covid-19 Survey Briefing Note: Home Schooling" (Essex: ISER, 2020), 15.

[80] Warren and Lyonette, "Briefing Note 2: Housework and Childcare", 11.

[81] Johnston, *Lessons Learned*, 17.

[82] See Johnston, *Lessons Learned* for a summary of evidence in early 2021.

[83] KCL, "COVID-19 Pandemic Significantly Increased Anxiety and Depression in the UK", Press Release, King's College London, 16 September 2020.

work, which women do disproportionately more of, boomed after March 2020. The pandemic drove 4.5 million more people into unpaid care work, 2.8 million of whom were juggling work and care.[84] This represents an exceptional intensification of the privatised regime of social reproduction as described by Nancy Fraser, which "externali[ses] carework onto families and communities while diminishing their capacity to perform it".[85] Two-earner households who cannot afford to pay someone to undertake this work are committed to radically overworking themselves. Wealth elites, on the other hand, drove demand for private tutors and nannies to mitigate the stresses of lockdown (see Chapter 5).

Housework and childcare demands have, accordingly, been borne by working-class women to a much greater degree. In June 2020, while over two-thirds of employed women in couples were mostly doing the housework, working-class women and female small employers/own account workers were doing the most housework hours. 19% of working-class women were doing 21 hours or more of housework a week, compared with 9% of women in managerial or professional roles.[86] They also had the least access to formal and informal flexible working arrangements in their workplaces and very few working-class women reduced their employed hours or were able to change their schedules. Surveys indicate that in June 2020, only 9% of working-class women (in routine and semi-routine jobs) were 'always' working from home, compared to around half of men

---

[84] Carers UK, *Caring behind Closed Doors: Six Months On* (London: Carers UK, October 2020), 6.
[85] Fraser, "Contradictions of Capital and Care", 112.
[86] Warren and Lyonette, "Briefing Note 2: Housework and Childcare".

and women in professional and managerial work.[87] Class divisions shape the way in which flexibility might even offer time for social reproductive work.

For employers, the substantial turn to homeworking raised the question of how managers would be able to control their remote workers, prompting some of the darker features of the crisis of space accelerated by Covid-19. A primary concern was that lack of proximity to managers and workspaces would erode productivity. Surveillance methods have adjusted to the pandemic and a variety of existing and novel online monitoring technologies have emerged to address this issue. As the household is embedded in the digital webs woven by platform capitalism, so it becomes a node of managerial surveillance as well as of production and consumption. In an example of extreme invasiveness, accounting firm PwC developed a facial recognition tool aimed at finance workers that logs when employees are not at their computer screens.[88] In a case that affected a broader part of the working population, it surfaced that the Microsoft 365 'productivity score' software package could allow managers to track individuals by counting the number of emails they were sending or how often they contributed to shared documents or participated in group chat conversations.[89] More generally, the pandemic represented an opening for tech companies to seize the opportunity to advance and develop their platform business,

---

[87] Warren and Lyonette, "Briefing Note 1: Employment and Mental Health", 9.

[88] Ashleigh Webber, "PwC Facial Recognition Tool Criticised for Home Working Privacy Invasion", *Personnel Today* (blog), 16 June 2020.

[89] Alex Hern, "Microsoft Productivity Score Feature Criticised as Workplace Surveillance", *The Guardian*, 26 November 2020.

increase control of emerging markets and cement their position at the heart of working life. As one research analyst said of Microsoft's newly developed app 'Teams': it "wants the captive portal through which you experience everything else ... They have tried this repeatedly. Teams is the closest they've come to it sticking".[90]

The proliferation of monitoring software has encouraged longer working hours and the further erosion of dividing lines between work and life, leading to fears about 'digital presenteeism'.[91] This kind of presenteeism might instead be understood as a sign of active resistance to monitoring. And the pandemic has also witnessed a boom in 'anti-surveillance software' that allows workers to seem like they are constantly switched on and engaged.[92] It has also boosted debates about legislating for the 'right to disconnect' from work demands, a right which already exists in law in an increasing number of countries.[93]

Furlough, Unemployment and the Misrepresentation of Official Statistics

For four decades, policy orthodoxy had viewed unemployment as an indictment of workers themselves: they were too expensive, too unionised, too well-protected by 'red tape' and

[90] Richard Waters, "Microsoft Looks to Make 2021 the Year of Teams", *Financial Times*, 5 January 2021.
[91] Neil Franklin, "Working from Home Surveillance Drives Rise of Digital Presenteeism", *Workplace Insight*, 8 April 2021.
[92] Alex Christian, "Bosses Started Spying on Remote Workers. Now They're Fighting Back", *Wired UK*, 10 August 2020.
[93] Angela Henshall, "Can the 'Right to Disconnect' Exist in a Remote-Work World?", *BBC*, 21 May 2021.

Brussels, insufficiently skilled or insufficiently motivated. How would policymakers react to an emergency that forced people out of work, in ways that were palpably not their fault? The furlough scheme was revealing, not only of how government functioned under duress, but of the kinds of alternative welfare paradigms that might be out there. The 'bridge' offered by public debt, through which so much else had been sustained over the previous years (most of all, asset prices), would now be deployed in the service of workers.

The government offered to step in and pay 80% of the salaries of employees eligible for furlough, up to a total of £2,500 per month, backdated to 1 March 2020. Employers would have to apply with HMRC to use the grant for their workers. The furlough scheme (Coronavirus Job Retention Scheme) was opened for an initial three months with provision to extend it further. A week later, a similar scheme to support the self-employed, the Self-Employment Income Support Scheme (SEISS), was unveiled. On 12 May, after a million businesses and 7.5 million workers had availed of it for some period of time, furlough was extended until the end of October, with provisions for 'flexible furlough' and employer contributions introduced from August to allow furloughed workers to return to work part time.[94] Across a series of phases from July 2020, the government grant element was due to be reduced and employer contributions increased.

At this point in autumn 2020 an alternative scheme was set to be introduced – the Job Support Scheme – which was due to run for six months and mitigate redundancies through a similar, but overall less generous, grant for salaries. Instead,

---

[94] HM Treasury, "Chancellor Extends Furlough Scheme until October", GOV.UK, 12 May 2020.

in a last-minute announcement and on the scheme's very last day, furlough was extended for another month and eventually to September 2021. The initial development of the government's strategic response to the labour market effects of lockdown was formed from limited experience of such economic contingency planning and relied in part on lessons from financial rescues following the financial crisis and on short-time working schemes in Germany.[95] The evident hesitancy around allowing the scheme to drag on, and the last-minute extensions, will have caused redundancies to be higher than if strong commitment had been shown to furlough across 2020–21. This bore striking contrast to the decisiveness with which the financial sector was supported through the various loan schemes detailed in Chapter 2.

Across the first lockdown (March–June 2020), roughly 9 million people were furloughed for at least one three-week period, with an estimated 7–8 million on furlough at a given time, or about 30% of the workforce (see Figure 3.3). This dropped across the summer to roughly 5 million people in July as lockdown restrictions eased, and further to 10% of the workforce or 2.5 million people in October.[96] Furlough then picked up again in the second national lockdown, rising back to 5 million in January 2021 during the third national lockdown.[97] By late July 2021, 11.6 million people had been furloughed and

---

[95] NAO, *Implementing Employment Support Schemes in Response to the COVID-19 Pandemic* (London: National Audit Office, 23 October 2020).

[96] Daniel Tomlinson, "The Government Is Not Paying Nine Million People's Wages", Resolution Foundation, 1 August 2020.

[97] ONS, "Comparison of Furloughed Jobs Data, UK", 5 March 2021.

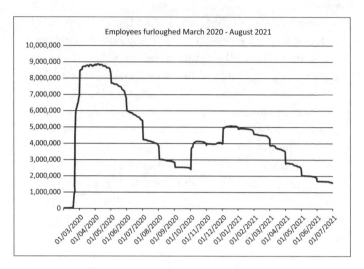

Figure 3.3   Employees furloughed March 2020 to August 2021
(HMRC CJRS statistics, 9 September 2021)

1.3 million employers had made use of the scheme, while just under 2 million people were still furloughed as the scheme began to be unwound with the intention of terminating it in September. Figure 3.3 shows the number of employees furloughed from the furlough's beginning in March 2020 through to August 2021 and Figure 3.4 shows employees furloughed in the year from July 2020 to 2021 by type of furlough.

Some workers were much more likely to be furloughed than others, and sector of employment was the greatest factor in explaining the employment effects of the pandemic.[98] By the third national lockdown, a quarter of all 18–65-year-olds had been furloughed or unemployed over the previous year

---

[98] Nye Cominetti et al., *Long Covid in the Labour Market* (London: Resolution Foundation, February 2021), 6.

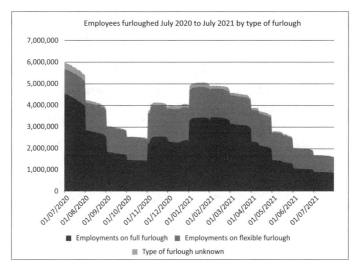

Figure 3.4 Employees furloughed July 2020 to July 2021 by type of furlough (HMRC CJRS statistics, 9 September 2021)

and nearly 2 million had been unemployed or furloughed for at least six months.[99] But at that point nearly half of all jobs furloughed had been in just two industries: accommodation and food services (24%) and wholesale and retail (20%). As a proportion of the sector's workforce, arts and entertainment also saw a high rate of furlough during lockdowns (55% at the end of January 2021), as did construction and manufacturing in the first lockdown.[100] These sectoral impacts of course contributed to the effects on younger workers, and those in more insecure employment, as already outlined.

[99] Ibid., 71.

[100] Alex Collinson, "A Year on from Furlough", *TUC* (blog), 20 March 2021.

It is important to note that the decision to use the furlough scheme, and how to do so, was ultimately at the employer's discretion. While it protected many millions of jobs, a major shortcoming of the scheme was that it did not guarantee that workers would be paid below the minimum wage while being furloughed, and employers had the flexibility to top up the wages of their furloughed workers, or not. This will have contributed to the situation in which a third of all accommodation and food workers were not earning the legal minimum wage in April 2020.[101] Research by the TUC also discovered that some groups struggled to access furlough. Seven in ten working mothers who applied for furlough following the school closures in the third lockdown had their requests turned down, underlining that there was no 'right to furlough', as a last resort for those in need.[102]

The furlough scheme appeared to be broadly effective at staving off a major unemployment crisis. In April 2020, the Office for Budget Responsibility (OBR) laid out a reference scenario for government designed to illustrate the anticipated impacts of a three-month lockdown on the economy and public finances. It envisaged a large but temporary shock in which the unemployment rate would reach 10% in the second quarter of 2020.[103] By the widely used (ILO) measure, unemployment instead peaked at 5.1% in the last quarter of 2020.

Yet labour market statistics presented a distorted and contradictory picture. The different means for reporting job

[101] Ibid.

[102] TUC, "TUC Poll: 7 in 10 Requests for Furlough Turned down for Working Mums", Trades Union Congress, 14 January 2021, 7.

[103] OBR, "Coronavirus Reference Scenario" (London: Office for Budget Responsibility, 14 April 2020).

losses – HMRC payee employee count, the Labour Force Survey count and the workforce employee count – pointed in different directions. And the relatively low unemployment rate, when set against the enormous (114%) increase in those claiming benefits principally for unemployment, suggests that official statistical means of capturing the effects of the crisis on jobs have been thwarted. One of the most striking figures was the number of people who said they were employed yet were not being paid, were working no hours and were not on furlough. Early in the pandemic this figure was at 776,000 people, and over summer 2020 it hovered between 200–300,000 people.[104] These were people who believed that they would be able to return to their employment at some point and so self-classified as 'employed'. The ONS suspected that many of them were young people who were working in casual employment and not eligible for furlough, but expected to be able to regain shifts when lockdown lifted.[105] This was one of many policy areas, which included schools, in which the pandemic saw a significant number of people slip between official classifications and out of the statistical purview of the state.

Due to these distortions, it is difficult to present reliable data for judging loss of employment across the pandemic. By the HMRC payroll data, it appears that 813,000 jobs were lost in the year to March 2021, 90% of these losses coming from four industries: accommodation and food services (41%),

[104] ONS, "X07: Labour Force Survey Weekly Estimates", 15 July 2021.

[105] Debra Leaker, "Painting the Full Picture: What Our Statistics Tell Us about the Labour Market", *National Statistical – ONS* (blog) 29 January, 2021.

wholesale and retail (21%), manufacturing (14%) and the arts, entertainment and recreation (14%).[106] Because of the prevalence of younger workers in some of these industries, the data show that 65% of the job losses between January 2020 and February 2021 were among those aged 25 and under.[107] The lockdowns also had devastating unemployment effects on those in insecure work. In the first lockdown, people on ZHCs or temporary contracts were four times more likely to lose their job, and self-employed people three times more likely to stop working compared to those in organisational employment. This meant the lowest paid were twice as prone to job loss compared to the highest paid.[108]

As we've noted, there are several intersecting inequalities that exist across these sectors characterised by insecure work, and consequently some groups are more at the mercy of employer discretion than others. Power imbalances are decisive. A typical expression of this discretion among precarious sectors of the labour market is the practice of 'firing and rehiring' workers on worse terms and conditions. This was rife throughout 2020–21 and estimates are that almost one in ten workers were subject to fire and rehire over this period.[109]

---

[106] Author calculation based on ONS, "Earnings and Employment from Pay as You Earn Real Time Information, UK", 20 April 2021.

[107] TUC, "Jobs and Recovery Monitor – Update on Young Workers", Trades Union Congress, 27 March 2021.

[108] Alina Şandor, "What the First COVID-19 Lockdown Meant for People in Insecure, Poor-Quality Work", Briefing (London: Joseph Rowntree Foundation, 29 March 2021).

[109] TUC, " 'Fire and Rehire' Tactics Have Become Widespread during Pandemic – Warns TUC", Text, TUC, 25 January 2021.

Once again, working-class, young and racialised minority workers are all much more likely to be impacted by this specific tactic, which effectively forces them to re-apply for their job on deteriorated terms.

The self-employed also experienced a particularly severe crisis in work and income across the pandemic, and job losses here are not represented in the PAYE data. Around one in seven of the self-employed, or 700,000 workers, stopped working entirely during the third national lockdown (up from one in eleven in the first lockdown). This group of workers also suffered a lack of support, despite a dedicated furlough scheme. Around 1.5 million of the self-employed were not eligible to access the SEISS, 1.3 million of whom because less than 50% of their income came from self-employment.[110] This latter category was much more likely to include the low-paid and female workers.

Conclusion: What Was Revealed?

The government intervened in the labour market in an extraordinary way with the furlough schemes for the employed and self-employed. In doing so it created a bridge to the future for millions of workers who continued to be paid and retained some connection to employment. The full cost of furlough, including for both employed and self-employed workers, was nearly £80 billion in the year to March 2021, which was the equivalent of adding 3.8% of GDP to 'welfare-like spending.'

---

[110] Jonathan Cribb, Isaac Delestre and Paul Johnson, "1.5 Million Currently Excluded from Claiming SEISS Could Easily Be Supported by Government at Modest Cost", Institute for Fiscal Studies, 27 January 2021.

As the OBR noted, "[a]dding that spending to the conventional definition of welfare spending in the UK would take the total to well above anything previously seen in the post-war period".[111] Yet furlough and other welfare measures have not prevented undue suffering for those in insecure work. A range of reports and surveys has revealed that the deep social and economic inequalities that beset the labour market before the pandemic – based on class, gender, ethnicity and age – have expanded even further. Mortality risks for some of these groups, heightened thanks to a decade of austerity, have been compounded by economic vulnerabilities and disregard for workers' safety during the pandemic.

The furlough scheme may have briefly disrupted the UK's flexible labour market model, but 'flexibility' appears to remain the policy orthodoxy in the longer term. The furlough scheme was abruptly unwound, while the Treasury was banking on a private sector-led recovery to allow the economy to rebound to its pre-pandemic state. In many sectors of the labour market, however, there is the prospect of long-term damage affecting provision of essential services. This is especially true in health and social care, where there are widespread reports of workers planning to leave the sector due to a year of 'unprecedented pressure' on top of longstanding issues of poor working conditions and low pay.[112] Without investment in 'social infrastructure', the risks to those important areas of the UK's foundational economy will be compounded.

---

[111] OBR, *Welfare Trends Report* (London: Office for Budget Responsibility, March 2021), 4.

[112] IPPR, "Commit to New Deal for Healthcare Workers or Risk 'Deadly Exodus', IPPR Warns Government", Press Release, IPPR, 30 March 2021.

While the pandemic offers the opportunity for more directed industrial policy and investment, such as towards jobs that support the transition to a low-carbon economy, the Johnson administration (and the Sunak Treasury in particular) has overwhelmingly retained a faith in supply-side policies – boosts to training, education and employability – to shape the labour market recovery. The pandemic, however, has revealed a need to fundamentally alter the rights, protections and conditions under which work is performed. Given our expanded understanding of 'key' work and the increasing dependency we have on platform-managed services and delivery, it would be a great loss if attempts were not made to reduce insecurity and improve workers' control over flexibility in these sectors. The platformisation and algorithmic management of work appears here to stay, so a reimagining of platforms for the public good, rather than in service to global corporations, needs to take place. As Ursula Huws has suggested, digital platforms for the public good should be community-led and democratically organised, and address issues of time poverty and care needs that are ignored in existing models.[113]

The UK labour market, as outlined above, has relied on an endless supply of cheap, flexible labour, and in significant part from foreign-born workers. The pandemic, the effects of Brexit and the UK Home Office's 'hostile environment' have stymied this, as we will explore further in the next chapter. The reassertion of the bordered nation as the territorial container of market activity is one of the most significant reconfigurations of economic space that is accelerated by Covid-19, though not initiated by it. In 2019–20 it was estimated that the number of non-UK-born workers resident in the UK fell by more than half

---

[113] Huws, *Reinventing the Welfare State.*

a million, and overall the number of non-UK-born residents fell by more than 1.3 million. This amounts to an 'unprecedented exodus' and the biggest drop in the UK resident population since World War Two.[114] London experienced a particularly acute fall of 700,000 residents, possibly heralding a longer-term shift in its population. The wells of informal labour that supply some of the sectors that have been worst affected by lockdowns have run dry, and will not necessarily refill when these parts of the economy reopen. As restrictions eased in summer 2021, retail and hospitality employers reported difficulties in filling vacancies. Estimates are that up to a quarter of the UK's hospitality workforce were EU nationals, and even greater proportions in some regions and sectors (EU nationals made up 75% of waiters and waitresses in London).[115]

Despite the acutely gendered inequalities around home-working and the often-adverse mental health impacts, the pandemic has also revealed an appetite for more homeworking in the future. Nine out of ten homeworkers who were surveyed expressed a wish to carry on working from home at least part of the week.[116] Given that those who have done so during the pandemic have been in more highly educated and

---

[114] Michael O'Connor and Jonathan Portes, "Estimating the UK Population During the Pandemic", *ESCoE* (blog), 14 January 2021.

[115] Hospitality & Catering News, "Study Shows Mass Exodus of Migrant Workers Due to Covid and Brexit", *Hospitality & Catering News* (blog), 6 April 2021.

[116] Alan Felstead and Darja Reuschke, *Homeworking in the UK: Before and During the 2020 Lockdown*, WISERD Report (Cardiff: Wales Institute of Social and Economic Research, 2020), i.

better paid or more prestigious occupations, this may have the effect of widening divides between a remote workforce and those expected to be present in workspaces. Higher rates of remote and 'hybrid working' (split between remote and workplace) will raise tensions around the issues of autonomy, surveillance, care responsibilities and the gendered balance of socially reproductive work.

Higher rates of working from home could yet politicise flexibility, bringing a large swathe of workers into contention with a model of flexibility based on employer discretion. This goes not just for those working remotely from home, but also working conditions and hours more broadly. Two-thirds of workers want some form of control over flexibility in their working times after the pandemic, including flexi-time, part-time work, predictable hours, compressed hours, term-time working and annualised hours. Yet only half of workers currently have a contract that would permit them to make a request for such changes (there is no right to flexible working conditions like these), and two-thirds of people in working-class occupations are locked out of the most popularly requested forms of flexibility such as flexi-time.[117] In spring 2021, the government reconvened the Flexible Working Taskforce, which is set to advise on how to make flexible working the default, unless employers have good reasons not to offer it.

The unprecedented government interventions, then, do not themselves address some of the longer-term pathologies of the UK labour market. It is evident that one-sided flexible labour market policies, and the deepening turn to employer discretion, have embedded insecurity into the labour market and revealed themselves in both financial and public health

---

[117] TUC, *The Future of Flexible Work* (London: TUC, June 2021).

impacts across the pandemic. We have an acute and public understanding, though, of who has suffered from one-sided flexibility, from austerity, from the inequalities of unpaid work, and how they have been left vulnerable to the pandemic as a result. Out of these revelations political efforts for change are being born, whether in demands for better pay and autonomy at work, social security and employment protections, investment in key workers, and recognition and valuing of the unpaid work on which society relies.

4

Confine and Track: The Politics of 'Protection'

Pandemics and epidemics have cleared the way for new technologies and political strategies of physical confinement and the regulation of human mobility. Each case reveals something distinctive about inequalities that already exist and that pandemics have enhanced and accelerated. The appearance of new infectious diseases has frequently provided the justification for the creation and enforcement of new racialised borders.[1] Specific cases also cast a light on the distribution and technologies of power: who holds it, how it is exercised, and who exploits it for their own gain. Freedoms are allocated and reallocated on different conditions, depending on a range of legal, medical, economic and political critieria, which are often weighed up and calculated in an opaque and contingent fashion that may be far messier than is publicly

---

[1] Alison Bashford, " 'The Age of Universal Contagion': History, Disease and Globalization". In Alison Bashford (Ed.), *Medicine at the Border* (London: Palgrave Macmillan, 2006); Kathryn Olivarius, "The Dangerous History of Immunoprivilege", *New York Times*, 12 April 2020; Lorna Weir and Eric Mykhalovskiy, "The Geopolitics of Global Public Health Surveillance in the Twenty-first Century". In Alison Bashford (Ed.), *Medicine at the Border* (London: Palgrave 2006).

acknowledged. Borders multiply and are tightened both around and within territories, though never rendered entirely sealed. The permeability of borders reveals hierarchies of human value. New patterns of geography and surveillance can be introduced at great speed, but then leave an enduring legacy.

National borders and surveillance infrastructures were at the heart of some of the deepest political controversies in the UK over the course of 2020–21. The inability of policymakers to bring infections under control in 2020 was held up by epidemiologists and the government's opponents as a reflection of inadequate forms of border control and surveillance, in contrast to some East Asian countries that deployed the full powers of the state to eliminate infections.[2] While many EU countries introduced strict mobility restrictions in 2020, and island nations such as Australia and New Zealand pursued a 'zero Covid' strategy of maximum constraints on international travel, the UK initially maintained a relatively soft approach to border closure.[3] A year later, however, it had imposed a rigid and yet also erratic entry–exit border control system. Taking inspiration from Australia and New Zealand, in February 2021 the UK government introduced a hotel quarantine system for travellers coming from countries on a 'red list', which was constantly updated.

Meanwhile, the failure to develop an effective 'test and trace' system, the extreme cost of the system that was built,

---

[2] David Wallace-Wells, "How the West Lost COVID: How Did So Many Rich Countries Get It So Wrong? How Did Others Get It So Right?", *New York Magazine*, 15 March 2021.

[3] Elspeth Guild, "Covid-19 Using Border Controls to Fight a Pandemic? Reflections From the European Union", *Frontiers in Human Dynamics*, 2 (2020): 1–13.

and the prominent role played by Serco also provoked widespread criticism. The so-called 'pingdemic' (the high number of people who were told to self-isolate through the NHS app as they had been in contact with someone who tested positive for Covid-19) triggered economic and logistical chaos in summer 2021. Supermarket provisions were subjected to shortages and huge delays due to the many truck drivers who were forced to self-isolate. Thus, digital technologies also turned into additional hurdles to people's movements and, relatedly, to the circulation and delivery of goods.

The reliance of the British state upon a handful of contractors and the ability of well-connected firms to acquire Covid-19 contracts at speed raised profound questions about accountability and privacy, given the amount of data that was generated by new surveillance and border infrastructures. The attempt to govern the pandemic via apps and data, often handled by commercial contractors, met with varying levels of public compliance plus understandable suspicion that these new infrastructures were being exploited for profit and future business opportunities. This disquiet was especially pronounced in relation to the planned creation of a national NHS patient database, which was expected to be made available to third party contractors. These developments cast the fusion of state sovereignty and corporate interests in an especially harsh light, seeing as the state was contracting out many of its most basic powers and duties.

The designation of national territorial borders, and the protection of citizens from harms, are historically foundational to the identity and purpose of the modern nation state. Precisely how borders and protections are introduced and maintained, by whom and for whom (and consequently, who they are protecting against), are more detailed questions, whose answers are often obscured from view. As the geographer Deborah

Cowen has argued, border infrastructures often remain invisible until they fail or are disrupted.[4] The effect of Covid-19, however, has been to shine a light on the technicalities of the British state, in particular its reliance on the private sector for the delivery of many of its most fundamental obligations and services, from border control to public health management. The use of violence is routinely outsourced, as witnessed in the expansion of a bordering industry and private sector detention of asylum seekers, which have been stretched under conditions of the pandemic. As we will discuss, these trends have been developing for many years, but the events of 2020 onwards drew attention to – and rapidly expanded – the panoply of technologies, surveillance and service industries that make up the UK border, not just in airports and ports but woven through everyday life.

In Chapter 1, we argued that the pandemic has hastened a 'crisis of space' that was already latent within the UK's model of capitalism, being driven by the rising power of digital platforms, the continued ascendency of housing as the key node in circuits of economic investment, production and consumption, and the re-bordering of the nation state that has been ongoing for several years. This chapter digs further into this crisis, and identifies the inequalities that condition and result from it. If there is anything distinctive about how this pandemic has been managed spatially, in contrast to previous health emergencies, it is the channelling of state sovereignty into the logic of the data platform: the combination of physical and digital borders, and the reliance on the private sector

---

[4] Deborah Cowen, *The Deadly Life of Logistics: Mapping Violence in Global Trade* (Minneapolis: University of Minnesota Press, 2014).

for the surveillance and management of populations. The outsourcing industry has, for many years, sucked revenue out of the state, often at very little risk and with little capital invested.[5] But Covid-19 has also increased commercial opportunities to suck *data* out of the population and its movements. The testing, tracing, monitoring and confining of populations are all functions of a state that promises 'protection', but which are in practice delivered for profit by the 'shadow state' of 'contract rentiers'. Together with that, a distinctive character of Covid-19 governance has been the multiplication of heterogenous bordering mechanisms: the 'crisis of space' has been inflected by the proliferation of economic, technological, social and political borders, some of which remained de facto invisible. The multiplication of heterogenous bordering mechanisms has been one of the key grounds of expansion of the 'franchise state'.[6]

At the same time, dominant political justifications for surveillance, confinements and restraints have changed, thanks to the pandemic. The 'protection' offered by the state to its citizens in the context of Covid-19 is not a traditionally nationalist one, even while it involves the raising of national borders. It is interwoven with arguments for public health management – not only the health of national citizens but (sometimes absurdly) of foreigners and migrants too. This shift in the logics of protection is what we name here 'contain to protect', in which the protracted confinement of migrants becomes defended on the basis that it is in their interests, as well as the host nation's. A form of health-based nationalism, which was

---

[5] Bowman et al., *What a Waste*.

[6] Claudia Aradau and Martina Tazzioli, "Covid-19 and the Re-bordering of the World", *Radical Philosophy*, 2:10 (2021).

already appealed to in populist rhetoric surrounding the NHS, sought to build common cause around the use of apps and restraints on movement.

Our key arguments in this chapter are threefold. Firstly, that Covid-19 has led social and economic inequalities to become further reflected in different mobility rights and freedoms. Mobility restrictions increased around the world over the course of 2020 and 2021, but these restrictions are not the same for all; they reflect underlying economic priorities and cultural hierarchies, not reducible to health risks. Secondly, that the re-bordering processes witnessed during this time did not occur only at national frontiers but in a multiplication of social, national and urban boundaries, underpinned by digital infrastructures. Indeed, rather than imagining the governance of the 'national border' as distinct from that of 'public health' (as a traditional liberal account might), we should think instead of the surveillance and control of populations as a single project enacted by overlapping national jurisdictions, who will inevitably build up greater capacities for multilateral cooperation in some (but by no means all) instances. And finally, and most pertinently for political economy, the sudden expansion in the political and market demand for the confining, testing and tracing of human bodies is a huge commercial opportunity, which is exploited by companies that specialise in the management of mobility and biodata.

The chapter is structured as follows. As in previous chapters, we start by laying out some of the conditions prior to 2020 that have shaped the expansion of lucrative re-bordering and surveillance industries. A crucial ingredient, which distinguishes the case of the UK, is Brexit, which had already generated the political need for more advanced border logistics. Indeed, the two 'crises' – Brexit and Covid-19 – have temporally overlapped and, as far as borders are concerned, they have also intertwined. That is, some border restrictions enforced due to Brexit have been justified as measures to tackle Covid-19. However, we also point to various ways in which borders and confinement facilities had long operated on a contractual basis where asylum seekers are concerned. Secondly, we introduce the concept of a 'confinement continuum', that is, a spectrum of constraints and infrastructures between the most restrictive (as are deployed for asylum seekers) and the most liberal (which are available at a cost to the traveller). Thirdly, we consider how this re-bordering merges into public health policy, enabled by a familiar set of outsourcing companies, many of whom are extracting data as well as rents. The influence of platformisation of health policy is to render the population a type of national 'asset' which can be made available to contractors. We conclude by identifying the particular hierarchies and inequalities that are revealed by these developments.

The Border-Industrial Complex

The backdrop to the restriction and surveillance of human mobility over the course of the pandemic lies in the rising public–private infrastructure, through which the UK state had operated its borders and detained migrants over the previous 30 years. In order to understand the political economy of the emergency infrastructures and measures introduced in 2020, we first need to look back at the steady rise of a border control and detention industry, in which the power to track and confine human movement was passed from the sovereign state to a set of para-state commercial firms, the same ones that have accumulated contracts across a range of public services. The kinds of mass quarantining and testing infrastructures that were developed at speed in 2020 may have been unprecedented, but states such as the UK had already been developing these kinds of capacities, often outside of the public eye, in order to govern flows of often vulnerable people. Consternation surrounding the use of hotels for confining travellers from 'red list' countries in 2021 was an awakening to a commercial and infrastructural politics that was already embedded. By considering the recent history of asylum and migration policy, we can see how a public–private capacity was in place for the enforced management of mobility.

The UK's public–private border control and detention infrastructure forms a major part of the broader 'public services industry' that we noted in Chapter 1. Within these contracted services, the UK has been a pioneer in the privatisation of migrant detention and in the housing of asylum seekers, something that can be traced back to the late 1980s.[7] A key policy shift, however, was introduced in 1998, when the Labour government released the White Paper *Fairer, Faster and Firmer, A Modern Approach to Immigration and Asylum*.[8] As part of this new agenda, not only did the UK government gesture sharply towards a tougher and exclusionary politics of asylum, it also highlighted the benefit of contracting with numbers of providers to secure accommodation, including private actors.[9] The outsourcing of asylum

---

[7] David Fée, "The Privatisation of Asylum Accommodation in the UK: Winners and Losers", *Revue Française de Civilisation Britannique. French Journal of British Studies*, 16:2 (2021).

[8] Home Office, *Fairer, Faster and Firmer – A Modern Approach to Immigration and Asylum*, 27 July 1998.

[9] In principle, asylum seekers should stay in temporary accommodation for no longer than 19 days – which is considered the time during which UK authorities should check whether the asylum applicant is economically destitute, on the

housing to private actors was justified in the name of rationalising immigration-related costs and relieving the burden on taxpayers. Outsourcing and privatisation of the asylum system expanded steadily from the 1990s onwards.[10] Between 2012 and 2019 accommodation for asylum seekers was provided through six regional *Commercial and Operational Managers Procuring Asylum Support Services* contracts, replacing 22 separate contracts with 13 different suppliers.[11] G4S, Clearsprings and Serco were awarded two contracts each, part of a trend towards the consolidation of contracted services. In 2019, these three contractors were awarded ten-year 'Asylum Accommodation and Support Service Contracts (AASC)' to house asylum seekers.[12] Serco had already been awarded a contract of £1.9 billion to cover asylum housing in the Midlands, North West and East of England. Mears covers Scotland, Northern Ireland, North East of England, Humberside and Yorkshire, while Clearsprings/Ready Home is in charge of Wales and Southern England.

---

basis of Section 95 law, and therefore shall be granted more stable accommodation or not. In reality, as reported by NGOs as well as by Reports of the House of Commons, asylum seekers end up living in temporary accommodation like hotels for much longer.

[10] Fée, "The Privatisation of Asylum Accommodation in the UK."

[11] Home Affairs Committee, *Asylum Accommodation Twelfth Report of Session 2016–17*, House of Commons, 31 January 2017.

[12] Home Office, "New Asylum Accommodation Contracts Awarded", 8 January 2019. www.gov.uk/government/news/new-asylum-accommodation-contracts-awarded (accessed 20 September 2021).

Far from constituting two distinct domains, the governing of 'illegalised' migrants and of asylum seekers are deeply intertwined in the UK.[13] Indeed, asylum seekers can be put in detention for 'security reasons' while they wait for the outcome of their asylum claims, and asylum applicants who have been denied refugee status can also be put in jail while they wait to be deported. At the same time, beyond formal detention, asylum seekers can be temporarily housed in hotels, as part of the Initial Accommodation (IA) system, or dispersed in apartments and accommodation centres across the country. This 'migrant dispersal' system had been in place long before the pandemic, and established a network of privately managed housing facilities across the country.[14] This is the key precedent for the quarantining measures that were introduced under duress thanks to Covid-19, which were innovative in their target populations, but not in their instrumental nature or the providers of such 'services', who were doing so for profit.

The global security company G4S has played a central role in the outsourcing of asylum housing in the UK: its first contract with the Home Office in the field of migrant detention was in 1989. Among its huge revenue in the field of migrant

---

[13] Nicholas De Genova, "Migrant 'Illegality' and Deportability in Everyday Life", *Annual Review of Anthropology* 31 (2002): 419–447.

[14] Jonathan Darling, "Asylum in Austere Times: Instability, Privatization and Experimentation within the UK Asylum Dispersal System", *Journal of Refugee Studies*, 29:4 (2016): 483–505; Nick Gill, "Governmental Mobility: The Power Effects of the Movement of Detained Asylum Seekers around Britain's Detention Estate", *Political Geography*, 28:3 (2009): 186–196.

detention, in the period 2012–18 it gained around £14.3 million exclusively from managing Brook House removal centre.[15] The company has been the focus of harsh criticisms due to the horrific and squalid conditions of the apartments where asylum seekers are housed, as well as due to systematic episodes of racism and abuses of G4S officers against refugees.[16] G4S's involvement in the immigration and refugee sector is internationally significant, as it operates in many refugee camps and detention centres across the world. For instance, in Greece the European Asylum Support Office (EASO) contracted G4S in 2016 to deploy security personnel at the gates of the hotspots, to tame migrants' protests and to provide 'security services' inside camps.[17] In September 2019, G4S ended its formal involvement in the immigration and asylum sector in the UK after journalistic investigations proved evidence of systematic violence perpetuated against migrants.[18] Yet, the evidence of the abuses did not end the outsourcing of immigration detention: rather, in 2020 another big private security

---

[15] Gurpret Narwan, "G4S Made £14m from Scandal-hit Immigration Centre", *The Times*, 22 July 2019.

[16] John Grayson, "G4S Promises (Again) to Repaint Asylum Seeker Red Doors and Relocate Families at Risk", *openDemocracy*, 25 May 2016.

[17] Apostiolis Fotiadis, "While Hotspots Become Chaotic, EASO Calls In G4S for Protection", 21 June 2016, https://apostolisf otiadis.wordpress.com/2016/06/21/while-hot-spots-bec ome-chaotic-easo-calls-in-g4s-for-protection/ (accessed 20 September 2021).

[18] Diane Taylor, "Immigration Detainee Allegedly Choked by G4S Guard Demands Public Inquiry", *The Guardian*, 25 September 2017.

contractor, Serco, took over the management of Brook House and of Yarlswood immigration removal centres. Even the opacity which underpins the Home Office's contracts with private security actors is not a novelty of Covid-19; rather, it has characterised the collaboration between the state and these private actors since its inception.

The hotels where people who seek asylum are temporarily housed are part of a wider network of humanitarian confinement and they are classified by the Home Office as 'initial accommodation'.[19] After being stranded in the hotels without being notified for how long, asylum seekers are often transferred to apartments or accommodation centres and are dispersed across the country. Serco runs many such accommodation centres and hotels, and – even before Covid-19 – had encountered numerous high-profile controversies over the years, such as that surrounding the use of 'no-key evictions' in Glasgow, whereby the contractor changed the locks on resident's homes, and cases of staff using their own keys to enter without permission. Serco's pivotal role in both digital and physical border infrastructures was notoriously boosted during the Covid-19 pandemic. It operated most of the hotels where migrants were housed and in 2020 managed 25% of the Covid-19 testing sites and contracted for Covid-19 contract tracing in the UK. This yielded the exceptional revenues and profits that we noted in Chapter 2.

The outsourcing of refugee governance to private actors is not circumscribed to housing and detention. The Home Office has been subcontracting different asylum services to

---

[19] Home Affairs Committee, "Home Office Preparedness for COVID-19 (Coronavirus): Institutional Accommodation", 28 July 2020.

the outsourcing agency Migrant Help since 2014.[20] Among other services, Migrant Help's main task is to provide asylum advice and interpreters to the asylum seekers, explaining the procedure and helping them complete paperwork. Yet, they do not provide legal aid. As for Serco, so for Migrant Help, the pandemic has been a moment of logistical chaos: "there are lot of asylum seekers ready to be dispersed across the country, and transferred to other accommodation centers but we cannot do it now, due to Covid-19. And, meanwhile, we don't know where to put them".[21] Covid-19 has substantially enhanced the intermediations and physical distance between Migrant Help officers and the asylum seekers, making it harder to access support and due process. In practice, the pandemic has strengthened the state's politics of 'organised abandonment' and the actual deprivation of infrastructures of support for migrants and people seeking asylum.[22] In the hotels where some asylum seekers have been transferred during Covid-19, they ended up completely isolated without knowing when they should expect the outcome of their asylum application nor if they will be transferred somewhere else. The violence of organised abandonment does not stem from a state's mere retreat and inaction; rather, it is the outcome of an active and deliberate strategy of migrants' legal and economic destitution and, as part of that, the UK government has mobilised huge resources for establishing partnerships with private tenders.

---

[20] Migrant Help website, www.migranthelpuk.org/ (accessed 20 September 2021).

[21] Interview with Migrant Help, 23 March 2021.

[22] Ruth Wilson Gilmore, "Organized Abandonment and Organized Violence: Devolution and the Police", 2015. https://vimeo.com/146450686.

This model of a complex 'franchise state', whose border infrastructure is delivered on a for-profit basis, was already being expanded and tested immediately prior to Covid-19, thanks to the intense difficulties presented by Brexit, which was itself an unprecedented challenge to the operation of borders, data management and migration. In November 2020, it was announced that the government had budgeted £1.41 billion for "new border infrastructure and systems and wider support for the border industry".[23] The crises afflicting UK borders over the course of 2020–21 were often a dense combination of Brexit-related and Covid-related challenges. This became most visible in late December 2020, when France closed the Channel for a few days to prevent the spread of the 'Alpha' variant of Covid-19 that was escalating rapidly in the UK. Long queues of trucks built up at Dover, and delays in food provisions arose.

As far as housing asylum seekers is concerned, the temporal conjuncture of Brexit and Covid-19 turned into a major logistical challenge for both the Home Office and its contractors. The logistical problem of managing, hiding and containing the presence of women, men and children seeking asylum during the pandemic took place in a new political and legal

---

[23] The NAO reported that "the total £1.41 billion for the border announced in 2020 comprises: a £50 million funding package to accelerate the growth of the UK's customs intermediary sector announced on 12 June 2020; a £705 million investment for GB-EU border ... and a £650 million investment for Northern Ireland ... (which includes support for peace, prosperity and reconciliation projects on the island of Ireland)". NAO, *The UK Border: Preparedness for the End of the Transition Period*. HC 371 (London: National Audit Office, 6 November 2020), 7 fn5.

scenario, when the Dublin Regulation could no longer be enforced in the UK to return migrants to European countries.[24] Thus, hotels appeared as the best logistical solution for temporarily housing and containing asylum seekers, and were presented at the same time as a measure for safeguarding both migrants – by not exposing them to Covid-19 – and citizens – by protecting them from migrants.

A system of hotel quarantining also served the government's aforementioned red list of countries, which were deemed unsafe and 'high risk' for travel to or from on the basis of shifting epidemiological criteria. Travellers were forced to pay £2,285 for the ten-day 'hotel quarantine package', which operated entirely through private providers. Corporate Travel Management was the sole 'booking agent' (CTM were also paid £26 million to repatriate tens of thousands of British people from across the world in 2020–21), while Novotel, Radisson Blu and Best Western were among the hotel chains where quarantining took place.[25] During the ten-day quarantine, security and enforcement of quarantining rules – which included short, accompanied breaks outside the hotel for fresh air and limited opportunities for exercise – was provided

---

[24] Since January 2021, the UK is out of the Dublin Regulation, which means that it cannot access the Eurodac database – which stores the fingerprints of asylum seekers and of unauthorised migrants apprehended on European territory; nor can it send asylum seekers back to the European country that, on the basis of the Dublin Regulation criteria, is responsible for processing their asylum claim.

[25] The figure for the CTM contract comes from the Tussell database, "Latest Updates on UK Government COVID-19 Contracts and Spending" (accessed 6 October).

by a familiar array of contract rentiers. G4S, Mitie, and Corps Security were in total paid around £97 million between them for border quarantine security.[26]

The prohibitive cost of the quarantine package for travellers enforced a hierarchy of mobility that was compounded by the global distribution of public health resources and Covid-19 vaccines.[27] In effect, it supported the UK's racialised and class-based border regime, locking out those without access to the vaccine, without access to adequate public health systems and unable to afford travel. The traffic light system that determined criteria for travel, testing and quarantine was wound down in autumn 2021, and the final countries removed from the red list not long after.[28] But these measures were politically revelatory. As well as representing another opportunity for contract rentiers, they expressed a system of differentiated mobility defined by class and racialised inequalities.

The 'Confinement Continuum' During Covid-19

In July 2021, a 24-year-old Sudanese asylum seeker was found dead at the Crowne Plaza hotel near Heathrow Airport. In 2020 the hotel, run by Serco, had been repurposed for temporarily housing and containing asylum seekers. Far from being an exceptional episode, 51 asylum seekers had died in Home

---

[26] Ibid.

[27] Department of Health & Social Care, "Booking and Staying in a Quarantine Hotel if You've Been in a Red List Country", 1 October 2021.

[28] Nazia Parveen, "England's Travel Traffic-light System Replaced and Testing Requirements to Change", *The Guardian*, 4 October 2021.

Office accommodation in the previous five years, including three babies, three who died as a result of Covid-19, and four who had taken their own lives.[29] The Crowne Plaza is one of the many hotels that are currently used for isolating asylum seekers in the UK. During the pandemic, many sites – such as barracks and hotels – were repurposed for containing asylum seekers in the name of hygienic-sanitary principles. Self-isolating measures were turned into ways for isolating migrants, by keeping them out of sight and by confining them to remote places.

Focusing on the multiplication of border restrictions and bordering mechanisms in the UK, it is worth noticing how different modes of containment overlapped. Both travellers from red list countries and people seeking asylum were sent to hotels upon arrivals and told to self-isolate there. Of course, the forced confinement of asylum seekers in hotels was very different from the quarantine hotel system for tourists and businesspeople. The former get sent to hotels as 'temporary' accommodation while they wait indefinitely for the outcome of their asylum application – or wait to be transferred to other accommodation – while the latter were people who could afford to spend thousands of pounds on the ten-day quarantine period in the hotels. Yet, the similarities in the use of hotels as a mechanism of containment in the name of citizens' protection against the global health threat tells us something about the nature of the contemporary border regime.

The entanglements and continuities between confinement of travellers and that of asylum seekers in hotels can

---

[29] Diane Taylor, "More Than 50 Died in Home Office Asylum Seeker Accommodation in Past Five Years", *The Guardian*, 25 July 2021.

be traced on a twofold level. Firstly, it is noticeable that confinement is used by state authorities as what Michel Foucault termed a 'political technology' for governing unruly movements under Covid-19. The pandemic witnessed the creation and expansion of a confinement continuum, characterised by hybrid sites – like the hotels. The spatial confinement of both travellers and migrants was justified on the basis of the 'contain to protect' logic: confinement has been presented as a spatial strategy to protect the health of both citizens *and* the people in isolation in hotels.[30]

Secondly, the hotel confinement system sheds light on outsourcing practices which have been at the core of the management of Covid-19. As far as asylum seekers are concerned, the use of hotels as a temporary accommodation solution did not start with the pandemic, as already noted.[31] However, additional facilities had to be swiftly requisitioned and established. In September 2020, the Home Office repurposed the former Napier Barracks in Folkestone into a temporary accommodation site for asylum seekers who were newly arrived to the UK. The same month, Penally army camp in Pembrokeshire was also converted into a housing solution for asylum seekers. After being repurposed into a temporary accommodation centre for asylum seekers – from where migrants from different nationalities were also deported in October 2020 – the Napier Barracks site has been managed by Clearspring. This

---

[30] Martina Tazzioli and Maurice Stierl, "Europe's Unsafe Environment: Migrant Confinement Under Covid-19." *Critical Studies on Security*, 9:1 (2021): 76–80.
[31] John Grayson, "Beyond English Borders: Asylum Hostels and Asylum Hotels in a Time of Covid-19", Institute of Race Relations, 6 May 2020.

represented merely one of the more visceral and graphic manifestations of how the contemporary UK state shares its monopoly on the legitimate use of violence with a host of out-sourcing contractors.

The humanitarian repurposing of military sites has a long history in migration and refugee governance, far beyond the UK; and, more broadly, hybrid sites of confinement have been used to house, control and detain migrants.[32] Yet, Pennally and Napier Barracks are not simply inadequate infrastructures for hosting asylum seekers: they soon turned into unsafe environ-ments and into actual Covid-19 hubs.[33] In the Napier Barracks, more than 200 migrants tested positive in January 2021 and cases quickly ramped up in a few days. Asylum seekers have been housed in cramped spaces where neither hygienic measures have been adopted nor physical distance among migrants has been guaranteed.[34] After that episode, and in response to the campaign launched by NGOs to demand the closure of the barrack site, the Home Office started to trans-fer some of the asylum seekers to hotels. Thus, the existing hotel system for asylum seekers was rapidly converted into a health-based confinement system. Most of these hotels have been, yet again, temporarily tendered to Serco.

---

[32] Tom Scott-Smith and Mark Breeze (Eds.), *Structures of Protection? Rethinking Refugee Shelter* (New York: Berghahn Books, 2020).

[33] Diane Taylor, "Inspectors Condemn Covid Safety of Barracks Used to House Asylum Seekers", *The Guardian*, 8 March 2021.

[34] William Walters and Barbara Lüthi, "The Politics of Cramped Space: Dilemmas of Action, Containment and Mobility", *International Journal of Politics, Culture, and Society*, 29:4 (2016): 359–366.

In addition to these confinements, economic and legal destitution have been actively enforced in the UK as part of the 'hostile environment' policy, the agenda introduced by then Home Secretary Theresa May in 2012. 'Hostile environment' designates a series of policies, physical infrastructures and administrative measures aimed at rendering everyday life unbearable for migrants, in part through restricting access to basic services. It also multiplies the instances of bordering practices within the UK, placing immigration checks around private rental agreements in housing and data sharing of immigration status between the NHS, schools, the police and the Home Office.[35] In so doing, the 'hostile environment' policy aims at encouraging migrants to leave the UK of their own accord and at deterring migrants from coming to the UK and claiming asylum in the first place.[36] The temporal conjuncture of Brexit and Covid-19 has in many ways made the UK yet more hostile to migrants and asylum seekers. This was exemplified by the thousands of migrants applying to repeal their 'No Recourse to Public Funds' (NRPF) status during the pandemic.[37] As part of the hostile environment logic, NRPF denies over 1 million people in the UK access to social security

[35] Amreen Qureshi, Marley Morris and Lucy Mort, *Beyond the Hostile Environment* (London: IPPR, 2021).

[36] Maya Goodfellow, *Hostile Environment: How Immigrants Became Scapegoats* (London: Verso, 2020); Lorenzo Pezzani, "Hostile Environments", *E-flux* (2020) www.e-flux.com/architecture/at-the-border/325761/hostile-environments/ (accessed 18 September 2021).

[37] Marley Morris and Amreen Qureshi, *Locked Out of a Livelihood: The Case for Reforming 'No Recourse to Public Funds'* (London: IPPR, 2021).

and other public services such as housing assistance because of their immigration status or visa conditions. This policy will have undoubtedly contributed to financial destitution and a higher number of deaths among migrants in the UK; destitution because migrants with NRPF status tend to work in industries such as hospitality where job losses were high, but they had no access to furlough or other mainstream welfare, and death because they will have continued to work if they could despite the health risks, because of lack of access to the social safety net.

Two of the most significant effects of Covid-19 on the asylum system are the greater distance separating migrants from support services, and the novel repurposing of infrastructure such as barracks for confinement. These were initially assumed to be temporary measures, but as with so much in the Covid-19 emergency, they look likely to leave a far more enduring legacy. Infrastructural investments cast a shadow over the future. A case in point is represented by the Napier Barracks: in August 2021 the Home Office declared that the Napier Barracks site might be actually used to 'house' asylum seekers until 2025.[38] Most of the places which had been repurposed for containing and housing asylum seekers in the name of a 'migration crisis' or emergency are often used longer term and become part of day-to-day governance. This is a familiar pattern across different nation states. For instance, with the outbreak of the pandemic the Italian government used 'quarantine ships' to self-isolate migrants upon arrival. Inside the ferries, migrants could not access

---

[38] Diane Taylor, "Controversial Napier Barracks in Line to House Asylum Seekers until 2025", *The Guardian*, 27 August 2021.

legal aid and were forced to live in overcrowded spaces.[39] But by the summer of 2021, this had become an integral part of Italian migration management: migrants who disembark in Southern Italy are transferred to the quarantine ships and kept there for two weeks.

On the one hand, the 'confinement continuum' refers to the partial overlapping between asylum seekers' 'carceral humanitarianism' and the hotel quarantine system for travellers coming from countries on the 'red list'.[40] On the other, it is important to stress that while the 'confinement continuum' was expanding, the other side of it was simultaneously accelerating: that is, business mobility and specific worker categories exempted from travel restrictions. This provides another context to the valuation of certain kinds of 'key worker' discussed in Chapter 3, this time, however, based on the calculation of a skills-based migration system that seeks to attract elite migrants who will not 'make recourse to public funds'. Among these workers, some were fully exempted from testing. This free-mobility umbrella included aerospace engineers, workers in the border security duties field, crown servants, defence personnel, visiting forces, government contractors, those on diplomatic missions, members of international organisations and people visiting for conferences, and representatives of a foreign country or territory or British Overseas Territories.

---

[39] ASGI, *Rights on the Skids. The Experiment of Quarantine Ships and Main Points of Criticism*, March 2021. https://inlim ine.asgi.it/wp-content/uploads/2021/05/Report-Rights-on-the-skids.-The-experiment-of-quarantine-ships-and-main-points-of-criticism-ASGI.pdf (accessed 20 September 2021).

[40] Kelly Oliver, *Carceral Humanitarianism: Logics of Refugee Detention* (Minneapolis: University of Minnesota Press, 2017).

Others have been granted facilitations, such as people working for BBC transmission networks, "business directors bringing significant numbers of jobs and investment to the UK", bus and coach drivers, civil aviation inspectors, clinical trials or studies, data infrastructure maintenance, downstream oil facility workers and elite sportspersons.[41]

The pandemic has therefore brought to public visibility, and at the same time enhanced, the privileges of elite mobility, and has further polarised the division between this elite and those individuals whose freedom of movement is subjected to different degrees of restrictions and conditions.[42] This is symptomatic of the often contradictory status of borders in the contemporary global economy, whereby they are constructed and governed so as to smooth the flow of one class of travellers, and to obstruct the flow of others, most of all those who have been illegalised by laws and policies.[43] Beyond a simple binary opposition, between the free and the unfree migrant, modern borders allow for a range of different levels

---

[41] For a full list, see: Home Office, "Coronavirus (COVID-19): Jobs That Qualify for Travel Exemptions", 2021, www.gov.uk/government/publications/coronavirus-covid-19-travellers-exempt-from-uk-border-rules/coronavirus-covid-19-travellers-exempt-from-uk-border-rules (accessed 20 September 2021).

[42] The lifting of restrictions for businesspeople and other categories triggered political quarrels, as documented by Aubrey Allegretti, "Business Leaders Arriving in England Granted Exemption from Covid Quarantine", *The Guardian*, 29 June 2021.

[43] Anderson, Bridget, *Us and Them? The Dangerous Politics of Immigration Control* (Oxford: Oxford University Press, 2013).

of inclusion and permission.[44] The 'confinement continuum' we have described here added new tiers of constraints and rights, on top of existing variegated border and visa regimes. What adds yet further complexity, however, is the entangling of these inequalities with those generated by digital health infrastructure.

Digital Health Infrastructures

The tightening of national borders by states such as the UK, which is frequently contradicted by economic dependency on overseas labour, is notionally facilitated by the creation of semi-permeable forms of bordering, which grant freedoms on the basis of potential economic contribution. The idea of a 'points-based' migration system has been celebrated across a significant swathe of the political spectrum in the UK, on the ostensible basis that it is able to distinguish between arrivals to the country using market criteria. Thus, forms of labour stratification are expected to determine freedoms to cross borders. The view of people as 'human capital' allows for a demographic perspective in which migration can be judged in terms of whether it adds or detracts from the overall asset value of the population as a whole.[45] The utopia of an economically rationalised border, which permits certain forms of

---

[44] Sandro Mezzadra and Brett Neilson, *Border as Method, or, the Multiplication of Labor* (Durham: Duke University Press, 2013).

[45] Michel Feher, "Disposing of the Discredited: A European Project". In William Callison and Zachary Manfredi (Eds.), *Mutant Neoliberalism: Market Rule and Political Rupture* (New York: Fordham University Press, 2019).

optimal migration (however understood), was further boosted following the Brexit referendum. It does, however, add significant complexity to bordering arrangements and increased demands on the forms of demographic oversight and audit, specifically in relation to which skills and qualifications people possess.

To this existing project of mobility stratification, Covid-19 added a further one of much greater complexity: to assess 'human capital' on the basis of the health risks it posed. Criteria of the market became wedded to criteria of epidemiology. The surveillance infrastructure that was necessary in order to track and manage infections, both nationally and internationally, inevitably amplified existing forms of inequality in rights, regarding the risks a person is perceived to pose, and the costs of mitigating those risks through tests and quarantining services. Moreover, as migration policies became entangled with questions of public health (in addition to issues of labour market needs), so the infrastructural challenge of tracking movement at the border joined up with that of tracking individuals throughout society. The 'crisis of space' we refer to in Chapter 1 sees borders and data extraction woven through everyday spaces and situations. And once again, the implementation of the technologies and services that facilitate bordering and data collection are, in practice, in the hands of the private sector.

One aspect of this, during the first 18 months of the pandemic, was the rapid expansion of a testing industry, able to charge often prohibitive prices for the use of tests on which mobility depended. This inevitably limited opportunities to travel to those able to pay, regardless of need to travel. In the first half of 2021, this could be as high as £225 for a single test. The mandatory test kit was introduced in February 2021, together with other anti-infection measures enforced at the border – among which the proof of a negative Covid-19 test taken no more than 72 hours prior to entering the UK border. Should travellers have wanted to end their quarantine period before day 10, they were offered a 'test to release' on day 5, but the cost varied depending on the provider and on the result timeline: if they wanted the outcome on the same day of the test, the price was as high as £200. A lucrative testing industry expanded rapidly over the months that followed. By July 2021, there were 990 private providers listed on the website of the UK Department of Health & Social Care, up from 400 a couple of months earlier – another whole sector whose revenue was implicitly guaranteed by force of state decree. Yet, as discovered by the *Financial Times*, only a small percentage – around 6% – of the providers listed have been accredited by the UK Accreditation Service (UKAS).[46] One particular testing firm, Immensa, was discovered to have been awarded a £119 million contract (without a standard tendering process) for offering PCR tests, just a few months after being incorporated in May 2020, with a single individual owner with a background in DNA testing.[47] By the autumn of 2021, the firm had been engulfed in multiple controversies, surrounding the non-delivery of test results, allegations of staff at a Wolverhampton lab sleeping, drinking and playing football, and – most seriously – the discovery of 43,000 possible false negatives being provided.

Like bordering and detention services, healthcare in the UK had also been subject to extensive outsourcing since the 1980s, with the involvement of the same handful of 'contract

[46] Sarah Provan, "Majority of Covid Test Providers Unaccredited, Says UK Assessor", *Financial Times*, 4 August 2021.

[47] Sam Bright, "£119 Million Covid-19 Testing Contract Awarded to Four-month-old DNA Analysis Firm", *Byline Times*, 9 November 2020.

rentier' firms. However, in the current context, mobility restrictions and hygienic measures have become mutually entangled, bringing bordering contracts and healthcare contracts closer together. Yet, while the border security industry has been traditionally justified on the basis of what the sociologist Didier Bigo terms an 'insecurity continuum',[48] coming from outside – formed by migrants, potential terrorists, criminals, traffickers – the test industry has been enforced in the name of a generalised threat: every individual who enters the country becomes in principle a vehicle of contagion and, therefore, people's right to move must be conditional upon (expensive) hygienic checks.

The conflation between (restricted) right to mobility and sanitary borders was further embedded by the UK government's use of the NHS app as part of a Covid-19 passport.[49] A similar project was enforced in Europe: the implementation of the Green Digital Certificate in summer 2021 as a sort of passport, predicated on the principle that freedom of movement as well as access to social spaces could be given back to those who have been vaccinated or who can demonstrate that they recently had Covid-19.[50] These 'passports to freedom' are

---

[48] Didier Bigo, "Security and Immigration: Toward a Critique of the Governmentality of Unease", *Alternatives*, 27:1 (2002): 63–92.

[49] The NHS app should not be confused with the NHS tracing app. The former was introduced before the pandemic, in 2019, and can be used to book an appointment with a GP or for requesting prescriptions. Zoe Kleinman, "Confusion Over Use of NHS App as Covid Passport", *BBC News*, 29 April 2021.

[50] Luiza Bialasiewicz and Alberto Alemanno, "The Dangerous Illusion of an EU Vaccine Passport", *openDemocracy*, 9 March 2021.

essentially based on the containment and immobilisation of some. The risk, as with so many infrastructures rolled out over the period we are describing, is that this becomes a permanent check on the mobility of people, both at an international and a domestic level, while at the same time further empowering the firms, platforms and security services that facilitate and exploit this new infrastructure.

As these policies and infrastructures were rolled out in the UK over 2021, they were characterised by considerable confusion and uncertainty surrounding costs, not to mention a period of constant updating of 'green', 'amber' and 'red' list countries, which generated havoc for travel plans. For a while, evidenced 'reasonable excuses' for travel had to be provided, or else travellers could be turned away at airports. One clear pattern throughout this, however, was the sudden raising of costs associated with travel: British holidaymakers spent an estimated £1.1 billion over the summer of 2021 on tests, with each test costing an average of £93.[51] Those who made a small error (for instance, taking one of their tests an hour or two outside of the required window prior to flying) could be refused entry to a plane and required to pay for a new test. The implied political priority was that, firstly, the growth of the testing industry should be incentivised through the opportunity of super-large profits, and secondly, that the cost of tests would be absorbed where necessary by business expenses. However, the interests of those with needs and 'reasonable excuses' to travel unconnected with business (or leisure) were entirely neglected.

Away from the border, the history of health mobile infrastructures during Covid-19 is also a history of health

---

[51] Ben Ireland, "Covid Tests 'Cost Travellers £1.1bn This Summer'", *Travel Weekly*, 10 September 2021.

surveillance systems and of the acceptance and refusal to be tracked for the 'common good.' Yet, while quite lot of focus has been dedicated in the media and in public debate to questions of surveillance and monitoring of the population through tracing apps, much less has been said about the political economy of digital health infrastructures. Indeed, outsourcing policies and private–public contracts stalk the increasing digitalisation of the health system in the UK. The country is home to one of the largest and highest-quality healthcare datasets in the world and Electronic Health Record (EHR) data-driven research represents a prime opportunity for private actors to develop this data as an asset from which they can both draw financial gain and expand their capture and capitalisation of data.[52] Sensitive patient data, in other words, is transformed from being a public asset into a private asset that circulates in a 'biomedical knowledge economy' populated by public health organisations, academia and biomedical industry actors.

During the pandemic, the contested and opaque role of Palantir, the US tech giant funded by the CIA, has exemplified this opportunity for the conversion of public data into a capital asset. In December 2020, Palantir was awarded a £23.5 million contract by the NHS for continuing to work on the provision of data management platform services until December 2022.[53] The first contract (£1 million) was awarded in March 2020 by

---

[52] Paraskevas Vezyridis and Stephen Timmons, "E-Infrastructures and the Divergent Assetization of Public Health Data: Expectations, Uncertainties, and Asymmetries", *Social Studies of Science*, 51:4 (2021): 606–627.

[53] Andrea Downey, "Cabinet Minister Owned £90,000 Shares in Faculty at Time of NHSX Contract", *Digital Health*, 18 November 2020.

the 'digital transformation arm' of the health service known as 'NHSX', to help the NHS develop its Covid-19 Data Store. As openDemocracy revealed, Palantir made £22 million in profits in 2020 and, overall, the UK government awarded the company about £46 million in public contracts.[54] However, as The Bureau of Investigative Journalism found out, negotiations between the NHS and the US tech giant were in place already in 2019. Among the concerns raised by organisations such as Foxglove and openDemocracy, there is again the worrying lack of transparency in the contract award procedure. Yet, thanks to Foxglove and openDemocracy's lawsuit, in March 2021 the UK government agreed to not continue the collaboration with Palantir in the longer term without public consultation, with the assurance in the interim that Palantir could not access NHS data other than for Covid-related purposes. A similar challenge was made to a contract between NHSX and Faculty, a British artificial intelligence startup who got access to patient data to build real-time predictive models of Covid-19 outbreaks.[55]

Alongside Palantir, Amazon, Google and Microsoft have been awarded contracts to work on the NHS Covid-19 Data Store.[56] Palantir's key role in digital health infrastructures has not been circumscribed to the UK. The company declares

---

[54] Martin Williams, "'Spy Tech' Firm Palantir Made £22m Profit After NHS Data Deal", *openDemocracy*, 23 August 2021.

[55] Paul Lewis, David Conn and David Pegg "UK Government Using Confidential Patient Data in Coronavirus Response", *The Guardian*, 12 April 2020.

[56] Mary Fitzgerald, "Under Pressure, UK Government Releases NHS COVID Data Deals with Big Tech", *openDemocracy*, 5 June 2020.

that it works for different "health agencies across the world to create national Common Operating Pictures" to manage responses to Covid-19, as well as to improve medical supply chains.[57] In Greece, Palantir was awarded a contract from the Greek government to manage the text system, through which Greek citizens had to communicate when and for which reasons they were leaving their home during the lockdown. Similarly to the UK experience, the involvement of Palantir in Greece triggered a harsh debate due to the lack of transparency about the contract award as well as about Palantir's access to biometric data. Despite the public outcry and privacy lawsuits putting obstacles in front of these tech companies, it is evident that aggressive forms of 'data rentiership' – involving "the extraction and capture of value through different modes of ownership and control over [data] resources and assets" – represent an accumulation strategy that is poised to feed off appeals to 'innovation' in areas such as healthcare (and education and remote working, as explored in Chapters 3 and 5).[58] An exceptional crisis like Covid-19 provides entry points to previously sheltered public data as well as the construction of new datasets. While the value of the contracts is important to data rentiers, the access and control of the data itself offers the potential to capitalise future streams of revenue off the back of these assets, offering

---

[57] Palantir, "Responding to Covid-19", www.palantir.com/covid19/ (accessed 20 September 2021).

[58] Kean Birch, Margaret Chiappetta and Anna Artyushina, "The Problem *of* Innovation in Technoscientific Capitalism: Data *Rentiership* and the Policy Implications of Turning Personal Digital Data into a Private Asset", *Policy Studies*, 41:5 (2020): 470.

services such as clinical risk prediction and recruitment subjects for research trials.[59]

The implementation of the NHS contact tracing app in September 2020 followed similar tracing apps which had been launched in other countries a few months before, without much success. For instance, Italy, the first European country severely hit by the pandemic, launched the contact tracing app Immuni in June 2020 and, yet, a few months later, in October, only around 24% of the population had downloaded it. The scepticism about the actual utility of tracing apps as well as about the use of the data collected was widespread across Europe. In the UK, the number of downloads registered by the NHS days after the launch of the app reached 10 million.[60] Nevertheless, this data does not tell us anything about the actual use of the app – the extent to which people who downloaded it actually became "users" and for how long.

Questions around data privacy and the enforcement of a 'digital hostile environment' towards marginalised communities, migrants and non-citizens took centre stage in the debate about the risks associated with the use of the NHS tracing app.[61] But much less has been said about people's actual use and non-use of the app, and how refusal might be linked to a

---

[59] Vezyridis and Timmons, "E-Infrastructures".

[60] Alisa Cowen, "Ten Million People Have Downloaded the NHS Covid-19 App", National Health Executive, 28 September 2020.

[61] Liberty, "Challenge Hostile Environment Data Sharing", 25 August 2021, www.libertyhumanrights.org.uk/campaign/challenge-hostile-environment-data-sharing/ (accessed 20 September 2021).

generalised scepticism about health-related measures shaped by tracking policies. This poses unanswered questions about the ultimate beneficiaries or commercial uses of the data. The NHS app has been backed up by Apple and Google – indeed it can only be downloaded from the Apple Store and Google Play. About seven months later, in April 2021, Google and Apple blocked the update of the NHS tracing app, accusing the UK government of gathering the location data of the users.[62]

The frontier of technological and biosecurity innovation in the UK moved rapidly due to the emergency needs of the Department of Health & Social Care. By the summer of 2021, the UK government was testing machine learning and AI tools for improving the NHS app. The NHS enrolled AI tools for updating and improving the NHS app in order to streamline the health system, not least to assist with the huge backlog of non-Covid-19 medical cases that had built up. Much faith was placed in increased digitisation of data and machine learning, which inevitably involves bringing the commercial technology sector further into the health service. For example, the NHS has worked with Israeli startup, Healthy.io, which is well known for using machine learning in the health sector. In 2020, the NHS started to partner with Healthy.io to provide 'smart' urine tests to patients and, soon after that, for developing the NHS app by introducing AI tools. During Covid-19, borders and health infrastructures have become more intermingled, while access to mobility and to private and public spaces increasingly depends on negative Covid-19 tests.

---

[62] Michael Behr, "NHS Covid-19 App Update Blocked by Apple and Google, Digit", 13 April 2021, https://digit.fyi/nhs-covid-19-app-update-blocked-by-apple-and-google/ (accessed 20 September 2021).

What Was Revealed?

The establishment of a 'red list' of countries in 2021 illustrates well how exclusionary infrastructures of health and mobility restrictions become entangled with each other, and how this clearly enhances class and nation-based inequalities in freedom of movement. The criteria through which countries were allocated onto different coloured 'lists' were never made entirely clear, resulting in bitter controversy and a collapse in the public legitimacy of the entire policy. According to a Global Travel Taskforce report, the UK 'traffic light system' included the rate of infection, the prevalence of variants of concern, the percentage of the population vaccinated and the country's access to reliable scientific data and genomic sequencing.[63] Only British citizens or residents were able to enter the UK from countries listed on the red list; and these latter were authorised for entry only if they self-isolated for ten days in a quarantine hotel at their own cost. By the summer of 2021, about 49% of the world population was de facto included on the UK's 'red list' if we consider their country of origin, but not one country from the Global North was included by this point.

The early management of Covid-19 in the UK was characterised by a multiplication of digital and physical border infrastructures, as well as by the acceleration of class and nation-based inequalities. Most of these border infrastructures have enhanced social and economic inequalities within

---

[63] Department for Transport, "Global Travel Taskforce Sets out Framework to Safely Reopen International travel", 9 April 2021, www.gov.uk/government/news/global-travel-taskforce-sets-out-framework-to-safely-reopen-international-travel (accessed 20 September 2021).

the UK and have put in place new forms of confinement, justified in the name of citizens' protection against a health threat that is unquestionably global. Yet, the UK is not an exception nor an exemplary case study to study the enforcement and management of border infrastructures during the pandemic. Rather, it is a hybrid case in point in which common global trends and peculiar border infrastructures coexist. On the one hand, the enforcement of a confinement continuum and the multiplication of hierarchies of mobility is a global phenomenon. On the other, the temporal conjuncture of Brexit and Covid-19 has influenced the ways in which multiple mobility restrictions have been enforced and might persist in the future.

As political theorists Sandro Mezzadra and Brett Neilson have pointed out, far "from serving merely to block or obstruct global passages of people, money, or objects", borders "have become central devices for their articulation. Borders play a key role in the production of the heterogeneous time and space of contemporary global and postcolonial capitalism".[64] The re-bordering of the world during Covid-19, this chapter has shown, did not stop movements as such: rather, it has strengthened class-based mobility and, at the same time, enforced a confinement continuum that has targeted both travellers and migrants according to a 'confine to protect' logic. Covid-19 has been turned into a fertile terrain for boosting outsourcing policies in the UK in the field of health, asylum and border controls. Where contractors are brought in primarily for their surveillance capacities, then it must be considered that the corporate purpose is extraction of data as well as profit.

If, on the one hand, it is worth stressing that outsourcing has a longstanding tradition in these sectors and did not

---

[64] Mezzadra and Neilson. *Border as Method*, ix.

start with the pandemic, on the other Covid-19 has been an occasion for fostering it and for testing border infrastructures that might remain in place in the future. The extent to which some of the border infrastructures here described will remain in place for the long term is impossible to know. However, an insight into the digital and physical infrastructures enforced during Covid-19 and new bordering mechanisms enforced in the name of 'confine to protect' sheds light, among other things, on outsourcing practices taking place at the border and in the health sector. The multiplication of border infrastructures in the UK foregrounds how the 'franchise state' has been reorganising border security industry and the digitisation of the health system during Covid-19.

5

Education without Context: The Politics of 'Learning'

For thousands of years, education has largely depended on face-to-face contact. Teaching and learning have occurred in particular enclosed physical spaces: the classroom, the lecture theatre and the seminar room. These might not serve every dimension of education, but they have historically been a necessary minimum. And since education involves the physical congregation of teachers and learners, it has also been an inescapably social phenomenon, inasmuch as it involves relationships, mutual understanding and an instinctive awareness of the context in which another person is speaking or writing. The possibility of things making sense in these enclosed spaces conditions how the world comes to make sense to us more broadly. The extra-curricular spaces of playgrounds, canteens, student unions and event spaces play a crucial role in enabling relationships and identities to be forged.

As a virus transmitted through face-to-face contact, especially indoors, Covid-19 unleashed rapid and unprecedented chaos in educational institutions around the world over the course of 2020–21. The closure of schools and universities affected 1.7 billion pupils and students around the world and over 9 million in the UK. Many children in the UK lost over a hundred days of learning between March 2020 and July 2021 due to school closures, while GCSE and A-level students in

England and Wales suffered the chaos and emotional turmoil of exams being cancelled, and their marks being algorithmically set and then reset.

The rapid and often messy 'pivot' to online learning, both at school and university level, would have been impossible only 15 years earlier, prior to the near-universality of broadband internet, smart phones and platforms such as Zoom and Google Classroom. This digital infrastructure enabled teaching and learning to continue in the absence of physical teaching spaces, but it also posed a whole new range of challenges to students, parents, teachers and policymakers, revealing and deepening various inequalities and class dynamics, not simply in availability of technology, but in the informal social resources on which education implicitly depends.

Higher education (HE) faced its own distinctive challenges and emergencies, rooted in the fact that, ordinarily, close to half a million students move around the country each year to study and live with one another, many in privately managed halls of residence. Over half a million overseas students were enrolled in UK universities when the pandemic struck, many paying fees at a level that are crucial for the cross-subsidisation of academic research. Had these living arrangements and enrolments been formally deferred or suspended, it could have triggered a financial crisis in the HE sector, parts of which were already facing economic threats on numerous fronts. The financial hit was nowhere near as bad as feared in the summer of 2020, but efforts to avoid it brought their own costs, not least for students suffering the effects of isolation in halls of residence, paying for accommodation they scarcely used, or paying for online tuition that many struggled to engage with. Academic workloads and stress levels rose severely at the same time.

As with so many other sectors and public services during the pandemic, the Covid-induced crisis of education was also an opportunity for profits. Beneficiaries included those firms that won government contracts for the provision of school meals, laptops and tutoring programmes, and the 'EdTech' sector, which supplies the platforms through which 'e-learning' can take place.[1] Private schools, tutors and universities that were already seeking to expand their 'market' to exploit the possibilities of online tuition also treated the pandemic as an opportunity. Amid the crisis, there were also political opportunities for those seeking to constrain the purpose and curriculum of education, but also countervailing forces – energised in 2020 by Black Lives Matter – aimed at expanding the scope of what was taught and how.

Covid-19 not only shone an unforgiving light on class and inequality in the UK, but also on the mechanistic expectations that have long been placed on education (buttressed by instruments of audit, league tables, digital platforms and student debt) to ameliorate and hide these social realities. The closure of schools and campuses not only revealed deep social and cultural inequalities in British society, but also served to highlight the importance of those contextual aspects of education – of place, history, family and community – that are largely eliminated from the account of education that shapes both government policy and the visions of the EdTech industry. A set of policies that strategically ignore the social qualities of a school, classroom or campus (because they are hard to capture or quantify) was suddenly exposed to the consequences of having to abandon those qualities altogether. The

---

[1] Ben Williamson, "New Pandemic EdTech Power Networks", *Code Acts in Education*, 1 April 2020; Ben Williamson, "Education Technology Seizes a Pandemic Opening", *Current History*, 120:822 (2021): 15–20.

results were brutal, though that brutality was heavily concentrated on those already disadvantaged.

Education is not ordinarily viewed as a central concern of political economists, even while it has become increasingly treated as an economic 'investment' by policymakers. Yet the unprecedented disruption of schools and universities over the period examined in this book still revealed – indeed 'photosynthesised' – many of the same political and economic patterns as we have explored in previous chapters. Firstly, there is the distinctive balance between centralisation and decentralisation that characterises the era of the 'franchise state'. A central priority of education policy over recent decades has been to wrest power away from professional educators and local authorities, and hand it to commercial or quasi-commercial entities, which exist in a symbiotic relationship with central government. The 'contract rentiers' who we have encountered in previous chapters are also a feature of the education landscape, and many have exploited the pandemic to their advantage. Once again, cultural and social proximity to the Conservative Party and central government represented a source of revenue for beneficiaries, while distance was a source of risk.

Secondly, the story of education in 2020–21 offers an additional glimpse of the traditionally unacknowledged 'well' of care, which is drawn upon in order to sustain households and communities without adequate monetary compensation or recognition. As we shall outline, the partial closure of schools and universities placed exceptional strains on teachers and parents, who faced onerous new social and educational responsibilities well beyond their formal duties. In orthodox economic jargon, this informal and unremunerated support is a type of 'externality' to the real work of 'delivering learning outcomes' as revealed by tests and league tables. But Covid-19 demonstrated its indispensable value, which is too often hidden. Students and pupils who lost that support suffered in manifold ways, some of which will cast an influence over their long-term future and that of society, quite aside from 'official' anxieties regarding the loss to the economy.

Thirdly, the 'crisis of space' that we diagnosed in Chapter 1 is scarcely more palpable than in the sphere of education. As the critical education scholar Ben Williamson has argued, "it is now clear that the dominant education policy preoccupation globally is how to deliver schooling without schools and degrees without campuses".[2] The key conditions of this new spatial settlement are, as we have outlined, 'hyper-domestication', which places greater and greater burdens upon the *home* as a space of value creation; and 'platformisation', which renders social and economic relations dependent on digital infrastructures and amenable to data extraction. While few could have predicted the full scale of the disruption to education over 2020–21 (and few would publicly celebrate it), it brought to light possibilities for a different spatial organisation of education, which undoubtedly offer lucrative financial opportunities to EdTech and private education providers.

This chapter is structured as follows. We start as before by mapping some of the key political and ideological trends in education policy over the years leading up to the pandemic. Secondly, we narrate the events of 2020–21 as they afflicted schools and universities in the UK, and the policies that were rolled out in response. Thirdly, we distinguish the main winners and losers from this historic interruption. We conclude by asking what in particular was revealed, which could have political consequences beyond the period of lockdowns themselves – consequences that we return to in the following chapter.

---

[2] Williamson, "New Pandemic EdTech Power Networks".

Before 2020

Inequality in the UK reached its lowest ever recorded level in 1977, but has been growing steadily since, both in terms of income and wealth.[3] In relation to education, the 1970s are often looked back on as a time of recession, when parent confidence in schools deteriorated and rising participation in HE went into reverse.[4] It was, however, a time of unusual politicisation of education and pedagogy, driven by comparatively high levels of autonomy for the teaching profession, allowing for considerable control over the curriculum and experimentation.[5] The ideological path away from that era, which promised both to constrain the political power of educators and to provide moral underpinnings for an era of rising inequality, is the one associated with the idea of 'meritocracy'.[6]

Following the example of the United States, the UK's turn towards markets and a more individualistic culture would, it was hoped, become underpinned by a system of educational credentialism, in which individuals would rise or fall to whatever level their talents deserved, with formal qualifications serving as a kind of signalling device to the market. A vigorous system of testing and audit, both of learners and the

---

[3] Thomas Piketty, *Capital in the Twenty-First Century* (Cambridge, MA: Harvard University Press, 2014).

[4] Peter Mandler, *The Crisis of the Meritocracy: Britain's Transition to Mass Education Since the Second World War* (Oxford: Oxford University Press, 2020).

[5] Ken Jones, *Education in Britain: 1944 to the Present* (London: Polity, 2016).

[6] Jo Littler, *Against Meritocracy: Culture, Power and Myths of Mobility* (London: Routledge, 2018).

institutions that taught them, would provide the alternative to a society organised around social class. Participation in HE would rise, delivering economic benefits to graduates and the broader economy. Academics and teachers would be expected to demonstrate the quality of their research and teaching in codified ways.

This ideal of a socially mobile, individualised culture was accompanied by closer attention to the economic benefits of education, both to the individual recipient and the economy more broadly. Visions of the 'knowledge economy', fuelled by investments in 'human capital', had been gathering momentum among economists and management gurus since the 1950s, but attained greater urgency following the de-industrialisation of the 1970s and early 1980s. This paradigm stressed that the true value of education was reflected in the labour market, productivity and GDP, but that realising this economic potential required an ideological reset across the educational establishment, which teachers, lecturers and local authorities were politically resistant to. If education could become valued in terms of quantitative evidence and outcomes, this would, it was supposed, release it from the grip of progressive pedagogical dogmas.

The major policy reforms that facilitated this shift in England occurred in the late 1980s, with the launch of the Research Assessment Exercise for universities in 1986, and the Education Reform Act two years later, which gave birth to a centralised 'national curriculum' and audit of school performance against the four 'key stages' of pupil progression. 1988 was also the turning point when participation in HE began its steady upwards climb from around 15% of school-leavers to 50%. The creation of Ofsted, which centralised school inspections, followed in 1992. Since this pivotal period, education policy in the UK has depended increasingly on instruments of statistical audit and league tables in order to drive up 'standards' and to inject a market-like competitive ethos into the running of schools and universities. While norms of academic freedom mean universities retain autonomy over the content of what they research and teach, the teaching profession and unions have been steadily constrained by curriculum reforms and the power of audit, which have seen more and more aspects of teaching governed by regimes of data collection and analysis.

The Labour government of 1997–2010 largely perpetuated the existing data-led approach to schools, expanding the range of data to be collected in various ways. The birth of 'City Academies' in 2000 (funded by and accountable to central government, rather than local education authorities) was justified on the basis that these would drive up standards in deprived areas of traditionally low attainment. Meanwhile, with rising participation in HE, and in view of the labour market returns of a degree, Labour introduced 'top-up fees' for university tuition in England and Wales. This initiated a process of marketisation in which questions of 'value for money' and 'return on investment' would soon become asked of university degrees, and which inevitably raised the profile of league tables and audits in the governance and image of the sector as a whole.

Governing via standardised audit and league table represents a distinctive formatting of the relationship between state and service delivery. Sociologists have used terms such as 'commensuration' and 'the audit society' to capture this ambition to quantify everything and render individuals and institutions comparable. In the case of schools, this model of governance hands considerable responsibility to headteachers and teachers to improve measured outcomes, but reduced levels of discretion regarding what to teach or what to value. In the case of universities, it forces attention towards various metrics of 'excellence' that divert managerial attention towards whatever indicators happen to influence league table position.[7] In any case, it threatens to devalue (and potentially defund) aspects of an educational institution that don't contribute positively to those scores, potentially leading to a narrowing of curricula and neglect of extra-curricular activities.[8]

Where competition becomes the dominant ethos of education, its value increasingly appears relative, that is, as a means of standing out from one's rivals. The mantra of 'excellence' in school and university audits suggests that success consists in *standing out from or above* others. The logic of private education (where fees trebled in real terms between the early 1980s and 2017) switches from mere cultural reproduction of class to victory in an ever more feverish game. A side-effect of the logic of competitive parenting and schooling is the growth of the private tutoring market, now viewed as essential by many parents who are already using private schools, but also relied upon by schools and parents in the state school system to enable children to keep up with others and boost grades.[9]

---

[7] See Wendy Espeland and Michael Sauder, *Engines of Anxiety: Academic Rankings, Reputation and Accountability* (New York: Russell Sage Foundation, 2016).

[8] See Alice Bradbury, *Pressure, Anxiety and Collateral Damage* (London: More than a Score, 2019).

[9] Mark Bray, "Shadow Education in Europe: Growing Prevalence, Underlying Forces, and Policy Implications", *ECNU Review of Education* (January 2020), doi:10.1177/2096531119890142; Judith Ireson and Katie Rushforth, "Private Tutoring at Transition Points in the English Education System: Its Nature, Extent and Purpose", *Research Papers in Education*, 26:1 (2011).

Private tutoring makes a mockery of the ideal of 'meritocracy': 35% of children from advantaged backgrounds have received private tutoring at some point, compared to just 18% from disadvantaged ones.[10] This industry would come to play a pivotal role in the policy response to the pandemic.

Rising competitiveness was accompanied by a distinctive turn within dominant pedagogical traditions, which the critical education scholar Gert Biesta has diagnosed as 'learnification'.[11] Biesta pinpoints the late 1990s as a moment when organisations such as the OECD and UNESCO began to speak habitually of 'learning' as the path to social cohesion, employment and economic growth. 'Learning', unlike 'education', was no longer something dependent on professional teachers or scholars, but an ongoing cognitive process that is 'lifelong' and can occur anywhere. By releasing more 'learning' in society, policymakers could therefore deliver on broader objectives, while also benefitting the individuals doing the learning. Education is not only instrumentalised by 'learnification' (becoming judged in terms of its economic and social outcomes), but educational specialists are potentially bypassed or forced to compete with rival providers, who are more attentive to the measurable outcomes of learning. This includes an expanding role for the 'shadow education' provided by private tutors and families in enabling individual learners to compete with their peers. The family

---

[10] John Jerrim, *Extra Time: Private Tuition and Out-of-school Study, New International Evidence* (London: Sutton Trust, 2017).

[11] Gert Biesta, "Interrupting the Politics of Learning", *Power and Education*, 5:1 (2013): 4–15.

becomes a crucial incubator of learning and 'human capital' appreciation.

The centralisation of the school curriculum and of testing regimes since the 1980s, together with this turn towards 'learning' as the measurable output of teaching, has led education to take on the qualities of training and behavioural control. With respect to English, for example, there has been a turn towards the teaching and testing of 'literacy' – also pushed by the OECD since the 1990s – as an attainment of an individual child that can be measured in a standardised way across a population, allowing for international comparisons.[12] With the turn towards 'learning', all the emphasis of education is on the ability to demonstrate a level of 'attainment' on paper (or on screen), which serves as an auditable data trail; the elements of teaching that involve oral communication, listening and reading are only valued to the extent that they deliver the ability to manipulate letters and numbers correctly. The relation between teacher and learner becomes a transactional one, in which a certain skill or item of knowledge is passed from one party to another. Within HE, this transactional ethos produces the uneasy situation of students being expected to evaluate the quality of programmes (via instruments such as the National Student Survey), as if they were the ultimate

---

[12] Mary Hamilton, Bryan Maddox and Camilla Addey, *Literacy as Numbers: Researching the Politics and Practices of International Literary Assessment* (Cambridge: Cambridge University Press, 2015); John Yandell et al., "Who Me? Hailing Individuals as Subjects: Standardised Literacy Testing as an Instrument of Neo-Liberal Ideology". In Seyyed-Abdolhamid Mirhosseini and Peter De Costa (Eds.), *The Sociopolitics of English Language Testing* (London: Bloomsbury, 2020).

authority on topics that they are simultaneously seeking to learn about.

This vision of education is driven by conflicting ambitions: to both ensure a 'dynamic' and 'meritocratic' society (in which the truly talented rise to the top), and to maximise the 'inclusion' of all, for instance by encouraging a rising number of people to go to university. This produces an unwieldy model of egalitarian elitism, which, through standardising and centralising tests and frameworks, seeks to judge all institutions and individuals according to a single set of benchmarks. On the one hand, this purports to give everyone a chance; on the other, it is potentially blind to the influence of culture, geography, class and history over education and life chances. The contextual aspect of education (the 'externality' to the test or league table) becomes airbrushed out, save for where it can be framed in psychological terms of individual 'resilience', 'growth mindset' or other cognitive and behavioural categories that might explain why the desire and aptitude for learning is unevenly distributed. So too does the unique contribution of an individual teacher.

Austerity Logics

Layered on top of these post-1980s developments, two further crucial trends were at work in England in the decade prior to the Covid-19 pandemic, both of which further constrained the social purpose of education and the autonomy of teachers. The first saw a deepening of trends towards quasi-market competition in education, both in schools and universities, unleashed by the reforms of the Coalition and Conservative governments. English schools suffered a 9% drop in real-terms funding per pupil over the decade leading up to 2020, the largest drop in over 40 years, and concentrated most heavily in deprived areas.[13] The number of children in classes of over 30 pupils rose by 20% in this time. Meanwhile, the gap between per-pupil spending in state schools and that in private schools doubled over this period.[14] The raising of university tuition fees to £9,000 per annum in 2010 completed a shift towards viewing HE as an 'investment', whose value was to be found in its future labour market returns.[15] This was followed by associated instruments (such as the Teaching Excellence Framework) and indicators (such as data on graduate earnings broken down by degree programme) that reinforced a financial view of HE. In late 2013, the government announced that the 'cap' on the number of students any institution could take would be abolished in 2015, opening the way for rapid expansion of higher-ranking universities. The government was clear that it wanted to see a fully competitive market between HE 'providers', which meant making it easier for popular institutions to grow, new ones to enter the 'market', and existing ones to fail and exit.[16]

---

[13] Luke Sibieta, "School Spending in England: Trends Over Time and Future Outlook", Briefing Note (Institute for Fiscal Studies, 2 September 2021).

[14] Luke Sibieta, "The Growing Gap Between State School and Private School Spending", Observation (Institute for Fiscal Studies, 8 October 2021).

[15] See Andrew McGettigan, *The Great University Gamble: Money, Markets and the Future of Higher Education* (London: Pluto, 2015).

[16] Department for Business, Innovation & Skills, "Higher Education: Success as a Knowledge Economy", Policy Paper, 26 May 2016.

Over the same period, with government funds shrinking, universities became increasingly adept at using their balance sheets in pursuit of rapid expansion. Often based on projections of uninterrupted growth of overseas students, levels of debt rose rapidly, including via the issuing of bonds, something that rose from a single deal worth £272 million in 2007, but had reached £2.4 billion a decade later.[17] To facilitate expansion plans, a vast programme of student accommodation construction has occurred, based on additional debt. This has become fertile territory for investment banks (such as Goldman Sachs), who have established student accommodation service providers, financed by pension funds, which contract with universities. A whole new asset class has been established, underpinned by the assumption of indefinite income in the form of student rental payments, which in many cases are guaranteed by the universities concerned, leaving them saddled with the risk of such a flow of students being interrupted. The scale of this financial industry was signified in 2020, when Blackstone acquired student accommodation firm iQ from Goldman Sachs for £4.7 billion, the largest property deal in UK history. The financial commitments woven through universities and accommodation providers would prove decisive in the progression of the pandemic. This is yet another instance of how housing's pivotal financial position would shape the course of the pandemic in the UK.

The notorious school reforms pushed through by Michael Gove between 2010–14 sought to further centralise the regulation of schools, through expanding the Academies programme

---

[17] Alex Katsomitros, "The Emerging University Bonds Market", *World Finance*, 20 April 2018, www.worldfinance.com/markets/the-emerging-university-bonds-market (accessed 5 October 2021).

(by 2020, the Department for Education was acting as the de facto regulator of 8,700 schools) and unleashing an even more exacting system of audit, 'Progress 8'. This new data specifically discounted the social challenges faced by schools in disadvantaged areas (which had been accounted for under Labour reforms via a measure of 'contextual value added'), and made individual teachers accountable for the progress of each individual pupil, as judged according to an 'expected' attainment score.[18] Gove also prioritised discipline, with several academies distinguishing themselves through enforcement of silence in corridors, punishment through isolation and rules such as 'no touching'. Encapsulating Gove's vision was the policy of fast-tracking soldiers into schools to offer guidance on behaviour.

Meanwhile, a highly controversial curriculum review conducted in 2011 resulted in a strict and centralised vision being imposed on teaching in key areas. This included a new emphasis on 'STEM' subjects, as areas that would have economic pay-off and yield innovations in the future. But it also included a reassertion of traditionalist visions of 'literacy' (demonstrated in the rote learning of grammar) and narrow nationalistic instructions for the teaching of history.[19] Gove

---

[18] Sharon Gewirtz et al., "What's Wrong with 'Deliverology'? Performance Measurement, Accountability and Quality Improvement in English Secondary Education", *Journal of Education Policy*, 36:4 (2021): 504–529.

[19] Matthew Watson, "Michael Gove's War on Professional Historical Expertise: Conservative Curriculum Reform, Extreme Whig History and the Place of Imperial Heroes in Modern Multicultural Britain", *British Politics*, 15:3 (2020): 271–290.

thereby helped revive a longstanding conservative campaign, dating back to the 1960s, against allegedly progressive, relativist or 'PC' values within the teaching profession and the local authorities that continue to oversee non-academised schools. These values, increasingly framed by the conservative media as 'woke', were also alleged to have stifled 'free speech' on campuses and to have drawn too many students towards 'low-value' degrees in the humanities and social sciences. The economistic attack on teachers and universities, that they don't deliver marketable outcomes, thereby works in tandem with a cultural attack, that they are disloyal to national traditions and 'Western' values.

This decade of Conservative policy reforms thus heaped unprecedented pressure on professional educators *and* on learners, further constraining the function of educational institutions and teachers through metrics, while adding cultural pressures to stick to certain nationally mandated narratives. The assumption that a teacher is simply an intermediary for the transmission of pre-accredited knowledge and skills to a recipient had steadily undermined the professional authority of educators since the 1980s (while the fear of knowledge and education being instrumentalised is a much longer-standing feature of modern critique), but was amplified under a Conservative regime that once again represented teachers, lecturers and local government as obstructive and ideologically motivated. Reforms that sought deliberately to individualise accountability, squeeze out space for creativity or experimentation, increase testing, narrow the curriculum, step up cultural attacks on educators and tie the value of education to the labour market were a recipe for deteriorating mental health rates among teachers, pupils and students.[20]

---

[20] Bradbury, *Pressure, Anxiety and Collateral Damage.*

The deterioration of the relationship between teachers and the government, manifest in mutual distrust and resentment, in the years preceding the pandemic would shape how its impact on education would be handled.

This relates to one of the most worrying developments in UK society of recent years, the dramatic increase in mental health problems among children, which was cast into even starker relief by the pandemic. A major NHS study published in the summer of 2020 reported that clinically significant mental health conditions among children had risen by a third over the previous five years, and that one in six children now had a probable mental health condition.[21] In the year immediately prior to the arrival of Covid-19, referrals to children's mental health services rose by an astonishing 35%, while the number of children actually accessing treatment rose by just 4%.[22] While there can be no straightforward causal link between education policy and psychiatric symptoms, these trends deserve to be seen in an educational context that has piled pressure on children (and teachers) via tests and exams, steadily reduced break time, and reduced unstructured social opportunities for children.[23]

---

[21] NHS Digital, "Survey Conducted in July 2020 Shows One in Six Children Having a Probable Mental Disorder", 22 October 2020.

[22] Children's Commissioner, "Damage to Children's Mental Health Caused by Covid Crisis Could Last for Years Without a Large-scale Increase for Children's Mental Health Services", 28 January 2021.

[23] UCL Institute of Education, "Break Time Cuts Could Be Harming Children's Development", 10 May 2019.

Platform Logics

The second trend, which shaped how educational institutions responded to the pandemic, was the rise of digital platforms and 'e-learning', facilitated especially by US technology companies, including the giant platform providers. The promise of online learning, as something that was both vastly more efficient than in-person teaching and potentially 'personalised' to the needs and behaviours of each individual learner, had been articulated by various technologists and innovation theorists since the early 2000s. The launch of successful 'MOOCs' (Massive Open Online Courses) by Stanford and MIT in 2011, with tens of thousands of students enrolled on individual modules, seemed to represent the actualisation of that vision. What was less recognised in this initial success was that the courses that worked online were those that taught codified, technical skills, which could be learnt in bitesize 'chunks' (such as maths and computing), and were taken by relatively affluent, self-directed students.[24] Many already worked in the technology sector, and were seeking to upgrade their credentials for the marketplace.

The apparent success of MOOCs led to a rush of investment into EdTech, with Amazon, Facebook, Microsoft, Google and Apple all expanding their e-learning services. Between 2012 and 2018, there was an explosion of new MOOCs or learning platforms, effectively partnerships between technology companies and universities to deliver online courses. Meanwhile, EdTech platforms started to provide the infrastructure on which schools operated in the US: by 2017, half of all American school pupils were using Google products in class, and Google Chromebooks made up 58% of all the mobile

---

[24] Justin Reich, *Failure to Disrupt: Why Technology Alone Can't Transform Education* (Cambridge, MA: Harvard University Press, 2020).

devices ordered.[25] Until 2020, this was far in advance of the reach of major EdTech platforms within UK schools, though private schools (such as Harrow, whose partnership with Pearson now has 75,000 overseas enrolments) and universities have deployed various e-learning tools for some time. Yet schools had widely adopted associated technologies aimed at steering 'learning behaviours' through 'gamifying' learning and rewarding positive behaviours, such as ClassDojo and Mathletics.[26]

To be sure, there are alternative visions and practices of online teaching that are not profit-driven, and resist instrumentalism.[27] The technology itself did not pre-ordain how EdTech would develop. What's crucial is how the business models and technological affordances of large platforms coincide with existing policies towards 'learnification', plus the conservative renewal of disciplinary norms, to generate a distinctive set of mechanised pedagogical practices. The promise of the EdTech sector is to enable each individual learner to be monitored, so as to algorithmically tailor tuition to their unique needs, pace and learning style.[28] The more utopian expectation

---

[25] Natasha Singer, "How Google Took Over the Classroom", *New York Times*, 13 May 2017.

[26] See Ben Williamson, "Decoding ClassDojo: Psycho-policy, Social-emotional Learning and Persuasive Educational Technologies", *Learning, Media & Technology*, 42:4 (October 2017): 440–453.

[27] See Sîan Bayne et al., *The Manifesto for Online Teaching* (Cambridge, MA: MIT Press, 2020).

[28] Jeremy Knox, Ben Williamson and Sian Bayne, "Machine Behaviourism: Future Visions of 'Learnification' and 'Datafication' Across Humans and Digital Technologies", *Learning, Media & Technology*, 45:1 (January 2020): 31–45.

is that optimal learning behaviours can be identified and triggered, thanks to real-time data analytics and 'nudges', all conducted automatically in real time. Teachers become more like coaches, who provide one-to-one support and assistance, plus the various forms of human contact that computers are unable to provide, but are generally released from the labour of transferring and evaluating knowledge.[29] Meanwhile, learning is broken down into short items of content and interactive tasks, which preclude the need for the learner to attend to something for more than a short period, but take the learner on a 'journey' through a series of discrete steps to be completed one by one. Marking and feedback is provided automatically and constantly, though this inevitably limits assessment to tests such as quizzes and numerical answers.

Empirical studies have cast doubt on whether students learn better from screens than from paper,[30] and whether digital monitoring of student progress relieves teachers of work, or actually creates *more* of it.[31] It is hard to see how humanities subjects, which traditionally involve long periods of unsupervised reading and writing, prosper under

---

[29] Malin Ideland, "Google and the End of the Teacher? How a Figuration of the Teacher is Produced Through an Ed-tech Discourse", *Learning, Media & Technology*, 46:1 (January 2021): 33–46.

[30] Lauren Singer and Patricia Alexander, "Reading on Paper and Digitally: What the Past Decades of Empirical Research Reveal", *Review of Educational Research*, 87:6 (December 2017): 1007–1041.

[31] Neil Selwyn, "The Human Labour of School Data: Exploring the Production of Digital Data in Schools", *Oxford Review of Education*, 47:3 (May 2021): 353–368.

these conditions, though of course there may be other more enlightening and emancipatory ways of using these technologies. However, we can see in the ideology and the promise of corporate EdTech another force for the reduction of education to 'learning', and the further downgrading of the professional vocation of teaching towards something more transactional and results oriented. Teaching and learning potentially collapse into a single stream of interactivity, leaving data in its wake. At the same time, the shift towards online interaction and digital environments can further isolate learning from meaningful social contexts. The advantages and disadvantages possessed by different students, which might be best understood sociologically, risk being reduced to largely invisible personal attributes ('aptitudes', 'mindsets'), reflected in divergent test scores, but otherwise left out of the sphere of education.

Education Under Lockdown

In a number of ways, Covid-19 exposed the limitations and the ideology of the model sketched out in the preceding section. Firstly, it demonstrated that, to the extent that schools and universities are engines of 'social mobility' (as the ideology of 'meritocracy' intends), this is heavily thanks to the supportive and stimulating social and educational environment they provide, outside of the family, which allows young people to expand their horizons and sense of possibility. It is not simply achieved through transferring chunks of knowledge from one party to another, under the eye of various audits, algorithms and tests. Reduced wholly to that mechanistic approach, mediated wholly by computers, the effects of social class and family background become overwhelming.

Secondly, it provoked overdue debate regarding the nature and value of education, beyond its economic outcomes. Many parents were bewildered by the senseless way in which 'literacy' was being taught as a type of alien grammatical code to be mastered, now that they could witness this at home.[32] Elsewhere, the emphasis on 'learning loss' (quantified in monetary terms by bodies such as the OECD) to be compensated for by 'catch-up' appeared blind to the emotional and social aspects of school closures and the extraordinary sacrifices young people had made.[33] Coinciding with the flowering of arguments over history that grew out of the Black Lives Matter protests of 2020, the posing of these questions was one political opening that resulted from the pandemic.

It also became clear early in the pandemic, but persisting over the course of the 18 months covered by this book, that education policy typified the shambolic style of the Johnson administration, in which the planning rarely extended beyond the limits of the present news cycle. The Education Secretary, Gavin Williamson, came to appear entirely out of his depth, performing U-turn after U-turn, while authority was frequently lost somewhere between his department and Downing Street.

---

[32] See John Yandell, "Learning Under Lockdown: English Teaching in the Time of Covid-19", *Changing English*, 27:3 (July 2020): 262–269; Michael Rosen, "Dear Gavin Williamson, Could You Tell Parents What a Fronted Adverbial Is?" *The Guardian*, 12 January 2021; Eliane Glaser, "Homeschooling Has Revealed the Absurdity of England's National Curriculum", *Prospect*, 28 February 2021.

[33] The OECD's work on this was led by Eric Hanushek of the free market Hoover Institution. See Eric Hanushek and Ludgar Woessman, *The Economic Impacts of Learning Loss* (Paris: OECD, September 2020).

One of many low points occurred in December 2020 when Williamson threatened local authorities with legal action if they attempted to close their schools (in the face of the rampant 'Alpha' variant), only to announce a few days later that they would be closed by central government. The lack of any contingency planning for (inevitable) future waves of the virus was arguably the worst failing.[34] But in general, the story of English education policy over 2020–21 can be seen as a reflection on an utterly dysfunctional political elite that had come to view its own particular sector as the problem, and even as the enemy. It was in education, as much as anywhere else, where Scotland and Wales successfully distinguished themselves, and where the seams of the United Kingdom frayed.

Attendance at schools and universities across the UK was already falling due to health fears over the course of March 2020, and was down by around 70–80% by the time the Prime Minister and Scotland's First Minister belatedly announced the closure of all schools on 18 March. Ofsted suspended all routine inspections the same day, though initially citing safety fears for their own staff. Universities had already been hastily shifting teaching onto Zoom. Schools would be open for children of 'key workers' and 'vulnerable' children. Headteachers were left with responsibility for ensuring the safety of their premises for the staff working on site, with no advice on how best to achieve this, nor on how best to pursue 'remote learning'.[35] A Department for

---

[34] Nicholas Timmins, *Schools and Coronavirus: The Government's Handling of Education During the Pandemic* (London: Institute for Government, August 2021).

[35] NAO, *Support for Children's Education During the Early Stages of the Covid-19 Pandemic* (London: National Audit Office, March 2021).

Education (DfE) Covid-19 helpline was overwhelmed. Instead, schools received a blizzard of 148 DfE guidance documents between mid-March and the end of May, often leaving teachers confused and more stressed.[36] Demand for key worker and special needs places was far lower in 2020 (just 2% of children were in school in May 2020) than during the lockdown of January–March 2021, and take-up of the places was heavily skewed by class, with working-class children (including 'vulnerable children') less likely to take up places that were actually available to them.[37]

Sooner than many experts were advising, the Prime Minister announced on 28 May 2020 that schools in England and Wales would now be expected to reopen. However, by this stage the government was in direct and open conflict with the teaching unions, who had made it clear that their members would not return to working in unsafe environments. The National Education Union reported that it had not been consulted on a plan for a phased reopening (with 15 children in a class) in June, and advised its members not to 'engage' with this plan. When primary schools did start phased reopening on 1 June (for Reception, Year 1 and Year 6), attendance was around 50% of what it might have been with parents citing

---

[36] Timmins, *Schools and Coronavirus.*

[37] "We find that disadvantage is a very strong predictor of the return to school; among children who had the option to go back for in-person learning, a child in the top percentile of the pre-COVID earnings distribution was more than 25 percentage points more likely to take up that offer than his or her peer in the bottom percentile." Sarah Cattan et al., *Inequalities in Responses to School Closures Over the Course of the First Covid-19 Lockdown* (London: Institute for Fiscal Studies, April 2021).

safety fears. University campuses remained closed throughout the summer, and – presciently – Cambridge University went as far as announcing in May that its entire 2020–21 academic year would be taught online, helping to focus attention on the ongoing challenges ahead.

The most urgent policy issue that arose from lockdown was the question of feeding the 1.4 million children who had previously received free school meals, many of whose parents were now facing additional financial difficulties brought on by the pandemic. Various solutions were considered, including an uplift in benefit payments (deemed impractical by the Department for Work & Pensions) and support for schools to use their own catering arrangements, but the DfE opted for a scheme of vouchers, worth £15/week per child, redeemable in participating supermarkets. The delivery of this service was rapidly contracted out to a private IT contractor, EdenRed, which DfE recognised was ill-suited to a project of this scale and which immediately struggled with service delivery.[38] Schools were responsible for registering eligible pupils and struggled to access the system; parents experienced great delays in receiving their vouchers; customer support was inadequate. DfE officials later reported that, had the situation arisen prior to the vast academisation expansion of 2010 onwards, the obvious solution would have been to work via local government (as was more feasible in Wales and Scotland), but that "my Ministers absolutely hate local government".[39] The eventual policy was therefore the consequence of a state that trusts

---

[38] NAO, *Investigation into the Free School Meals Voucher Scheme* (London: National Audit Office, 2021).

[39] Timmins, *Schools and Coronavirus*, 7.

a small oligopoly of 'contract rentiers' more than devolved political powers.

The DfE paid the face value of the vouchers that were used, while EdenRed's revenue stream came from buying the vouchers from the supermarkets at below that value. The initial expectation was that this would cost £288 million, but following a successful campaign by the footballer Marcus Rashford to continue the scheme over the summer holidays, the total cost had risen to £384 million by the end of 2020. Yet the initial difficulties that EdenRed had in delivering this service meant that families became all the more dependent on schools and individual teachers to provide meals, alongside other forms of support that went entirely unrecognised by DfE. Especially in more deprived areas, teachers suddenly found themselves in the role of frontline social workers, delivering food parcels to families, checking on the emotional wellbeing of children, and offering various forms of social support and contact that were far less essential in more advantaged areas.[40] Many teachers found themselves confronting problems such as domestic abuse and serious mental health events, which lay well beyond the curriculum or their own professional expertise. Others delivered breakfasts and clothing to children.[41] As we highlighted in Chapter 1, many public sector workers (such as teachers) had been silently leant upon frequently over the decade prior

---

[40] Gemma Moss et al., *Primary Teachers' Experience of the Covid-19 Lockdown – Eight Key Messages for Policymakers Going Forward* (London: UCL Institute of Education, June 2020).

[41] TES Reporter, "Teachers Feed and Clothe Pupils Hit by Covid Pandemic", *TES*, 7 April 2021.

to Covid-19 to identify and meet informal social needs. But the pandemic exacerbated and clarified the fact that the fabric of British, or at least English, society was being sustained via goodwill, unpaid overtime and basic empathy, which was politically and economically taken for granted.

The switch to online teaching initially depended heavily on the resources and capacity of individual schools, which were simultaneously struggling with challenges of on-site staff safety and the extra-curricular needs of children. Teaching Assistants (on a median income of less than £14,000 a year) became pivotal in liaising with families, cleaning classrooms and equipment, and taking in-person classes while teachers focused on online content.[42] Schools that had fewer extra-curricular demands to meet were better able to focus on providing an online curriculum, plus middle-class children had greater access to laptops.

One early DfE intervention in providing an online curriculum was the provision in April 2020 of £500,000 to support National Oak Academy, an online teaching portal initially created by a free school in North London. An additional £4.3 million was given to Oak to establish a full curriculum for all school years for 2020–21. This served as a kind of government-endorsed standard for how online teaching should be conducted, while also offering another step towards centralisation of curriculum content.[43] Critics have pointed out that the key parties in the development of

---

[42] Gemma Moss et al., *Unsung Heroes: The Role of Teaching Assistants and Classroom Assistants in Keeping Schools Functioning During Lockdown* (London: UCL Institute of Education, March 2021).

[43] NAO, *Support for Children's Education.*

Oak, including a number of academy trusts, have actively
sought to increase private sector involvement in schooling
over the years.[44] The government also announced in April
2020 a £100 million partnership with Google and Microsoft
to provide support in using their platforms in schools.[45] The
Coronavirus Act passed in October 2020 did later place a
duty on all schools in England and Wales to provide remote
teaching, should it become necessary again, as transpired
the following January.

---

[44] "Despite its self-presentation as teacher-created, Oak
National Academy is in fact headed up by staff from many
of its supporting organisations, many of which have overtly
reformatory aims, private sector links, and governmental
connections. Its principal, for example, is a government advi-
sor on teacher professional development and founder of the
Ambition Institute. The various academy trusts involved in
Oak National Academy are all part of longstanding reform
efforts in England to publicly fund private bodies to run
schools and displace local authority control or local governors
from involvement in public education. In addition, Teach First
lists Oak National Academy as a key resource supporting its
response to the Covid-19 emergency. Teach First approaches
teacher education as a career development opportunity for
business leaders rather than an embedded academic discipline, and was originally conceived by the consultancy
group McKinsey and Company." Ben Williamson and Anna
Hogan, *Commercialisation and Privatisation in/of Education
in the Context of Covid-19* (Brussels: Education International
Research, July 2020).

[45] Department for Education, "Schools to Benefit from
Education Partnership with Tech Giants", Press Release, 24
April 2020.

At the same time, the DfE announced a scheme to distribute laptops (typically Google Chromebooks) to disadvantaged children, though this was beset by problems in the speed of delivery and calculations regarding where the need was located. Despite 540,000 pupils being eligible for the scheme, only 220,000 had received them by the end of August 2020.[46] Schools found that the money for the purchase of laptops arrived unpredictably in lumps, right through to the following summer. It was later discovered that the contract for supplying the majority of laptops (worth £198 million) was handed without competitive tendering to a firm called Computacenter, founded by a major Conservative Party donor.[47] The depth of the 'digital divide' became acutely visible over this time: just 5% of state schoolteachers reported that *all* their pupils had adequate access to a device, compared to 54% in private schools.[48] However the differences in social and environmental support for home schooling during the lockdown may have been just as significant. The ability of children to motivate themselves to learn, to hand in work, to have quiet time and space in which to work was predictably determined by the economic background of their parents. Loss of school routine meant that children became dependent on the stability of family life to provide it instead. Such

---

[46] Rachel Wearmouth, "Exclusive: 27 Academy Trusts Given Just ONE Free Laptop Each from Government", *Huffington Post*, 18 August 2020.

[47] Good Law Project, "Firm Founded by Tory Donor Provided Substandard Laptops for Vulnerable Children", 24 January 2021.

[48] Sutton Trust, *Remote Learning: The Digital Divide*, 11 January 2021.

discrepancies had already been observed in the context of online university tuition, as provided by MOOCs, as reflected in the higher drop-out rates of disadvantaged and disabled students.[49] Disengagement of already deprived children from learning habits was severe, with one study suggesting that the 2020 school closures had increased the attainment gap within Year 3 (7–8 year-olds) by 52%.[50] At the other end of the class spectrum, demand for online private tutors – and even in-house governesses! – shot up, as middle-class parents sought commercial means to keep their children engaged while themselves working from home.

In general, the effect of the class divides meant that less privileged children received less curriculum-based teaching (because schools lacked the means to provide it to them) and did fewer hours of school work every day over the course of both the 2020 and 2021 closures. For example, 40% of state school pupils continued to do a day of school work every day during the 2020 closures, compared to 70% of private school pupils.[51] The signs are that, for older children with good technology, no special needs and spacious homes, it was generally possible to engage with school work relatively autonomously, with many receiving live lessons over Zoom and Microsoft

---

[49] Eric Bettinger and Susanna Loeb, "Promises and Pitfalls of Online Education", *Evidence Speaks Reports*, 2:15 (Washington, DC: Brookings, June 2017).

[50] John Dickens, "The Cost of Lockdown: Attainment Gap Widens by up to 52% for Primary Pupils", *Schools Week*, 24 July 2020.

[51] Lee Elliot Major, Andrew Eyles and Stephen Machin, "Denied Jobs and Schooling, 'Generation Covid' Faces a Struggle to Catch Up", *LSE Blog*, 27 October 2020.

Teams. While children in more deprived families did fewer hours' work than average, their parents spent *more* time than average assisting them with it,[52] and primary school teachers reported having to come up with more imaginative tasks from outside the core curriculum so as to engage pupils who lacked good technology.[53] No doubt the discrepancies in learning time and curriculum deepened class divides, but it's also worth thinking critically about what sort of 'privilege' was involved for those children who spent whole days alone in front of a screen. Reading for pleasure among children, which had been dropping steadily prior to 2020, *rose* during school closures, another indication of possible benefits of relaxation of curriculum constraints.[54]

Policy Challenges

As the 2020 lockdown receded, the summer was dominated by a number of unprecedented educational problems. Firstly, there was the question of how to produce GCSE and A-level results in the absence of any exams. Governments of Scotland, England and Wales had all planned to use algorithms to calculate grades, a challenge made tougher by the decline of coursework assessments over previous years. The algorithm that was adopted in England by Ofqual relied heavily on

---

[52] Eemer Elvers, Jack Worth and Anusha Ghosh, *Home Learning During Covid-19: Findings from the Understanding Society Longitudinal Study* (Slough: National Foundation for Educational Research, July 2020).

[53] Moss et al., *Primary Teachers' Experience.*

[54] Alison Flood, "Children Read More Challenging Books in Lockdown, Data Reveals", *The Guardian*, 29 April 2021.

Unprecedented?

the past performance of the school, while individual pupils were only differentiated by their ranking within that context. Young people were being subjected to what Louise Amoore described as "a deeply political idea: that a person is only as good as their circumstances dictate".[55] Over 40% of predicted grades in England were downgraded from teacher predictions, clustered (by design) in lower-performing schools.

In Scotland, where the downgrading of Scottish Highers scores was not as widespread as that of A-levels in England, the government had reverted to teacher-predicted grades within a week of the publication of grades on 4 August. In England, the government was ready for an outcry, but dug its heals in. DfE officials later admitted that the 'totemic' political priority of ministers was to avoid 'grade inflation'.[56] The public reaction included the extraordinary and indicative spectacle of protesters chanting 'fuck the algorithm' outside the DfE, and holding up signs saying 'your algorithm doesn't know me'.[57] Within this movement was the glimmer of resistance to teacherless platform-based education. Williamson held out for just four days after the publication of English results on 13 August, before U-turning to teacher-predicted grades.

Secondly, there was the looming question of university re-openings in September, and the prospect of a devastating loss of income should large numbers of students defer, claim fee rebates or decline their places altogether. When the pandemic

---

[55] Louise Amoore, "Why 'Ditch the Algorithm' is the Future of Political Protest", *The Guardian*, 19 August 2020.

[56] Timmins, *Schools and Coronavirus*, 21.

[57] Daan Kolkman, "'F**k the Algorithm'? What the World Can Learn from the UK's A-level Grading Fiasco", *LSE Blog*, 26 August 2020.

broke, the government had initially reimposed the cap on university admissions to prevent a destructive competition for students, but this had to be lifted once more in response to the A-levels U-turn, which resulted in an above-average number of students meeting their grade requirements. The government repeatedly ignored pleas from the HE sector for financial support, although it transpired by October that the shortfall in students had not materialised on anything like the scale imagined, and international student registrations actually increased by 9%.

Meanwhile, the government refused to act to prevent students travelling to universities in September and taking up places in halls of residence. The suspicion was that ministers and universities were both afraid of the financial consequences should students have not taken up and paid for the accommodation that now plays such an important role in the balance sheets of universities and asset managers such as Blackstone.[58] Universities stuck to offering 'blended' learning (as opposed to entirely online courses) for fear that they would then be liable for fee reimbursements, which many couldn't afford. Before the end of September, several halls of residence had suffered Covid-19 outbreaks, with students forcibly confined to their halls – most notoriously at Manchester University, where students encountered fences erected around their buildings and private security guards employed to prevent them escaping. Many abandoned their accommodation when they could, or never took it up, meaning that by January 2021 an astonishing £1 billion had been spent on unused student accommodation.

---

[58] Alessio Kolioulis and Rahel Suss, "Why Does Finance Care So Much About Students?", *Greater Manchester Housing Action* (blog), 28 September 2020.

This was the income that universities were depending on and which the government was unwilling to underwrite.[59] As with the algorithm, this also met with resistance, with a wave of rent strikes and protests taking place in campuses across the country. Two rounds of funding were made available to help students in England in financial difficulties, one of £20 million in December and a further £50 million in February 2021, though this worked out at just £25 per student, compared to £78 in Scotland or £302 in Wales.

The announcement in July 2020 of an imminent 'Higher Education Restructuring Board' set out plans to offer loans to universities in trouble, but with conditions attached that suggested the government saw an opportunity to pursue its 'cultural' mission against 'low-quality' degrees (calculated in terms of graduate income) and 'niche activism and campaigns' by student societies. The board consisted of finance directors and management consultants, and its remit was sufficiently interventionist as to dissuade any universities from ever taking up such loans. This was coupled with the less fearsome Sustaining University Expertise package, which offered a combination of loans and grants to support research activities, which had otherwise been funded through international student tuition fees. In addition, three English universities turned to the Bank of England's Covid Corporate Financing Facility for loans.[60]

Finally, there was the question of how to compensate for the exceptional loss of education over 2020 and early 2021.

---

[59] Rachel Hall, "UK University Students Wasted £1bn in a Year on Empty Accommodation", *The Guardian*, 17 February 2021.
[60] These were Roehampton, Leicester and London School of Economics.

The economistic view of education as 'human capital' investment, which had become hegemonic across so many capitalist economies over the previous 30 years, successfully framed the problem in terms of 'learning loss.'[61] With predictions of lifelong consequences for 'learning loss,' including costs to personal earnings and the macro economy, the DfE swiftly introduced a programme of 'catch-up' with a budget eventually totalling £3.1 billion in England, far lower than education specialists had insisted was necessary, and a fraction of what other national governments had provided per pupil.[62] The majority of this would be a 'recovery premium' that would be money directed at schools to help students who had fallen behind with additional support, including summer schools for secondary school pupils. The rest was to fund a flagship National Tutoring Programme (NTP), which created an authorised list of tutoring agencies that schools could draw from to help individual pupils who had fallen behind. Oversight of the NTP was contracted out to the Dutch human resources firm, Randstad, at a cost of £218 million.

---

[61] Ben Williamson, Felicitas Macgilchrist and John Potter, "Covid-19 Controversies and Critical Research in Digital Education", *Learning, Media & Technology*, 46:2 (April 2021).

[62] The Institute of Fiscal Studies calculated that total loss of income due to the loss of a half year of schooling would amount to £350 billion in total, and an associated loss of £100 billion of tax revenue. The government's 'Catch-up Tsar', Kevan Collins, resigned in June 2021, less than four months after being appointed, after his request for £15 billion was turned down. The DfE budget amounts to £100/pupil/year, compared to £2,500 in Netherlands or £1,600 in the US. See Luke Sibieta and Ben Zaranko, "HM Treasury: Stingy and Short-sighted, or Prudent and Practical?", *IFS Blog*, 4 June 2021.

Here again there was conflict between the teachers and government. Schools were compelled to use the NTP-accredited tutors, rather than being given money to spend as they saw fit (for instance, employing supply teachers as the NEU suggested), and the partnering agencies were largely for profit. *The Observer* revealed that some were charging DfE £72–84 for an hour's tuition, while paying the tutor £15.[63] *The Guardian* discovered a case of an online tutoring provider using tutors in Sri Lanka, who were paid just £1.57 an hour.[64] NTP was evidently another means through which DfE could centralise regulation of education while increasing the role of private providers and circumventing the teaching profession. But as with so many of the exceptional measures that have been introduced over 2020–21, there are doubts as to whether NTP has reached the children with the greatest need.[65]

The challenge of gauging the scale and key locations of lost learning was also met in familiar fashion, with a turn towards digital data collection and analytics. In September 2020, the EdTech firm Renaissance Learning won a DfE contract to assess learning loss on the basis of data already being collected via the use of its 'Star Reading' and 'Star Mathematics' digital assessments in schools. This, combined with the commercialised and centralised nature of

---

[63] Donna Ferguson, "England's 'Catch-up' Tutors Are Being Short-changed by Private Employers", *The Observer*, 28 February 2021.

[64] Sally Weale, "UK Tutoring Scheme Uses Under-18s in Sri Lanka Paid as Little as £1.57 an Hour", *The Guardian*, 19 March 2021.

[65] NAO, *Support for Children's Education*.

NTP, demonstrated the continuation of the pre-pandemic pedagogy and ideology, in which 'learning' is something to be delivered and accelerated via a range of 'providers', and measurable audit.

Coinciding with these unprecedented events was a series of parallel battles for control over the culture and politics of education and knowledge. On top of the exceptional policy challenges presented by Covid-19, the government chose to engage in seemingly frivolous conflicts: barring 'anti-capitalist' thinkers and speakers from the school curriculum, legislating against the 'no-platforming' of speakers in universities, and declaring a crisis of 'discipline' in schools wrought by lockdown to be tackled with new 'behaviour hubs'. In no case was there evidence of a problem warranting this level of political attention. However, it seemed that the rising autonomy of schools and teachers during the lockdown, the suspension of Ofsted inspections, the loss of traditional exams, and the extraordinary new movements to recognise historic harms enacted by empire and slavery had provoked the Conservative government into a new raft of centralisation and 'culture war' tactics. This was further evidence of how Covid-19 had re-politicised the governance and purpose of education.

Winners and Losers

English schools were only *forced* to close for 40 days in the spring and summer of 2020 (compared to an OECD average of 60 days) and then an additional 40 days in early 2021. However, due to the geography of the virus, children living in deprived regions were much more likely to lose further days over the autumn 2020 and summer 2021 terms due to their 'bubbles' registering an infection, forcing them back into remote learning.[66] These were also the same children who lacked adequate technology access and who were more likely to have overcrowded homes and less predictable routines. For many children from disadvantaged backgrounds, the net effect of Covid-19 was to provoke a general withdrawal from education over the course of a whole year. This included the already-noted tendency of children from lower-income families not to take up in-school places that were available to them during school closures; the difficulty schools faced in recreating the curriculum via remote means, especially where laptops and bandwidth were limited; and the struggle to engage the neediest pupils in the NTP. The result of this was not simply a major 'learning loss' across the whole population, but a disproportionate impact on disadvantaged pupils, whether assessed at the level of the individual, school or neighbourhood.[67] Teachers expressed concern that a large number of vulnerable children were now outside of any professional purview, as reflected in the sharp drop-off in referrals to children's services.[68]

Tackling this became the major focus of the DfE from the summer of 2020 onwards. Yet the focus on 'learning', 'attainment', 'literacy' and test scores (all tacitly fuelled by anxiety regarding the longer-term economic consequences) excluded

---

[66] The 2020–21 school year ended with 1 million children off school in England, due to positive cases in their 'bubbles', including many leavers who missed out on the normal send-offs and goodbyes.

[67] Education Endowment Foundation, "Best Evidence on Impact of Covid-19 on Pupil Attainment", June 2020.

[68] Committee of Public Accounts, "Covid-19: Support for Children's Education" (26 May 2021).

the other dimensions of education and educational institutions, whose absence represented a more serious social and psychological cost for children and young people. School closures also led to rising mental health problems, loneliness and increased risk of exposure to abuse, neglect and domestic violence.[69] For teenagers, closure of school represented the loss of a hugely important social world and source of identity, and pushed even more of their social lives into digital environments. The loss of early years (aged 4–6) schooling is especially harmful in terms of the development of social, communicative and emotional abilities, potentially with lifelong consequences, and again clustered among disadvantaged children.[70] Some in this age group were observed to have become anxious about physical exercise and less confident in their play, while others had lost basic abilities such as independent use of the toilet.[71] Early years provision is widely recognised to be especially important in combating inequalities, and its loss cannot be easily compensated for.

The social and psychological costs to university students are also significant: the loneliness of studying away from home without a normal social life, the loss of in-class discussion and interaction with teachers, the absence of cultural, political and communal activities, as provided by societies and student unions. According to research by the Higher Education Policy Institute in April 2021, around two-thirds of undergraduates reported that their mental health had suffered as a result of

---

[69] Sarah Lewis et al., "Closing Schools is Not Evidence Based and Harms Children", *BMJ*, 372:521 (February 2021).

[70] Marmot et al., *Build Back Fairer*, 52.

[71] Ofsted, "COVID-19 Series: Briefing on Early Years, November 2020", 15 December 2020.

the pandemic, while only 19% had received any reimburse-
ment related to accommodation, and 13% related to tuition.[72]
E-learning may be more attainable for university students (who
are expected to possess greater self-direction) than for school
pupils, but all the evidence on MOOCs and associated forms of
e-learning is that inequalities emerge around motivation and
concentration, which are reflective of underlying inequalities
related to social class and disability. There is no in-built reason
why online education must be inferior to in-person education,
so long as the differences are properly appreciated by teachers
and students.[73] Yet a rapid 'pivot' online, as occurred in 2020,
is scarcely the best way to think through the manifold ways
in which pedagogy needs to change to exploit the distinctive
affordances of online spaces and relationships. Moreover, it
was not what the majority of students or teachers aspired to.

'Learning loss' may indeed have major consequences for
individuals and economies, and the losses are most severe for
those who have received the fewest days of schooling and most
limited online curriculum: the children of poorer families. But
the loss of the social context provided by school and university –
a context that is different from home and family, whose value
can't be measured, and which offers a crucial psychological
and social holding environment for personal and intellectual
development – did the more immediate harm to young people. Its absence threw them back upon the resources of their
own families, homes and self-motivation, with all of the inequalities that go with that, and with nothing but screen-based
interactions to offset that. (Referrals for gaming addiction

---

[72] HEPI, "Students' Views on the Impact of Coronavirus on
Their Higher Education Experience in 2021", 1 April 2021.
[73] Bayne et al., *Manifesto*.

treatment among children and young adults tripled over the first year of the pandemic.)[74] 'Learning' is *in principle* something that can be recovered through more one-to-one tuition, extending school over the summer and the evening, and more time spent in online tutorials. But how might the unrecoverable losses associated with childhood, development, play and free time be recognised?

Who were the beneficiaries? The obvious ones were those firms who won commercial contracts to oversee the provision of free school meals, laptops, teaching platforms, tutoring services and an online curriculum. The profit margins being made by some of the NTP partners, and the general demand for private tutoring over the course of the pandemic, suggest that Covid-19 was a lucrative opportunity for providers in this market. Within HE, the A-levels fiasco in the summer of 2020 ended up with more students than expected achieving their desired grades, meaning that (with the cap on university recruitment removed) there was – unexpectedly – an overall increase in tuition income to universities, but which flowed particularly towards upper-ranking institutions. Many universities were unable to cope with student numbers and responded in 2021 by making far fewer offers, out of fear that A-level results would again exceed pre-Covid-19 levels, given they would again be set by teacher prediction.

Where the pandemic created the greatest commercial opportunities, as with so many other areas of social and economic life, was in the reach of digital platforms, that is, the EdTech industry. As Ben Williamson has explored in detail, school closures were viewed enthusiastically by EdTech and

---

[74] Tobi Thomas, "Referrals to UK Gaming Addiction Clinic Triple in Year of Lockdowns", *The Guardian*, 20 June 2021.

its cheerleaders as a huge global 'experiment', which might irreversibly transform the nature of learning and embed platforms as a basic condition of education.[75] As Williamson notes, active users of Google Classroom doubled between the dawn of the pandemic and mid-April 2020 to 100 million, and by the summer Google was working in tandem with UNESCO and the International Society for Technology in Education to produce what it called an Anywhere School. In the UK, the government's education partnership with Microsoft and Google saw the creation of 2.4 million new user accounts with the two platforms. On top of the distribution of Google Chromebooks, this represents a significant penetration of giant platforms into schools that is unlikely to be reversed. EdTech software packages, which promise to 'accelerate' learning in literacy and maths, and which become necessary during school closure or for 'catch-up', risk becoming a normal part of school. Meanwhile, major commercial EdTech specialists, such as K12 and Pearson, expanded rapidly over the summer of 2020.[76] Interest in online-only schools soared, offering a boost to private platform schools such as the Valenture Institute, founded by the EdTech pioneer Robert Paddock, which aims to teach 100,000 pupils by 2030.

While EdTech providers benefitted directly, this enforced global experiment in e-learning represented an acceleration in

---

[75] Ben Williamson, Rebecca Eynon and John Potter, "Pandemic Politics, Pedagogies and Practices: Digital Technologies and Distance Education During the Coronavirus Emergency", *Learning, Media & Technology*, 45:2 (April 2020); Williamson, "Education Technology Seizes a Pandemic Opening".

[76] Williamson and Hogan, *Commercialisation and Privatisation*.

a direction that many had already wanted to go, for reasons of profit, cost-cutting or simple techno-utopianism. Andreas Schleicher, Head of Education at the OECD and a tireless advocate for EdTech, described the pandemic as 'great moment' for learning, and the OECD was quick to celebrate this new awakening. As they wrote in March 2021:

> The opportunities that digital technologies offer go well beyond a stop-gap solution during the pandemic. Digital technology allows to find entirely new answers to what people learn, how people learn, where people learn and when they learn. It can elevate the role of teachers from imparting knowledge towards working as co-creators of knowledge, as coaches, as mentors and as evaluators. Already today, digital learning systems cannot just teach students, but simultaneously observe how students study, the kind of tasks and thinking that interest them, and the kind of problems they find boring or difficult.[77]

A more gushing eulogy to e-learning it would be hard to find. Similar sentiments were expressed by university Chief Finance Officers, who (according to a survey by PwC) saw the enforced use of digital platforms (as an alternative to lectures, seminars, meetings and conferences) as one of many positive behavioural changes, together with a welcome increase in understanding of financial constraints among academic staff.[78]

The longer-term vision of education, which has potentially been accelerated by the pandemic, is of a significant concentration in the number of 'providers', or at least far greater

---

[77] OECD, *The State of School Education: One Year into the Covid Pandemic* (Paris: OECD, March 2021), 4.

[78] PWC, *Covid Recovery and Improvement: Locking in the Benefits and Overcoming the Challenges* (January 2021).

reliance on a small handful of platforms and content creators, further reducing the autonomy of individual institutions and teachers, and further standardising the 'learning experience' so as to produce measurable and comparable outcomes. Boosters for the EdTech industry have long predicted that, within a few decades, the world would have a fraction of the number of universities, with hundreds of thousands of students enrolled in each one. Schools could also become platform based, with teachers primarily working as one-to-one coaches to help motivate children to engage with an online curriculum, over which they had scant influence. While the depths of the Covid-19 emergency witnessed a sudden reassertion of teacher autonomy, DfE policy has pushed hard in the opposite direction, and partnership with a small handful of EdTech suppliers will aid the centralisation of control. In April 2021, the Education Secretary announced a further push towards conglomeration of school governance, by seeking to pull the remaining third of non-academised English schools into academy trusts, where they would be accountable to central government.

Also emerging from this crisis is the ascendent figure of the tutor, who targets a specific learner, with a specific learning deficiency, as identified in the data, and 'accelerates' their progress relative to their peers. Part of the appeal of tutoring, from the perspective of policy elites, is that it allows for easily quantifiable inputs and outputs, which can be economically calculated. The logic of NTP and of DfE-funded summer schools is to target learning loss individually, and to bring pupils back to their expected level of performance as quickly as possible. Tutoring is one of the countless ways in which commercial contractors have extended their reach within public services and government thanks to Covid-19; however, in this instance it also reflects on a broader process of marketisation and competition in education. Outside of the pre-modern traditions of Oxbridge, the purpose of tutoring is rarely education as such, but to increase an individual attainment level, either because a tutee has fallen behind (the function of NTP), but equally so as to enable them to get ahead or keep up with a peer group who may themselves be being tutored. This latter scenario is the one already present in many private schools, but it is also one that follows from the logic of 'learnification' and 'human capital', where education becomes conceived as a transfer of knowledge and skill to a recipient, to be achieved as efficiently as possible, and with the greatest outcome.

Conclusion: What Was Revealed?

The political–economic events afflicting education in the UK, and especially in England, over the course of 2020–21 followed a pattern that is by now familiar, reflecting on the centres of economic power within the UK economy and state more generally. A cluster of firms hovering around the state, offering to fix particular policy problems at speed, extracted revenue from the public balance sheet. Some of these were established outsourcers (such as Randstad), others were friends of the Conservative Party (Computacenter), others were global technology giants (Google et al.). But this rapid turn to commercial entities, and the chaos that repeatedly engulfed schools, was also a symptom of a longstanding ideological project in education policy: to disempower local authorities, unions and teachers themselves. An alternative form of decentralisation would involve trusting those who are vocationally invested in education as such, but such are the pathologies of English government.

Then there is the spatial reconfiguration of education, which preceded 2020 but was pushed to new limits by the pandemic. The tendencies that we referred to in Chapter 1 as 'hyper-domestication', in which greater and greater economic value and decision-making become clustered within the household, were already manifest in the steady rise of private tutoring, the vast financial investments in student accommodation made by the likes of Blackstone, and the efforts of EdTech to push 'learning' into the home. School and campus closures obviously took things much further, and laid bare the inequalities in informal, non-monetary social resources available to children at home. The corollary of these spatial trends and platformisation sustained education through lockdowns, but also exacerbated tendencies towards the privatisation of education provision and surveillance. It has the potential to further centralise the oversight of curriculum content and assessment, as the example of National Oak Academy indicates.

But we should not lose sight of the specificities of the education story of 2020–21, which concerned the dysfunctional place of class stratification in British society, which is officially disavowed while shaping so much. The 'meritocratic' and economistic ideology that has driven English education policy since the 1980s places a huge responsibility upon schools and universities to deliver 'social mobility', and counteract the influence of family, place and culture in reproducing past inequalities. Largely overlooked in this ideology is the fact that schools, universities and their staff play a fundamental role in providing their own community, place and culture, within which young people can develop beyond the limits of their family background and homes. Educators provide relationships, recognition and emotional support that necessarily exceed the limits of 'learning' and measurable 'outcomes'. This failure to see that education offers an invaluable social holding environment, within which learning (among other things) can occur, means that policymakers have for decades overlooked the immeasurable conditions of 'social mobility' and 'learning' in favour of those narrowly defined measurable outcomes.

The enforced removal of these contextual components of education, in favour of a grand experiment in remote learning, revealed the crucial role of community and place in education, and quite how unevenly distributed the social resources for learning in the home are. These don't only include technology, but also time, space, emotional support (often the very basis of self-esteem) and self-motivation. Simultaneously, the relational dimension of teaching was briefly expanded in new ways, such that teachers and lecturers found themselves having to support disadvantaged pupils and students in ways that extended well beyond learning and the curriculum. But the crucial lesson was that, reduced to a combination of platforms, self-motivation, centrally mandated curriculum and family, the weight of social advantages and disadvantages becomes overwhelming. The consequences of the school closures for inequality will be huge and long-lasting, regardless of the DfE's 'catch-up' agenda.

The suspension of Ofsted routine inspections for 18 months represented a potentially useful hiatus in the direction of education and policy. However, the government's ambition since summer 2020 has been to simply make up the lost learning, targeting the children who have fallen most behind, and to do so as efficiently as possible. The flaw in this vision is that children and young people lost something of immeasurable value over 2020–21, while the government only focuses on the measurable losses. As a result, the government policy effectively produces yet further stress and anxiety, with dozens of additional school tests held in 2021 (to establish GCSE and A-level results) and extending school via tutoring and summer schools. The informal, unstructured, social dimensions of school are thus shrunk even further. What's unclear is how the already-rising burden of mental health problems among young people will be tackled, in a context where the primary aim is to return to a regime of inspection and standardised testing as quickly as possible.

How far and how rapidly this 'experiment' leads towards platform-based education in the future remains to be seen. Where it does, this will also alter the nature, meaning and curriculum of education because the technology is far from neutral. Not only will audit, evaluation and curriculum setting become potentially more centralised, but new commercial opportunities will open up for services offering to further 'personalise' learning, analyse data on 'learning behaviours', provide consultancy on 'student engagement' and so on. Those universities under greatest financial pressures at the moment, or those simply seeking to exploit their brand further, will look again to MOOC-type services, which don't require in-person attendance. At the same time, education risks becoming more concentrated on the auditable skill to manipulate symbols on a screen (varieties of literacy and numeracy) and less concerned with dialogue, understanding and culture. The implicit reliance of this model on forms of self-motivation and self-direction, which are unevenly distributed, became much clearer over 2020–21, but won't necessarily derail it.

6

Escaping Rentier Nationalism

This book began from the intuition that a violent rupture in the status quo must surely reveal certain aspects of political and economic reality that are otherwise papered over. Our analysis has been an evolutionary one, resting on the assumption that the character of a crisis or emergency is shaped by the policies, politics and institutions that precede it. Events and decisions may well be unprecedented, but the tools, ideas and resources that are mobilised *in extremis* will already be lying around. Some of these are likely to become more dominant or visible over the course of a crisis. The longer-term policy challenges of Covid-19, and how the economy adapts to accommodate the virus, is a much larger question that is beyond the scope of this book. But the events of 2020–21 that we have detailed here will certainly leave a legacy, in how patterns of power, wealth, inequality and exploitation have been deepened.

Covid-19 has photosynthesised various tendencies of British capitalism that pre-existed the pandemic, but are now rendered more acute. How might we distil these? What *type* of capitalism can we point to, in a comparative sense? It is widely accepted that a likely consequence of the pandemic is a growth in the size of many states relative to the rest of their economies. In the UK, the size of the state (relative to GDP) had fallen steadily in the decade leading up to the pandemic thanks to austerity measures, with cuts to public spending concentrated especially in local government and the benefit system, something that played a demonstrable role in the country's catastrophic mortality rate over 2020–21.[1] Covid-19 saw public spending immediately leap from around 35% to over 45% of GDP, and is likely to leave it at over 40% for the foreseeable future. But these sorts of headline indicators still conceal questions of power: what kind of state, what sources of profit and what types of exploitation are underway?

By rewarding, empowering and amplifying key centres of economic power, Covid-19 has helped coalesce a certain model of capitalism that we term 'rentier nationalism'. The roots of this model lie in the wreckage left by the global financial crisis: the austerity measures introduced across Europe, the 'unconventional' monetary policies that sought to mitigate them, and the subsequent democratic upheavals that sought to reclaim national sovereignty from the global economy. But the pandemic has cast it in a new light, creating exceptional new opportunities to expand political and corporate control over strategic areas of the economy. The term 'rentier nationalism' seeks to highlight the reassertion of the nation as an economic unit and 'imagined community', but also to specify the main beneficiaries of this mutation: asset-owning households, financial elites, platforms and outsourcing contractors. A distinctive type of national capitalism is emerging, based around an unashamedly larger state with higher levels of public borrowing and spending, especially on healthcare; an electoral base made up of older homeowners

---

[1] Marmot et al., *Build Back Fairer*; Paul Johnson, Robert Joyce and Lucinda Platt, *The IFS Deaton Review of Inequalities: A New Year's Message* (Institute for Fiscal Studies, January 2021).

and ultra-high-net-worth donors; para-governmental industries of public service providers and digital platforms; and an
unstable combination of labour market 'flexibility' and tight
immigration control.

The growth of the state, which was already becoming ideologically mandated in certain corners of the political Right
prior to 2020, does not automatically imply reduced power or
autonomy for capital, as if in some zero-sum game between
'public' and 'private'. On the contrary, it is – as the health crisis
has made clear – a huge opportunity for certain forms of capital and certain sectors to expand and profit. Political scien-
tists first began to describe the 'hollowing out' of the state and
the rise of public–private centres of 'governance' in the early
1990s, with the UK as the pioneer of many techniques of privatisation and 'new public management'.[2] Outsourcing in the
UK has gathered pace ever since. But the post-2020 version of
public–private collaboration adds several distinguishing features that characterise 'rentier nationalism'.

Distinguishing 'Rentier Nationalism'

Firstly, the relationship between the state and private businesses has become even more intimate as the ideological
veneer of 'competition' and 'the market' for contracts is abandoned. The greater willingness of the state to deploy the full
potential of its sovereign balance sheet (or, ultimately, the

---

[2] See Rod Rhodes, "The Hollowing Out of the State: The
Changing Nature of the Public Service in Britain", *The Political
Quarterly*, 65:2 (1994): 138–151; Rod Rhodes, "The New
Governance: Governing without Government", *Political
Studies*, 44:4 (1996): 652–667.

Bank of England's) also produces more money to be diverted towards Serco, G4S et al. Rising public debts once produced fear of inflation, leading interest rates to be raised in response. But the indebtedness of the contemporary state has led primarily to inflation of asset prices, including house prices, which is politically celebrated. Meanwhile, the emergency procurement practices of 2020 onwards frequently abandoned all pretence of competitive tendering or due process, at little political or electoral cost. The proximity of certain wealthy individuals or firms to the Conservative Party and the state translated into contracts, something that is typically viewed as a hallmark of illiberal or 'populist' regimes.

The first priority of the state in an economy based around the extraction of rents is to defend the sanctity of property rights and contracts, which are the sole basis of revenue where firms and individuals are dedicated to controlling assets rather than production.[3] The second priority is to do whatever's possible to prop up the value of assets. Quantitative easing has contributed greatly to this internationally, and especially during the pandemic, but the UK Treasury threw further petrol on the fire in 2020 by announcing a stamp duty holiday, which then got extended repeatedly out of fear of prompting a housing crash. As we will discuss, Covid-19 *did* temporarily introduce a limit to some rentier rights in the UK, in the form of the eviction ban. But in general, those who can demonstrate a property right to as-yet-unrealised income streams in the future can rely on the power of the state to ensure they are delivered.

Secondly, rhetorical and symbolic appeals to the nation have become increasingly integral to state legitimacy claims. The dawn of the pandemic coincided with numerous 'culture

---

[3] Christophers, *Rentier Capitalism.*

war' interventions, against universities, charities, the BBC and museums, who have been routinely accused of censorship, 'wokeness' or 'rewriting the past'. The field of education, which has featured a familiar pattern of cultural conflicts between Left and Right since at least the 1960s, witnessed heated battles over 2020 and 2021 regarding 'free speech', curriculum content and fidelity to British values – as if the DfE, schools and universities didn't have enough else to be worrying about over this time. Coinciding with rising media panic surrounding Channel crossings by asylum seekers, this rhetorical agenda contributed to a nationalistic mood which presented 'Britain' and its values as under threat from various internal and external sources. The need for the state to control national borders was central to how the argument for Brexit was made in 2016, as with so many other populist reactions of the time. The Nationality and Borders Bill, introduced to Parliament in 2021, aimed to deter asylum seekers, alongside Home Office plans to process asylum claims offshore. Covid-19 has added great momentum to this re-bordering agenda, including on the Left, where the 'zero Covid' policies of countries such as New Zealand and Australia were often held up as a model for social democracy. Efforts to reassert the sovereignty of nations do, of course, present a particular problem for the UK, which is not one nation but four, and Covid has undoubtedly made this reality harder to conceal, despite rising government investment in union flags.[4]

While these appeals to nationhood and territory tend to be made in cultural and ethnic terms, they also have economic implications that are crucial to the model we are seeking to

---

[4] Ben Quinn, "UK Government Spends More Than £163,000 on Union Flags in Two Years", *The Guardian*, 6 August 2021.

distinguish. They contribute to keeping certain forms of work 'cheap', either because it is expected that they are performed for the greater national good (paid for in claps), or because they have been performed by migrants, or both. It may be, as we have explored, that a combination of Brexit and a generalised care crisis have led the UK to the limit of its 'flexible' labour market model. However, the rhetoric of nation and 'protection' of an indigenous population works to conceal how society is actually sustained and whose work is actually indispensable. In the arena of education and the cultural sector, this rhetoric also plays a key role in ostracising centres of professional expertise who are perceived to be 'disloyal' or 'woke', such as teachers, academics and curators, hastening the ascendency of private platform-based alternatives to traditional schools, campuses and cultural institutions.

Thirdly, Covid-19 has elevated the significance of the platform business model to new heights, meaning that the extraction of data is often just as significant to business strategies as the extraction of profit. In aiding this extraction of data, states wield crucial economic power. Governments, after all, are often still needed to unlock access to populations, especially in sensitive areas such as health. The kinds of 'partnership' that exist between central government and data-hungry firms such as Palantir and Google produce networks of demographic control, in which the state helps to break down or disregard privacy barriers or other regulatory constraints, while the contractor helps to algorithmically sift, distinguish and rank populations. The NHS becomes a financial resource, but not one that necessarily requires privatisation or marketisation to be realised as such. Instead, it becomes the entry point to a vast treasure trove of medical, behavioural and social data. Similarly, schools, which were far more platform based by the autumn of 2021 than they had been two years earlier, provide a mine of behavioural data for EdTech to scrutinise, and then potentially sell their findings back to the DfE.

The national population therefore becomes a type of national asset that exists as a kind of property of the sovereign state and is made available to private firms to mine, for both intelligence and profit. Covid-19 *could* signal the beginning of a whole new era of public–private partnerships, in which states and platforms strike deals over access to different forms of population data. In its list of '10 Tech Priorities', the government makes the ambiguous claim that "by removing barriers to responsible data sharing and use, we aim to become the world's number one data destination."[5] This also represents the dawn of a new era of demographic government, in which nurturing and analysing population – in pursuit of security, biosecurity and human capital appreciation – is a constant concern, which also shapes migration policies. The intellectual historian Quinn Slobodian coined the term '*volk capital*' to capture a conservative view of population as both ethnic community and financial asset.[6] In the contemporary UK, the state does not necessarily seek to upgrade this capital through public investment (Chapter 5 noted that the decade leading up to the pandemic saw the largest fall in per-pupil spending in schools in 40 years), but the Johnson administration committed to creating new routes for technological elites and 'global talent' to live and work in the UK, promising to "actively market our visa offering ... in global talent hotspots", while at the same time

5 Department of Culture, Media & Sport, "Our 10 Tech Priorities", 2021.
6 Quinn Slobodian, "Hayek's Bastards: The Populist Right's Neoliberal Roots", *Tribune*, 15 June 2021.

making it even harder to claim asylum.[7] Similarly, with serious labour shortages afflicting supply chains, retail and the hospitality sector over 2021, this was not seen as a problem to be corrected by the market, but as a problem requiring direct demographic intervention by the state. Temporary visas represented a supposed demographic–economic fix to a shortage of HGV drivers, the analogue of the zero-hours contract, where overseas labour would be available to the nation only to the *precise extent* that it was needed.

These, in our view, are the key contours of a model of capitalism and the state that was emerging prior to 2020, and which then coalesced over the first 18 months of the pandemic; this is the politics of our economy. And yet, the pandemic has also energised more hopeful and less predictable political practices. Not only has it indicated new realms of political possibility, by exposing the economy and state in a new light, it has also prompted new forms of protest and resistance. Power and inequality have been revealed in new ways and to new publics. Many of the dysfunctions and injustices covered in this book long predate Covid-19, yet it is of great political significance whether or not they are seen and identified as such. One of the strangest and most exciting features of 2020 was the flowering of political mobilisations that occurred. In the rest of this final chapter, we explore the political economy of Covid-19 from a different angle altogether: not in terms of how power is successfully mobilised in pursuit of exploitation and extraction of value, but in the *questioning* of that success and the huge broadening of political and economic horizons. In the following section, we identify areas

---

[7] HM Treasury, *Build Back Better: Our Plan for Growth* (3 March 2021).

where governing economic orthodoxies were abandoned thanks to Covid-19. We then explore how these ascending heterodoxies might be channelled towards an economy that granted care its full social value. Finally, we consider some of the extraordinary social movements that blossomed over 2020 and 2021, which took direct aim at centres of rentier nationalist power. Regardless of how the pandemic and how capitalism evolve from here on, the widespread sensing of possibilities and of injustices that were at large over 2020–21 should be preserved.

Heterodoxy Reigns

Policies are not only significant in what they achieve or 'deliver', but in what they signify and show.[8] Moreover, even if a policy is quickly reversed or cancelled, the collective memory of it survives and serves as a political resource. In some cases, it leaves a more material residue: infrastructure, debt or data, for example. The need to maximise social distancing over the spring of 2020 prompted a range of policy decisions that would have been politically almost unimaginable only a few months earlier. The purported justification was that the health emergency would be brief, a hiatus to be bridged, even while it did not turn out that way. And while the circumstances of these decisions were obviously crucial and sometimes fleeting, they had certain irreversible consequences in terms of how problems of policy would be framed in future. The exceptional actions of states during world wars, for example, significantly altered

---

[8] Dvora Yanow, *How Does a Policy Mean?: Interpreting Policy and Organisational Actions* (Washington, DC: Georgetown University Press, 1996).

economic possibilities and demands in subsequent peace-time. It is worth keeping note of what these were in the early stages of Covid-19.

In Chapter 1, we stressed the importance of two deep 'wells' of debt that have been drawn on time and again to keep the vision of the market economy alive, often without full public acknowledgement. The science of economics and the idea of 'the economy' both depend partly on *not* seeing the full importance of these entities.[9] The first is the balance sheet of the sovereign state and central bank; the second is the unpaid and underpaid commitments of care in the household and community. What changed thanks to Covid-19 was partly the *scale* of the commitments that became made between sovereign and bondholders, and between care providers and those in need. But there was also a new *visibility* about these basic preconditions of economic life, which holds great political potential. The idea of 'the market' as a separate and self-sustaining entity, so long criticised by political economists on the Left, became ideologically untenable.

In the case of sovereign debt and macroeconomics, Covid-19 signalled the final death of the austerity logic that stipulated some arbitrary limit to the size of government debt, an idea that had resulted in such terrible social harm over the decade prior to Covid-19. The sharp rise in debt over 2020 and 2021 was not accompanied by any increase in the cost of borrowing, greatly widening economic possibilities. For the Left, this confirmed the once-heterodox notion that governments could and should seize the possibilities of cheap credit to pursue social and environmental goals to the maximum of their capacity. Of course, the Right also has goals of its own, and

---

[9] Mitchell, "Fixing the Economy".

there is no reason to assume that the evaporation of austerity logic necessarily leads to more socially and environmen-
tally progressive outcomes, or that certain morally mandated
austerity measures – such as continued cuts in areas such as
welfare and education – will not continue. Nevertheless, the
heterodox became orthodox.

Secondly, the politics of work and the labour market
were dramatically overhauled in 2020 out of necessity. As we
detailed in Chapter 3, the state flipped from a role of seeking
to push people into work to one of seeking the opposite. The
most dramatic feature of this was the furlough scheme, but
conditionality was also temporarily removed from Universal
Credit, just as a record 2.4 million people started on it in the
two months after lockdown began. The success of the furlough
scheme may have enduring effects on expectations around
government intervention in the labour market, at least in
future episodes of economic crisis. The assumption that the
government would offer a form of furlough every time there
is economic turbulence would run fundamentally against the
flexible labour market model that is so firmly entrenched. But
there were calls for just this from the TUC, in the form of a 'permanent furlough scheme' in the UK, who noted that in 23 other
OECD countries permanent short-time working schemes were
already in place.[10]

The pandemic-induced shutdowns of the labour market
and the recognition of an expanded range of 'key workers' lent
promise to a re-evaluation of welfare and work amid a moment
of national solidarity. Yet initial evidence was that public attitudes towards welfare experienced extremely 'muted change',

---

[10] TUC, "Beyond Furlough: Why the UK Needs a Permanent
Short-time Work Scheme", August 2021.

and where they became more positive, this suggested a 'Covid exceptionalism' reserved for Covid-19 claimants rather than pre-pandemic claimants.[11] However the public and political outcry at the government's plans to scrap the £20 pandemic raise in Universal Credit simultaneously suggested an acknowledgement of the inadequacies of the existing welfare system and public appetite for changing it. There was widespread acknowledgement of the fact that key workers who were praised through the first phases of the pandemic are overwhelmingly in poorly paid and insecure work. The test of the legacy of key worker solidarity is whether it can translate into meaningful political and legislative change and ultimately change in the workplace itself. The introduction to Parliament in May 2021 of the 'Status of Workers Bill' – pledging to "abolish insecure work" and offer "true flexibility, for both workers and employers" – signalled positive steps in this regard.[12] The Bill created a single category of 'worker', constraining employer discretion and seeking to end the creative manipulation of workers' legal status, especially in the gig economy. The rhetoric of the Conservative government over the autumn of 2021 pivoted unexpectedly towards celebrating wage inflation (partly as a smokescreen to distract from, or even justify, supply chain chaos), which may yet herald a shift in policy paradigms, albeit one that is likely to further deepen the distinction between rights of indigenous workers, and those of 'foreigners'

---

[11] Rob De Vries et al., *Solidarity in a Crisis? Trends in Attitudes to Benefits during COVID-19* (Salford: Welfare at a Social Distance, September 2021).

[12] IER, "New Bill Will Abolish Insecure Work", Institute of Employment Rights, 26 May 2021, www.ier.org.uk/press-releases/new-bill-will-abolish-insecure-work/.

whose rights are only ever contingent on a narrowly calculable economic contribution.

Then there was a range of other measures in which the political and economic orthodoxy of the previous 40 years was abandoned, virtually overnight. A ban on the eviction of commercial tenants was introduced in March 2020, which lasted until May 2021. Even after that date, tenants were granted more time to make up their rent arrears before landlords were permitted to use bailiffs. The *Everyone In* initiative, which sought to get homeless people off the streets in March 2020, initially aimed to get 5,000 people into emergency accommodation. Yet by May 2021, it had achieved far more than this: 37,500 people had been helped not only off the streets, but from unsuitable housing into Covid-secure units.[13] This was an entirely unprecedented and unexpected success story of how concerted action – especially involving coordination between central and local government – could alleviate unnecessary social distress if the political will was there.

In the sphere of education, 35 years of creeping centralisation of audit, testing and curriculum were instantly undone when the first lockdowns were introduced. Ofsted inspections were cancelled straight away, and SATs, GCSEs and A-levels soon after. With the DfE struggling to achieve any coherent strategy, schools and teachers suddenly found themselves with more autonomy and social responsibility than they had done in a generation. While this experience was a hugely stressful one for teachers, pupils and parents alike, it also confirmed what teachers and unions had long argued: that, in spite of decades of onerous quantitative audit, schools and teachers retain an informal role in the social health of their

---

[13] Christine Whitehead and Martina Rotolo, "Everyone In: The Numbers", *LSE Blog*, 10 May 2021.

local communities that is irreplaceable, but devalued under regimes of quantitative audit. Whether in the sustaining of a curriculum or in the awarding of A-levels and GCSEs, policymakers were suddenly thrust into the position of having to trust the judgement and duty of care of a profession that had frequently been viewed with suspicion, as ideological and obstructive. The anxiety this must have generated among conservative educationalists, whose central purpose had been to wrest power *away* from the local level, must have been acute, and goes some way to explaining why the pandemic coincided with such frivolous new mandates in England surrounding the singing of patriotic songs and the ban on 'anti-capitalist' speakers in schools.

What did these various policy heterodoxies have in common? If there was one thing that Covid-19 forced policymakers to accept, against everything that had been argued since the ascendency of the 'New Right' in the 1980s, it was that people were not responsible for the circumstances that had befallen them, that they were doing their best, but that some things were outside of their control. People's ability to work, raise a family, pay their rent, meet public sector targets, and so on, was periodically undermined by circumstances which left them in need of support. In a country such as the UK, which had developed a steady current of hatred towards dependency, manifest in tabloid headlines and cultural products such as Channel 4's 2014 *Benefits Street* depicting poor people as ugly and lazy, Covid-19 resulted in an extraordinary cultural and psychological *volte face*.[14] While (as we show in

---

[14] On the media production of dependency discourses see Tracey Jensen, "Welfare Commonsense, Poverty Porn and Doxosophy", *Sociological Research Online* 19(3) (2014): 277–283.

Chapter 4) this attitude did not extend towards some of the most vulnerable, namely asylum seekers, a discernible shift arose in relation to social and labour market policy, of suddenly seeing the needy individual for what they were, that is, as a victim of circumstance. Public sector workers, meanwhile, were suddenly assumed by default to be motivated by altruism and professionalism, and not by self-interest as the governing ideology had once presupposed. It remains to be seen what kind of residue this aspect change may leave, but it is possible that, having suddenly seen the world from a different angle, voters and policymakers could more easily do so again in future.

Searching for a New Paradigm

This sudden disintegration of long-held orthodoxies was astonishing, generating new political uncertainties and possibilities. In the absence of time to think through policy options, the unthinkable was simply enacted. For many conservatives, this produced serious 'moral hazard' in the sense that claims upon the state and arguments for mutual dependence might now escalate. The ideal of 'the market' had lost its hold as a moral paradigm of valuation. But it wasn't immediately clear what alternative basis for the valuation of activity might emerge instead, nor what such an alternative might mean for policy. Once we recognise the economy as constituted by commitments (debts, both monetised and unmonetised) rather than transactions, very different priorities loom into view. Here we trace the contours of some of these alternative goals that became more visible in the wreckage of 2020–21. The major question, we suggest, concerns how the two 'wells' of debt outlined in Chapter 1 might be reassembled and recombined.

When the Bank of England put its balance sheet behind sovereign debt and the debts of the largest corporations it was an exercise of political power. A central bank was less an 'independent' check on the sovereign than, at the crunch moment, it *was* the sovereign itself, able to guarantee the (financial) futures of state and market alike. This power to sustain the life of public and private institutions largely worked to sustain the status quo, and as such the interests of those on the right side of the k-shaped economy. The question arose as to why it could not do more. Was it not possible to defund rentier capitalists and put the power of the public balance sheet to better use? The dramatic opportunity of 2020 derived not only from the discovery of what was financially possible at a macroeconomic level, but simultaneously from the panoply of new measures and intuitions of economic value that were at large in society, often at a very micro level.

Alternative value systems broke through during the pandemic and the wartime-like sacrifices it entailed. Amid the conditions of collective scarcity during the first lockdown there were glimpses of a new kind of abundance that a functioning public politics could help foster. For some, the lockdowns granted an unexpected richness of time unlike any experienced in years. The normal working rhythms that swallow up the hours of the week were upended. Sudden new resources of time were used for cooking, for exercise, for online art, dance and music classes, for online gaming; for doing nothing in particular. For some, gardening and home improvement became sources of joy, creativity and accomplishment. For others, municipal parks became sites of relief, conviviality and occasional transgression. These hinted at what philosopher Kate Soper describes as 'an alternative hedonism' that could guide societal change after the pandemic and would not simply be focused on kickstarting economic growth.[15] As we have tried to show, these were pleasures felt unevenly. Undergirding their very possibility was the labour of others and the deep wells of care and debt that were drawn upon day after day. The pandemic suspended the ruling orthodoxies of previous decades, and as such opened up the question of what it could really mean to 'build back better' afterwards.

For those in and around the government, rebuilding had to continue the rentier nationalist project unleashed through Brexit and secured by the 2019 election. This included a promise of 'levelling up' regional inequalities and an accentuated focus on regions 'left behind' by globalisation, though that promise was refracted via the cultural and electoral priorities of the Johnson administration. The rhetoric of national renewal involved 'freeports' (special economic zones offering tax relief and discounted labour costs), investment into roads to bolster the construction sector, and an airy promise of new high-tech manufacturing like 'gigafactories' to produce batteries for electric cars.[16] What separated much of this from familiar Conservative missions was the much greater mobilisation of public finance. Fiscal austerity was abandoned in favour of debt-led investment into the regions, causes and demographics deemed electorally strategic.

---

[15] Kate Soper, *Post-Growth Living: For an Alternative Hedonism* (London: Verso, 2020).

[16] Peter Campbell, "UK in Talks with Six Companies over Battery 'Gigafactories' for Electric Cars", *Financial Times*, 16 June 2021; Hannah Finch, "The Plans for All Eight Freeports in Rishi Sunak's Spring Budget", *Business Live*, 3 March 2021.

The clearest alternative to rentier nationalism centred on proposals for a Green New Deal. This would also involve expansive state investment and the active use of the central bank balance sheet, but be directed to confront the environmental crisis instead. For its advocates, a Green New Deal could reprogramme the economy away from fossil fuel dependency and also build a fairer society that focused the rewards of economic growth on work rather than wealth. Practically, this meant creating 'good-quality jobs' in the manufacturing industries that had been destroyed by Thatcherism. Its more mainstream advocates talked up big infrastructure projects like 'building flood defences', installing heat pumps and insulation into homes, and greening the automotive industry.[17] In recognising the urgency of a just transition to a carbon-free future, the Green New Deal at the very least grounded itself in climate science.

In many visions of 'building back better', 'the economy' is the guarantor of social wellbeing. Only increasing economic growth can generate the resources with which to 'level up'. In some articulations of the Green New Deal, government funding of infrastructure and public goods would work to counter rentier capture of the economy and allow useful investment to help raise productivity and 'green growth'.[18] The 'good-quality, unionised jobs' and associated wage increases are the social dividends of an economy returned to health. The aggregate objects of governance – GDP, unemployment, investment,

---

[17] Ed Miliband, "How Labour Would Invest in Jobs through Our Green Economic Recovery", Speech, The Labour Party, 25 March 2021.

[18] Robert Pollin, "De-Growth vs a Green New Deal", *New Left Review*, 112 (1 August 2018): 5–25.

productivity – are those that have undergirded politics for almost a century. Productivity and a growing economy the solvent to distributive conflict. It is a governing imaginary that lies in stark contrast to Marmot's diagnosis that societal wellbeing is best organised by outcomes in public health. Moreover, it necessarily ignores the crucial importance of the care economy.

Precisely because of the historic marginalising of care economy labour, it has never counted as part of the 'productive' economy that anchors grand visions of economic transformation. Long cast aside as 'women's work' that takes place outside the labour market, and outside labour-market social struggle, the care economy has never fully been part of the valuation practices that end up in economic indicators.[19] Moreover, labour-intensive sectors such as care, education and the arts cannot easily be made more 'productive'. Producing more 'care per hour' can only mean providing less care per hour, as care's value is found in the time spent giving it. This is described by economists as a 'cost disease', whereby rising wage bills relative to more productive sectors of the economy are locked in. Truly valuing care, therefore, might mean explicitly rejecting economic growth and productivity as ends in themselves.[20]

For that reason, unlike freeports and gigafactories, care is often excluded from grand industrial strategies. Yet the need was clear. The NHS had built a backlog of over 5 million patients, while adult social care was still blighted by high cost,

[19] The classic text is Waring's *If Women Counted*, but see also Hoskyns and Rai, "Recasting".

[20] Tim Jackson, *Prosperity without Growth*, 2nd edition (London: Routledge, 2016), 170.

low pay and underfunding. Schools, meanwhile, were struggling to retain exhausted and under-supported teachers, just as hospitals were losing nurses and midwives. There were very few calls in the UK to mobilise the potency of public finance for the very areas – social care, education, healthcare, social work, childcare, food preparation – that had strained carrying society through the pandemic.

Expelled from the valuation practices and the related categories of governance, recognition of the care economy's vital importance only comes in the debate of 'how are we going to pay for it?' Rather than the vital constituent to societal flourishing, it is cast, at best, as a necessary cost. When the UK government proposed a tax rise in September 2021 to 'fund' the NHS and social care provision it was an acknowledgement of the sector's needs. But it retained the idea that the care economy was the receiver rather than creator of societal wealth. There was, as such, no offer of 'unlimited' liquidity support, nor the fiscal indulgence provided to the companies 'of strategic importance'. Instead, the government proposed a tax on earned income that helped leave familial wealth and its inter-generational transfer intact. Taxing hoarded wealth would do much more to revive aggregate economic fortunes, but would break the electoral coalition of homeowners that is the government's 'heartland'.

Rather than a narrow focus on how best to finance a minor uptick in fiscal support, the care economy could be the basis for a more expansive vision of national renewal after the pandemic. It is the backbone of working-class employment across the country, and the shared interest between the providers and receivers of care should cut across racial, gender and generational divides. This harnesses a solidaristic social basis that is absent from fantasies of both rentier nationalism and moon-shot industrial strategies. The ballast of the public balance sheet could be deployed to support an expansion and transformation of the social infrastructure whose abundance was glimpsed briefly, and unequally, during the pandemic. For social care it would mean more than just extra funding. The sector is dominated by rentiers whose profit is predicated on immiserating life-giving workers and extracting as much wealth as possible out of the most basic human relationships. Without more substantial overhaul, more funding could see public money channelled into private hands in just the way the pandemic exposed. The UK has one of the most privatised care systems in the world, and bailout money would increase the £1.5 billion in 'leakage' that flows to rentiers rather than finding its way to frontline care.[21]

A fuller investment in social and physical infrastructure that supports a caring economy is needed, but so is the requirement to revalue the place of care in our society and economy more broadly.[22] This might entail funding universal and free public care services, the recognition of unpaid work and an ambitious reimagining of care's social and environmental value. It would need innovative ways to redistribute, organise and deliver care that prioritise democracy and the relationships that sustain care, rather than efficiency, productivity and financial return. Plans for the basis of this care economy are already emerging and can draw on many sources – from think

---

[21] Allyson Pollock, "Multinational Care Companies Are the Real Winners from Johnson's New Tax", *The Guardian*, 14 September 2021.

[22] Sara Stevano et al., "Hidden Abodes in Plain Sight: The Social Reproduction of Households and Labor in the COVID-19 Pandemic", *Feminist Economics* 27:1–2 (2021): 271–287.

tank research to trade union advocacy to decades of research in feminist political economy.[23] They are built on critiques of the existing value and provisioning of care – particularly in its marketised and financialised form – but also on a positive vision of collective and public care economies. For care work and the social care system more specifically, this looks like new models of public–social partnerships that are not for profit and that operate both within *and with* local communities in a democratically accountable way.[24] These models have to be built around improvements to care workers' professional agency and autonomy – and therefore, their power – to value the time and standards which adequate care requires.[25] The overarching system might combine localised, democratic care services within the framework of a universal and free at the point of use National Care Service.

The Biden administration has broken some new ground by asserting that 'care' *is* infrastructure, on which the rest of

---

[23] Recent reports include: Laura Bear et al., *Social Infrastructures for the Post-Covid Recovery in the UK* (London: LSE Covid and Care Research Group, 2021); Women's Budget Group, *Creating a Caring Economy: A Call to Action* (London: Women's Budget Group, 2020); Jerome De Henau and Susan Himmelweit, *A Care-Led Recovery from Coronavirus* (London: Women's Budget Group, June 2020). See also Care Collective, *The Care Manifesto: The Politics of Interdependence* (London: Verso, 2020).

[24] Daniel Button and Sarah Bedford, *Ownership in Social Care* (London: New Economics Foundation, 2019); Isaac Stanley, Adrienne Buller and Mathew Lawrence, *Caring for the Earth, Caring for Each Other: An Industrial Strategy for Adult Social Care* (London: Common Wealth, 2021).

[25] Paul Cotterill, "Carers' Agency: Power and Professionalisation", *Renewal*, 30 April 2021.

the economy depends. Pushed by the economist and member of Biden's Council of Economic Advisors Heather Boushey, Biden's $2.3 trillion infrastructure package initially included $400 billion to be spent on the 'care economy', plus $25 billion to be spent on upgrading childcare provision. Boushey's analysis is an economic one, focused on the productivity gains that are possible in the labour market once care responsibilities are met, but the very notion of care being 'infrastructure' represents a significant paradigm shift at the highest level of US policy thinking.[26]

Supporting social infrastructure more broadly is also about reclaiming time for caring for oneself and for others. This could take the form of more extensive and generous parental leave schemes, or carers' leave and allowances, which are designed to address the gender inequalities in unpaid care. Radical proposals for a universal basic income – where unconditional payments are made to every citizen – would be another way to value the mass of unpaid work that sustains life on an everyday and inter-generational basis. Another radical proposal to carve out time for care and begin to address gendered inequalities is for a reduction of the working week and an emphasis on good-quality part-time work that gives greater flexibility to workers rather than employers.[27] Though it may sound radical, a pilot programme has recently been trialled in Scotland for a four-day week with no loss of pay.[28]

---

[26] Heather Boushey, *Finding Time: The Economics of Work-life Conflict* (Cambridge, MA: Harvard University Press, 2016).

[27] Will Stronge and Aidan Harper (Eds.), *The Shorter Working Week: A Radical and Pragmatic Proposal* (London: Autonomy, January 2019).

[28] Douglas Fraser, "Scotland to Trial a Four-Day Week", *BBC News*, 1 September 2021.

These are questions, ultimately, of valuation rather than economy: what we choose to count and how. But they reflect on a set of commitments that came to the fore over the course of 2020–21, both those made by the state to its creditors and its citizens, and those made by people to one another. At some point, these must trump commitments to asset owners, which put the appreciation of asset prices and guaranteed rents above all else. The political economy currently planned to sustain asset prices and aggregates of consumption, employment and GDP could be re-programmed to grow and sustain a flourishing collective care infrastructure.

Reclaiming of Public Space

The period reviewed in this book saw exceptional and unprecedented restrictions of basic liberties – in particular, freedoms of movement and of the utilisation of shared space. While these restrictions (like many of the heterodox economic policies that coincided with them) were deemed necessary and temporary, they nevertheless embedded and accelerated spatial processes that we have described as the 'crisis of space', manifest in the further valorisation of housing and domestic space, the expanded role of platforms for the coordination of all forms of social activity across space, and the re-bordering of nations and everyday life. By the time freedoms were somewhat restored, property values had risen further, home working had become normalised for many, platforms had extended their reach further into everyday life (including schools, workplaces, hospitality and civil society), surveillance was more endemic, national borders remained far tighter, and legislation was being tabled seeking to make asylum claims even tougher. None of these shifts counts as a brief hiatus, but constitutes the embedding of the spatial facets of rentier nationalism.

As we argued in Chapter 1, these multiple spatial tendencies combined as a pincer movement against the openness and indeterminacy of public space, as a political resource and a 'public thing'. And yet, 2020–21 was also a period in which spaces were occupied in unpredictable and transformative ways, not least due to the heightened importance of public parks and other outdoor spaces as crucial conditions of social activity and health. The role of the street as the 'holding environment' for democracy was often dramatically restored and reasserted, even while countervailing pressures sought to squeeze it. The largest and most historic of these were the Black Lives Matter (BLM) protests that escalated following the murder of George Floyd in Minneapolis on 25 May 2020, becoming the largest protest movement in US history and sweeping the world over that summer. This was undoubtedly the catalyst for a host of related movements, demands and reforms – but not the sole one.

Two prominent cases of successful protests, both resulting in government U-turns, concerned the use of data: the algorithmic calculation of A-level grades, and the plan to make NHS patient records available to researchers and companies. Both of these controversies witnessed high-profile campaigns and mobilisations against a form of 'platformisation' of public institutions. In the first case, the righteous anger of pupils and parents towards an algorithm that judged individuals according to where they were from, rather than what they'd done, forced a government U-turn, and the restoration of teacher-predicted grades. In the second case, privacy campaigns, such as medConfidential, worked effectively to raise awareness of the government's plan, and to direct people towards opting out of the scheme. The government subsequently cancelled a deal with Palantir, which would have let the controversial data analytics firm host and analyse data on adult social care, but was fiercely attacked by privacy campaigners.[29] Where surveillance capital and algorithms have steadily expanded their power over decades without mass political reactions, perhaps the sudden jolt of additional surveillance triggered by the pandemic was enough to prompt resistance, like the proverbial frog jumping straight out of the boiling water.

Then there were the strikes against exploitative financial practices, in areas of the economy not typically organised sufficiently to resist. Students, who had been effectively told to return to campuses in September 2020, only to be subjected to harsh policing of their social behaviour and receive the vast bulk of their tuition online, engaged in a series of rent strikes over the 2020–21 academic year. As of January 2021, rent strikes had occurred in 55 of 141 UK universities – the largest nationwide tenant action in 40 years – and many of these were successful in their demands for rent rebates of 30–50% for the year.[30] Questions remain, however, as to the role of private accommodation providers, many of which are owned by asset managers and investment banks, who are able to lock universities into rigid contracts guaranteeing future rental streams. Of the 32,000 new beds created in the sector in 2019, 90% were owned and operated by private providers.

Although many workers in the 'key worker' category became much more visible during the pandemic, this didn't

---

[29] Adam Bychawski, "UK Health Department Ends Data Deal with 'Spy Tech' Company Palantir", *openDemocracy*, 11 September 2021.

[30] Mollie Simpson, "Britain's Historic Wave of Student Rent Strikes", *Tribune*, 21 January 2021.

fundamentally change their everyday conditions. In many instances, the intensity of work increased. Flexibility allowed employers to shirk obligations to provide workers that they claimed were 'self-employed' with adequate protective equipment, as well as entitlements such as sick pay. One consequence of key workers' deadly workplace conditions, though, was to spark resistance. This developed around health and safety concerns in relation to social distancing at work, provision of personal protective equipment (PPE) and support for self-isolating workers. Given the ever-tightening restrictions on trade unions in balloting for industrial action, and the immediacy of the threat, worker resistance often took the form of what are, effectively illegal, 'wildcat' strikes.[31] These who went on strike in this way included: Royal Mail staff; local government workers; refuse, warehouse, construction and meat processing workers; and even cleaners at the Ministry of Justice. Strikes were particularly prominent among gig economy delivery workers too, who complained that they were not only lacking protections from Covid-19, but also that their employers were driving down rider fees, leaving many workers well below minimum wage.[32] Epidemiological injustice, combined with exploitative work and pay, drove many to fight conditions through refusal of work.

The 2021 labour shortages offered workers some leverage to demand increases in wages and employers responded with higher salary offers and recruitment bonuses in sectors such as the haulier industry. In the US, President Biden's response

---

[31] Gregor Gall, "Britain's Coronavirus Wildcat Strikes", *Tribune*, 1 May 2020.

[32] TBIJ, "Deliveroo Riders Can Earn as Little as £2 an Hour during Shifts, as Boss Stands to Make £500m", *The Bureau of Investigative Journalism*, 25 March 2021.

to questions about worker shortages was: "pay them more, this is an employee's bargaining chip now".[33] These demands may point to a heightened class conflict around pay and conditions in sectors affected by supply chain problems and Brexit. Yet a deeper malaise affects work in these industries, driven by decades of erosion to collective regulation of the labour market and of labour's bargaining power. In some cases, the efforts to bend production to the whims of increasingly globalised supply chains – chiefly via automation and platformisation – have only intensified and degraded the jobs that service them. The social settlement that remedies these problems will need to go beyond wage rises to tackle the deeper power imbalances in the organisation and management of work.

And yet in scale and legacy, the most significant mobilisations of 2020–21 were undoubtedly those that took aim at racism and state violence, both in the past and the present. Although lockdown measures were still in place and gatherings were not allowed, during the first week of June 2020, thousands of people gathered in Parliament Square and Trafalgar Square as well as in many cities across the country to protest against racism and police brutality. From that moment on and for a few months, BLM mobilised every week in the UK, both locally and responding to national calls.[34] Around the world, the claims of BLM extended to demands for equal access to

---

[33] Danielle Zoellner, " 'Pay Them More': Biden Uses Stage Whisper to Tell Business How to Fix Staff Shortages", *The Independent*, 24 June 2021.

[34] One of the most important protests was the demonstration held in front of the US Embassy in London. Reuters, "Thousands Join Black Lives Matter Protest Outside US Embassy in London", 7 June 2020.

care and public health: the struggle over care and health was at the same time an anti-racist mobilisation. This link was made on the basis of evidence of much higher infection and death rates among racialised minorities.[35] Indeed, access to public health is, as BLM stress, underpinned by racialised practices that often remain invisible. 'Now it's time to act': this was the slogan that circulated widely in the streets across the world among BLM demonstrators. In so doing, BLM started from the assumption that mobilisation should not be procrastinated further, due to the Covid-19 emergency. Thus, BLM challenged "the temporality of 'incompatible priorities' between freedom of movement and health. Freedoms relegated to an indefinite future only reinforce a present of inequality and injustice".[36] Struggles over public space and against the temporality of postponement (to an indefinite future) converged in BLM's mobilisations and claims. Starting from such a convergence, other claims emerged – such as the importance of teaching black history at school and decolonising the curriculum and of removing statues of slave traders and slave owners.[37]

BLM could be seen as a collective attempt to overturn the spatial crisis which, as this book demonstrates, was deepened over 2020–21. At the same time, it prevented the foreclosure of politics through the temporality of emergency, which prioritises 'necessary' actions over others. On 7 June 2020 the statue

---

[35] Layal Liverpool, "Why Coronavirus Hit People from BAME Communities So Hard", *Wired*, 25 August 2020.

[36] Aradau and Tazzioli, "Covid-19 and the Re-Bordering of the World".

[37] David Batty, "Only a Fifth of UK Universities Say They Are 'Decolonising' Curriculum", *The Guardian*, 11 June 2020.

of the 17th-century slave trader Edward Colston was toppled and thrown into Bristol harbour by BLM protesters.[38] Two days later, thousands of people gathered in Oxford demanding the University of Oxford decolonise its curriculum and remove the statue of the white supremacist and British imperialist Cecil Rhodes. The two events triggered a revival of the 'Rhodes must fall' movement – which started in Cape Town in 2015[39] – both in the universities and in public spaces.

The momentum of BLM helped to enthuse and mobilise a wave of parallel protests against border and policing strategies that successfully revealed the latent authoritarianism in the policies of the British Home Office. A year after the first big BLM protests, a wave of protests took place in the UK to oppose the new Police, Crime, Sentencing and Courts Bill that establishes new police powers to tackle and disperse peaceful demonstrations. More precisely, the Bill hands over power to the police for shutting down protests and marches if these might turn into 'too noisy' or 'disruptive' events.[40] These mobilisations unfolded across the country under the slogan 'Kill the Bill', which also became the name of the heterogenous composition of individuals and groups that gathered multiple times

---

[38] Damien Gayle, "Toppled Edward Colston Statue Goes On Display in Bristol", *The Guardian*, 4 June 2021.

[39] Rahul Rao "On the Statues", *The Disorder of Things*, 2 April 2016.

[40] Home Office, "Police, Crime, Sentencing and Courts Bill 2021: Protest Powers Factsheet", 7 July 2021, www.gov.uk/government/publications/police-crime-sentencing-and-courts-bill-2021-factsheets/police-crime-sentencing-and-courts-bill-2021-protest-powers-factsheet (accessed 20 September 2021).

in the squares and in the street across the UK between April and August 2021. The collective resistance against the new Bill was more broadly a mobilisation against the authoritarian drift that the pandemic had accelerated. Then there was the vigil for Sarah Everard in March 2021, which was planned to mark the death of a woman murdered by a police officer, but which escalated into conflict following forceful policing. But most extraordinary, perhaps, was the protest against the deportation of two men in Glasgow in May 2021, which successfully halted their deportation through the unrelenting intervention of the crowd. The activist network that instigated the protest had already successfully forced Serco to cease the use of 'lock-change evictions', which saw asylum seekers unable to get into their homes.

Protesters also took aim at what we've termed the 'confinement continuum' of asylum seekers over 2020-21. In particular, the situation of protracted confinement in the Napier Barracks in Folkestone as well as the overcrowded and unhealthy spaces in which they were forced to live pushed migrant solidarity networks to organise demonstrations against semi-detention enforced in the name of Covid-19. Asylum seekers themselves mobilised collectively, protesting against the unbearable living conditions of the barracks and the fact that they were not informed by the Home Office of their future destination.[41] The campaign against the unhealthy and overcrowded living conditions in the Napier Barracks took place simultaneously with protests against the multiplication of detention sites in the UK during the pandemic.[42] Thus, the

---

[41] BBC News, "Folkestone's Napier Barracks Asylum Seekers Stage Protest", 12 January 2021.

[42] The Home Office plans to turn the former Hassockfield Detention Centre in Durham into a Category 3-style prison to

temporal conjuncture of Brexit and Covid-19 and the enforcement of migrants' confinement boosted calls and collective mobilisations against the detention of migrants and asylum seekers. Such movements took the impetus of BLM, which had popularised the demand to 'defund the police' (that is, to divert funds towards the social infrastructure on which people depend, and which prevents such a *need* for police), and directly targeted the illiberal and violent practices of the Home Office, to often spectacular effect.

To understand why this was such a fertile political moment, despite the clampdown on public space generated by the pandemic, we should also note the connections between heterogenous struggles that happened in different countries. A case in point is constituted by the global feminist movement 'Ni Una Menos'[43] that during the global feminist strike on 8 March 2020, a few weeks after the outbreak of the pandemic, pointed to the mutual connections *between* social reproduction, racialised border restrictions and unequal access to healthcare. "The same border regime which kills women and men", they argued, "confronts us with the constitutive nexus between freedom of movement and conditions of social reproduction". The pandemic foregrounds that "freedom of movement should be at the centre of our struggles for an equal access to welfare, rights and income".[44] In so doing,

---

detain people whose application for UK residency has been denied. Several big mobilisations took place in 2021 against the plan.

[43] 'Ni Una Menos' (Not one less) started in Buenos Aires in 2017 and then spread across the world. It has a strong presence in Italy and Spain.

[44] Non una di Meno, "La vita oltre la pandemia", *Dinamopress*, 2020.

Non una di Meno has foregrounded the heterogenous bordering mechanisms which have multiplied and been enforced
during Covid-19: within such a context, they contend, equal
access to freedom of movement and to public health are goals
that cannot be object of compromises and that require a joint
struggle. According to the feminist movement, the class-based
and racialised mobility restrictions shape the current conditions for social reproduction and, at the same time, make or let
(some) people die while hamper others from travelling.

We don't aim to provide an exhaustive list of all the mobilisations that happened in 2020 and 2021. Rather, what matters here is to foreground the common denominator of some
of these mobilisations and the new political avenues they
opened, namely the occupation of public space in opposition
to the crisis of space triggered by Covid-19. As Judith Butler
pointed out speaking about the Occupy movement in 2011,
"these demonstrations or, indeed, these movements, are char-
acterized by bodies that come together to make a claim in public space, but that formulation presumes that public space is
given, that it is already public, and recognized as such" while,
in fact, "assembly and speech reconfigure the materiality of
public space, and produce, or reproduce, the public character
of that material environment".[45]

At the same time, what distinguishes the mobilisations
during the pandemic from previous collective movements
that were characterised by the occupation of the public space –
such as the Occupy movement in the US and Los Indignados
in Spain – was the centrality of claims for racial justice,

---

[45] Judith Butler, "Bodies in Alliance and the Politics of the
Street", *European Institute for Progressive Cultural Policies*, 9
(2011): 1–29.

intertwined with claims for equal access to care and public health. That is, the way in which these movements unsettled the 'crisis of space' was through alliances against racialised and exclusionary spatial 'enclosures' of Covid-19. In more explicit or implicit ways, these movements challenged racialised borders – showing how these are not narrowed to national frontiers nor to travel restrictions but, rather, shape and affect the urban space as well. Overall, on the one hand at a first glance Covid-19 has foreclosed political spaces, and rendered collective mobilisations more difficult to organise – also due to the protracted lockdown measures. On the other, the pandemic did not successfully shut down uprisings and mobilisations. To the contrary, 2020 and 2021 were prolific years of struggles and unexpected political convergences that did not simply replicate mobilisations that happened before Covid-19, but rather invented new ways of holding together different social justice claims and have unfolded through a very diversified social composition. This political moment is far from over.

These various examples pose fascinating and complicated questions about the connection between the pandemic and popular mobilisations. At a quite superficial level, there were clearly pent-up frustrations and desires for physical gatherings after so many months spent indoors and without physical congregation. More subtly, the uprisings of 2020–21 suggested that the politics of public space was less settled and more democratically fertile than one might fear. The emptying of the streets during lockdowns, and the additional time spent interacting online, had a dual effect. On the one hand, it added fuel to cultural and symbolic controversies, surrounding ideas, images, statues, songs, which for a while existed wholly on screens. On the other, it produced a spatial vacuum – abandoned streets – which was waiting to be filled once the pressure valve was released. Efforts to organise society via private space, platform surveillance and physical force nevertheless run into the ambiguity and possibilities of public space.

Sustaining Anger

In their book, *Angrynomics*, the political economists Mark Blyth and Eric Lonergan distinguish between 'righteous anger' (that reflects real failures and injustices in society) and 'tribal anger' (that is stoked by demagogues to divert anger towards enemies and others).[46] For Blyth and Lonergan, the fall-out from the global financial crisis generated considerable 'righteous anger' over the years that followed, especially in Europe, which could and should have translated into political overhaul of economic policies. The danger is that if left unheard, 'righteous anger' generates a set of sentiments that nationalist movements and leaders can swiftly divert into 'tribal anger', in which a scapegoat is found. This provides some political and psychological insights into the decade following the financial crisis, in which elite refusal to acknowledge the scale of social distress experienced from 2009 onwards eventually played into the hands of 'populist' insurgents. Anger that is ignored or forgotten does not evaporate, but turns toxic and reappears in new forms.

The desire to move on from a crisis swiftly, and paper over the conflicts and suffering that was revealed, may be understandable in some ways, but carries considerable political and psychic risks. If, instead, a rupture is treated as a moment of truth – if it is recognised as offering rare insights into political

---

[46] Mark Blyth and Eric Lonergan, *Angrynomics* (London: Agenda Publishing, 2020).

economy – then it is worth trying to keep its lessons and conflicts alive, to prevent them from being suppressed, only to return years down the line in an uglier guise. For various reasons, some obvious and others less so, the dawn of the pandemic spawned a considerable degree of 'righteous anger', expressed in the streets and online, mobilising people around new causes and to new ends. 2020–21 may end up being seen as the beginning of a long wave of activism, in spite of legislative restrictions on the right to protest. Alternatively, it might be seen as a temporary political eruption provoked by the unprecedented pressure cooker of lockdowns. Either way, and *especially* if it turns out to be the latter, it is worth reflecting on and remembering the instances of alternatives, resistance and protest that emerged during this time, and what they reveal about the possible vulnerabilities of the 'rentier nationalist' model we sketched out in the previous section.

In the first instance, the pandemic cast a terrible light on the moral economy of contemporary capitalism in the UK. The sudden discovery of which work was 'essential', and the discrepancy with its valuation by the labour market, provoked a sudden awakening to the social injustices of work and employment practices, not to mention the luxury of so many of what David Graeber famously classified as 'bullshit jobs' that continued to be done from home for ample remuneration. The reliance of society on care workers, often employed on low-wage precarious contracts, and other essential frontline service professionals, in education, health and local government, became publicly and dramatically apparent once the first lockdowns got under way in the first half of 2020. That many of the most essential workers, notably those in much of the social care sector, had become exploited for profit due to the rise of outsourcing and the entry of private equity (where profits are heavily derived from applying downward pressure on working conditions) represented a form of 'slow violence' against the social fabric, mental health and individual wellbeing that long pre-dated 2020 but became a belated matter of public concern thanks to Covid-19.

If there is anything deserving of 'righteous anger' through all of this, it is the epic and unignorable demonstration that this level of poverty and political vulnerability kill people. This, too, is very far from unprecedented; indeed, Michael Marmot has consistently argued that mortality statistics are among the most revealing indicators of a society's broader cohesion, prosperity and fairness. Growth in life expectancy had already been stalling or going into reverse in many parts of the UK due to the impact of austerity measures over the post-2010 period. Covid-19 predominantly killed members of those communities – disproportionately low-income, racialised minorities living in overcrowded and multigenerational housing – who were *already* suffering higher rates of morbidity and mortality due to their socio-economic circumstances.[47] As Marmot demonstrates, this cannot be understood other than through confronting the intersecting harms of poverty, structural racism and under-investment in various sources of care.

Part of the purpose of this book is to document and narrate extraordinary events, but also to try and demonstrate how they were shaped by political decisions, policies and ideologies that had become sedimented over the previous decades. Despite the sense of radical transformation, terror and possibility that swept the world in March 2020, it now looks safe to say that the pandemic has not occasioned any kind of dramatic change in political consciousness or ideological direction, at least not yet. But by keeping in mind the memory of

[47] Marmot et al., *Build Back Fairer.*

what occurred during periods of the greatest stress – both the good and the bad – we might sustain a political resource and a sense of 'righteous anger' that could still be drawn upon when future opportunities for change arise. Things that become visible, for a while, can leave a residue. The main weapon in the nationalist armoury is a slow occlusion of empirical evidence by mythology. In the UK as elsewhere, this process is greatly aided and accelerated by particular corners of the media and unscrupulous politicians, which seek to distort and paper over inconvenient facts, and to amplify convenient threats. In the face of these cultural forces, merely to remember and assert the basic political, economic and social facts is to offer some hope that there might finally be proper recognition of injustices.

References

Adams-Prassl, Abi, Jeremias Adams-Prassl and Diane Coyle. *Uber and Beyond: Policy Implications for the UK*. Cambridge: Bennett Institute for Public Policy, 2021.

Adkins, Lisa, Melinda Cooper and Martijn Konings. *The Asset Economy*. Cambridge: Polity Press, 2020.

Alakeson, Vidhya, and Conor D'Arcy. *Zeroing In: Balancing Protection and Flexibility in the Reform of Zero-Hours Contracts*. London: Resolution Foundation, 2014.

Allegretti, Aubrey. "Business Leaders Arriving in England Granted Exemption from Covid Quarantine." *The Guardian*, 29 June 2021.

Amato, Massimo, and Luca Fantacci. *The End of Finance*. Cambridge: Polity, 2013.

Amoore, Louise. "Why 'Ditch the Algorithm' is the Future of Political Protest." *The Guardian*, 19 August 2020.

Anderson, Bridget. *Us and Them? The Dangerous Politics of Immigration Control*. Oxford: Oxford University Press, 2013.

Anderson, Elizabeth. *Private Government: How Employers Rule Our Lives*. Oxford: Princeton University Press, 2017.

Aradau, Claudia, and Martina Tazzioli. "Covid-19 and the Re-bordering of the World." *Radical Philosophy*, 2:10 (2021): 3–10.

Arnold, Martin, Colby Smith and Matthew Rocco. "House Prices Climb to Record Levels in US and Europe." *Financial Times*, 22 June 2021.

ASGI. *Rights on the Skids: The Experiment of Quarantine Ships and Main Points of Criticism*, March 2021, https://inlimine.asgi.it/wp-content/uploads/2021/05/Report-Rights-on-the-skids.-The-experiment-of-quarantine-ships-and-main-points-of-criticism-ASGI.pdf (accessed 20 September 2021).

Baccaro, Lucio, and Chris Howell. *Trajectories of Neoliberal Transformation*. Cambridge: Cambridge University Press, 2017.

Baker, Andrew, Colin Haslam, Adam Leaver, Richard Murphy, Len Seabrooke, Salia Stausholm and Duncan Wigan. *Against Hollow Firms: Repurposing the Corporation for a More Resilient Economy.* Sheffield: Centre for Research on Accounting and Finance in Context, 2020.

Baker, Carl. "NHS Staff from Overseas: Statistics." Briefing Paper. House of Commons Library, 4 June 2020.

Bakshi, Haksan, Alex Bowyer, Richard Dorsett and Jessica Hug. "How Differently Has the Creative Workforce Fared under COVID-19?" *ESCoE* (blog), 10 May 2021.

Bales, Katie. "A Labour Market Divided: COVID-19 and Employment Regulation." *Futures of Work* (blog), 1 October 2020.

Bank of England. *The Distributional Effects of Asset Purchases,* 12 April 2012.

Bank of England. *Interim Financial Stability Report (May 2020),* 5 May 2020.

Bank of England. "Seven Moments in Spring: Covid-19, Financial Markets and the Bank of England's Operations – Speech by Andrew Hauser", 4 June 2020.

Bank of England. *IEO Evaluation of the Bank of England's Approach to Quantitative Easing.* Independent Evaluation Office, 13 January 2021.

Bank of England. "Covid Corporate Financing Facility (CCFF)", 20 August 2021.

Bashford, Alison. "'The Age of Universal Contagion': History, Disease and Globalization." In Alison Bashford (Ed.), *Medicine at the Border.* London: Palgrave Macmillan, 2006.

Batty, David. "Only a Fifth of UK Universities Say They are 'Decolonising' Curriculum." *The Guardian,* 11 June 2020.

Bayne, Sîan, Peter Evans, Rory Ewins, Jeremy Knox, James Lamb, Hamish Macleod, Clara O'Shea, Jen Ross, Philippa Sheail and Christine Sinclair. *The Manifesto for Online Teaching.* Cambridge, MA: MIT Press, 2020.

BBC News. "Covid: Bus Drivers 'Three Times More Likely to Die' Than Other Workers", 19 March 2021.

BBC News. "Folkestone's Napier Barracks Asylum Seekers Stage Protest", 12 January 2021.

Bear, Laura, Nikita Simpson, Caroline Bazambanza, Rebecca Bowers, Atiya Kamal, Anishka Gheewala Lohiya, Alice Pearson, Jordan Viera, Connor Watt and Wuerth Milena. *Social Infrastructures for the Post-Covid Recovery in the UK*. London: LSE Covid and Care Research Group, 2021.

Beckert, Jens. *Imagined Futures*. Cambridge, MA: Harvard University Press, 2016.

Behr, Michael. "NHS Covid-19 App Update Blocked by Apple and Google." *Digit*, 13 April 2021, https://digit.fyi/nhs-covid-19-app-update-blocked-by-apple-and-google/ (accessed 20 September 2021).

Bell, Torsten. "Feel Poor, Work More – the Real Reason behind Britain's Record Employment." *Resolution Foundation* (blog), 13 November 2019.

Benanav, Aaron. "Service Work in the Pandemic Economy." *International Labor and Working-Class History*, 12 October 2020, 1–9.

Bentham, Justin, Andrew Bowman, Ismail Ertürk, Peter Folkman, Julie Froud, Sukhdev Johal, John Law, Adam Leaver, Mick Moran and Karel Williams. *Manifesto for the Foundational Economy*. Manchester: CRESC, November 2013.

Berry, Christine, Laurie Macfarlane and Shreya Nanda. *Who Wins and Who Pays? Rentier Power and the Covid Crisis*. London: IPPR, 13 May 2020.

Bessant, Judith. *The Precarious Generation: A Political Economy of Young People*. Abingdon: Routledge, 2017.

Bettinger, Eric, and Susanna Loeb. "Promises and Pitfalls of Online Education." *Evidence Speaks Reports*, 2:15. Washington, DC: Brookings, June 2017.

Bevan, Stephen, Beth Mason and Zofia Bajorek. *IES Working at Home Wellbeing Survey: Interim Findings*. Brighton: Institute for Employment Studies, 7 April 2021.

Bhattacharya, Tithi (Ed.). *Social Reproduction Theory: Remapping Class, Recentering Oppression*. London: Pluto Press, 2017.

Bialasiewicz, Luiza, and Alberto Alemanno. "The Dangerous Illusion of an EU Vaccine Passport." *openDemocracy*, 9 March 2021.

Biesta, Gert. "Interrupting the Politics of Learning." *Power and Education*, 5:1 (2013): 4–15.

Bigo, Didier. "Security and Immigration: Toward a Critique of the Governmentality of Unease." *Alternatives*, 27:1 (2002): 63–92.

Birch, Kean, Margaret Chiappetta and Artyushina Anna. "The Problem *of* Innovation in Technoscientific Capitalism: Data *Rentiership* and the Policy Implications of Turning Personal Digital Data into a Private Asset." *Policy Studies*, 41:5 (2020): 468–487.

Birch, Kean and D.T. Cochrane. "Big Tech: Four Emerging Forms of Digital Rentiership." *Science as Culture* (2021), doi:10.1080/09505431.2021.1932794.

BIS (Bank for International Settlements). "BIS Statistics Explorer: United Kingdom Debt Securities Issues and Amounts Outstanding: Table C3." *Bank for International Settlements*, 14 September 2021.

Blanchflower, David G. *Not Working: Where Have All the Good Jobs Gone?* Oxford: Princeton University Press, 2019.

Blyth, Mark, and Eric Lonergan. *Angrynomics*. London: Agenda Publishing, 2020.

BNP Paribas. "BNP Paribas Investment Partners Temporaly Suspends the Calculation of the Net Asset Value of the Following Funds." BNP Paribas Press Release, 9 August 2007.

Borrett, Amy. "Why Big Tech Stocks Boomed in the Pandemic." *Tech Monitor*, 16 December 2020.

Bourquin, Pascale, and Tom Waters. *Jobs and Job Quality between the Eve of the Great Recession and the Eve of COVID-19*. London: Institute for Fiscal Studies, 25 June 2020.

Boushey, Heather. *Finding Time: The Economics of Work-life Conflict*. Cambridge, MA: Harvard University Press, 2016.

Bowman, Andrew, Ismael Ertürk, Peter Folkman, Julie Froud, Colin Haslam, Sukhdev Johal, Adam Leaver, Micheal Moran, Nick Tsitsianis and Karel Williams (Eds.). *What a Waste: Outsourcing and How It Goes Wrong*. Manchester: Manchester University Press, 2015.

Bradbury, Alice. *Pressure, Anxiety and Collateral Damage*. London: More than a Score, 2019.

Bray, Mark. "Shadow Education in Europe: Growing Prevalence, Underlying Forces, and Policy Implications." *ECNU Review of Education* (January 2020), doi:10.1177/2096531119890142.

Brenner, Neil, Bob Jessop, Martin Jones and Gordon Macleod (Eds.). *State/Space: A Reader*. London: Wiley, 2003.

Brenner, Robert. *The Economics of Global Turbulence: The Advanced Capitalist Economies from Long Boom to Long Downturn, 1945–2005*. London: Verso, 2006.

Bright, Sam. "£119 Million Covid-19 Testing Contract Awarded to Four-month-old DNA Analysis Firm." *Byline Times*, 9 November 2020.

British Business Bank. "Our Programmes", 2021, www.british-business-bank.co.uk/ (accessed 25 September 2021).

Bunting, Madeleine. *Labours of Love: The Crisis of Care*. London: Granta Books, 2020.

Burns, Diane, Luke Cowie, Joe Earle, Peter Folkman, Julie Froud, Paula Hyde, Sukhdev Johal, Ian Rees Jones, Anne Kilett and Karel Williams. *Where Does the Money Go? Financialised Chains and the Crisis in Residential Care*. Manchester: CRESC, 2016.

Butler, Judith. "Bodies in Alliance and the Politics of the Street." *European Institute for Progressive Cultural Policies*, 9 (2011): 1–29, https://scalar.usc.edu/works/bodies/Judith%20Butler:%20Bodies%20in%20Alliance%20and%20the%20Politics%20of%20the%20Street%20%7c%20eipcp.net_thumb.pdf (accessed 2 November 2021).

Butler, Sarah. "John Lewis to Close Eight More Stores, Putting 1,500 Jobs at Risk." *The Guardian*, 24 March 2021.

Butler, Sarah. "Firms Selling UK Travellers Covid Tests Not Charging VAT – Investigation." *The Guardian*, 13 August 2021.

Button, Daniel, and Sarah Bedford. *Ownership in Social Care*. London: New Economics Foundation, 2019.

Bychawski, Adam. "UK Health Department Ends Data Deal with 'Spy Tech' Company Palantir." *openDemocracy*, 11 September 2021.

Byline Times and The Citizens, "£121.7 Million Increase in Profits for Covid Contract Winners with Conservative Links", 12 October 2021.

Cabinet Office and Department for Education. "Children of Critical Workers and Vulnerable Children Who Can Access Schools or Educational Settings." GOV.UK, 9 March 2021.

Campbell, Peter. "UK in Talks with Six Companies over Battery 'Gigafactories' for Electric Cars." *Financial Times*, 16 June 2021.

Care Collective. *The Care Manifesto: The Politics of Interdependence.* London: Verso, 2020.

Carers UK. *Caring behind Closed Doors: Six Months On.* London: Carers UK, October 2020.

Carlyon, Tristan. *Food for Thought: Applying House Price Inflation to Grocery Prices.* Shelter, February 2013.

Cattan, Sarah, Christine Farquharson, Sonya Krutikova, Angus Phimister, Adam Salisbury and Almudena Sevilla. *Inequalities in Responses to School Closures Over the Course of the First Covid-19 Lockdown.* London: Institute for Fiscal Studies, April 2021.

Cheng, Jeffrey, Tyler Powell, Dave Skidmore and David Wessel. "What's the Fed Doing in Response to the COVID-19 Crisis? What More Could It Do?" *Brookings* (blog), 30 March 2021.

Children's Commissioner, "Damage to Children's Mental Health Caused by Covid Crisis Could Last for Years Without a Large-scale Increase for Children's Mental Health Services", 28 January 2021, www.childrenscommissioner.gov. uk/2021/01/28/damage-to-childrens-mental-health-caused-by-covid-crisis-could-last-for-years-without-a-large-scale-increase-for-childrens-mental-health-services/ (accessed 27 August 2021).

Christian, Alex. "Bosses Started Spying on Remote Workers. Now They're Fighting Back." *Wired UK*, 10 August 2020.

Christophers, Brett. *Rentier Capitalism: Who Owns the Economy, and Who Pays for It?* London: Verso, 2020.

Christophers, Brett. "Mind the Rent Gap: Blackstone, Housing Investment and the Reordering of Urban Rent Surfaces." *Urban Studies*, August 2021, doi:10.1177/00420980211026466.

Chung, Heejung, Hyojin Seo, Sarah Forbes and Holly Birkett. *Working from Home During the Covid-19 Lockdown: Changing Preferences and the Future of Work.* University of Kent and University of Birmingham, 2020.

Clark, Pilita. "The New In-Demand Jobs: Delivery Drivers and Tax Specialists." *Financial Times*, 13 December 2020.

Collinson, Alex. "A Year on from Furlough". *TUC* (blog), 20 March 2021.

Collinson, Alex. "Self-Isolation Support Payments: The Failing Scheme Barely Anyone's Heard Of." *TUC* (blog), 21 June 2021.

Cominetti, Nye, Kathleen Henehan, Hannah Slaughter and Greg Thwaites. *Long Covid in the Labour Market.* London: Resolution Foundation, February 2021.

Committee of Public Accounts. "Covid-19: Support for Children's Education", 26 May 2021, https://publications.parliament.uk/pa/cm5802/cmselect/cmpubacc/240/24005.htm (accessed 28 August 2021).

Cook, Tim, Emira Kursumovic and Simon Lennane. "Exclusive: Deaths of NHS Staff from Covid-19 Analysed." *Health Service Journal* (April 2020).

Cooper, Melinda. *Family Values: Between Neoliberalism and the New Social Conservatism.* New York: Zone Books, 2017.

Corlett, Adam. "The Benefit Freeze Has Ended, but Erosion of the Social Security Safety Net Continues." *Resolution Foundation* (blog), 16 October 2019.

Corlet Walker, Christine, Angela Druckman and Tim Jackson. *Careless Finance: Operational and Economic Fragility in Adult Social Care.* Guildford: Centre for the Understanding of Sustainable Prosperity, 23 March 2021.

Cotterill, Paul. "Carers' Agency: Power and Professionalisation." *Renewal*, 30 April 2021, https://renewal.org.uk/carers-agency-1/ (accessed 23 August 2021).

Cowen, Alisa. "Ten Million People Have Downloaded the NHS Covid-19 App." National Health Executive, 28 September 2020.

Cowen, Deborah. *The Deadly Life of Logistics: Mapping Violence in Global Trade.* Minneapolis: University of Minnesota Press, 2014.

Cribb, Jonathan, Isaac Delestre and Paul Johnson. "1.5 Million Currently Excluded from Claiming SEISS Could Easily Be Supported by Government at Modest Cost." Institute for Fiscal Studies, 27 January 2021.

Daon, Yair, Robin Thompson and Uri Obolski. "Estimating COVID-19 Outbreak Risk Through Air Travel." *Journal of Travel Medicine*, 27:5 (July 2020): 1–8.

Darling, Jonathan. "Asylum in Austere Times: Instability, Privatization and Experimentation within the UK Asylum Dispersal System." *Journal of Refugee Studies*, 29:4 (2016): 483–505.

Davies, Paul, and Mark Freedland. *Towards a Flexible Labour Market: Labour Legislation and Regulation since the 1990s.* Oxford: Oxford University Press, 2007.

De Genova, Nicholas. "Migrant 'Illegality' and Deportability in Everyday Life." *Annual Review of Anthropology*, 3:1 (2002): 419–447.

De Henau, Jerome, and Susan Himmelweit. *A Care-Led Recovery from Coronavirus*. London: Women's Budget Group, June 2020.

De Vries, Rob, Ben Baumberg Geiger, Lisa Scullion, Kate Summers, Daniel Edmiston, Jo Ingold, David Robertshaw and David Young. *Solidarity in a Crisis? Trends in Attitudes to Benefits during COVID-19*. Salford: Welfare at a Social Distance, September 2021.

De Waal, Alex. *New Pandemics, Old Politics: Two Hundred Years of War on Disease and Its Alternatives*. London: Wiley, 2021.

Department for Business, Innovation & Skills. "Higher Education: Success as a Knowledge Economy." Policy Paper, 26 May 2016.

Department of Culture, Media & Sport. "Our 10 Tech Priorities", March 2021, https://dcms.shorthandstories.com/Our-Ten-Tech-Priorities/index.html (accessed 5 October 2021).

Department for Education. "Schools to Benefit from Education Partnership with Tech Giants." Press Release, 24 April 2020, www.gov.uk/government/news/schools-to-benefit-from-education-partnership-with-tech-giants (accessed 27 August 2021).

Department of Health & Social Care. "Booking and Staying in a Quarantine Hotel if You've Been in a Red List Country", 1 October 2021, www.gov.uk/guidance/booking-and-staying-in-a-quarantine-hotel-when-you-arrive-in-england (accessed 1 October 2021).

Department for Transport. "Global Travel Taskforce Sets Out Framework to Safely Reopen International Travel", 9 April 2021, www.gov.uk/government/news/global-travel-taskforce-sets-out-framework-to-safely-reopen-international-travel (accessed 20 September 2021).

Dickens, John. "The Cost of Lockdown: Attainment Gap Widens by Up to 52% for Primary Pupils." *Schools Week*, 24 July 2020.

Digital, Culture, Media and Sport Select Committee. "Culture, Tourism and Sport Bring Us Together in a Shared Experience." House of Commons, 23 July 2020.

Dorling, Danny. "The Unprecedented Rise of Mortality across Poorer Parts of the UK." *Glasgow Centre for Population Health* (blog), 11 November 2020.

Dowling, Emma. *The Care Crisis: What Caused It and How Can We End It?* London: Verso, 2020.

Downey, Andrea. "Cabinet Minister Owned £90,000 Shares in Faculty at Time of NHSX Contract." *Digital Health*, 18 November 2020.

Duggan, James, Ultan Sherman, Ronan Carbery and Anthony McDonnell. "Algorithmic Management and App-Work in the Gig Economy: A Research Agenda for Employment Relations and HRM." *Human Resource Management Journal*, 30:1 (2020): 114–132.

Durand, Cedric. "1979 in Reverse." *Sidecar*, 1 June 2021.

Edgerton, David. *The Rise and Fall of the British Nation: A Twentieth-Century History*. London: Penguin, 2018.

Education Endowment Foundation. "Best Evidence on Impact of Covid-19 on Pupil Attainment", June 2020, https://educationendowmentfoundation.org.uk/covid-19-resources/best-evidence-on-impact-of-school-closures-on-the-attainment-gap/ (accessed 1 October 2021).

Elliot Major, Lee, Andrew Eyles and Stephen Machin. "Denied Jobs and Schooling, 'Generation Covid' Faces a Struggle to Catch Up." *LSE Blog*, 27 October 2020, https://blogs.lse.ac.uk/covid19/2020/10/27/denied-jobs-and-schooling-generation-covid-faces-a-struggle-to-catch-up/ (accessed 27 August 2021).

Elson, Diane. "The Economic, the Political and the Domestic: Businesses, States and Households in the Organisation of Production." *New Political Economy*, 3:2 (1998): 189–208.

Elvers, Eemer, Jack Worth and Anusha Ghosh. *Home Learning During Covid-19: Findings from the Understanding Society Longitudinal Study*. Slough: National Foundation for Educational Research, July 2020.

Espeland, Wendy, and Michael Sauder. *Engines of Anxiety: Academic Rankings, Reputation and Accountability*. New York: Russell Sage Foundation, 2016.

Fair Work. *The Gig Economy and COVID-19: Looking Ahead*. Oxford: The Fair Work Project, September 2020.

Federal Reserve. "Federal Reserve Announces Extensive New Measures to Support the Economy." Board of Governors of the Federal Reserve System, 23 March 2020.

Fée, David. "The Privatisation of Asylum Accommodation in the UK: Winners and Losers." *Revue Française de Civilisation Britannique. French Journal of British Studies*, 26:2 (2021): 1–17.

Feher, Michel. "Disposing of the Discredited: A European Project." In William Callison and Zachary Manfredi (Eds.), *Mutant Neoliberalism: Market Rule and Political Rupture.* New York: Fordham University Press, 2019.

Felstead, Alan, and Darja Reuschke. *Homeworking in the UK: Before and During the 2020 Lockdown.* WISERD Report. Cardiff: Wales Institute of Social and Economic Research, 2020.

Ferguson, Donna. "England's 'Catch-up' Tutors Are Being Short-changed by Private Employers." *The Observer*, 28 February 2021.

Financial Times Money Reporters. "Bank of Mum and Dad 'Tenth Biggest Mortgage Lender.'" *Financial Times*, 31 August 2019.

Finch, Hannah. "The Plans for All Eight Freeports in Rishi Sunak's Spring Budget." *Business Live*, 3 March 2021, www.business-live.co.uk/ports-logistics/more-eight-freeports-rishi-sunaks-19956704 (accessed 1 October 2021).

Fitzgerald, Mary. "Under Pressure, UK Government Releases NHS COVID Data Deals with Big Tech." *openDemocracy*, 5 June 2020.

Flood, Alison. "Children Read More Challenging Books in Lockdown, Data Reveals." *The Guardian*, 29 April 2021.

Florida, Richard, Andrés Rodriguez-Pose and Michael Storper. "Cities in a Post-COVID World." *Urban Studies* (June 2021), doi:10.1177/00420980211018072.

Folbre, Nancy. *The Invisible Heart: Economics and Family Values.* New York: The New Press, 2002.

Fotiadis, Apostiolis. "While Hotspots Become Chaotic, EASO Calls in G4S for Protection", 21 June 2016, https://apostolisfotiadis.wordpress.com/2016/06/21/while-hot-spots-become-chaotic-easo-calls-in-g4s-for-protection/ (accessed 20 September 2021).

Foucault, Michel. "The Politics of Health in the Eighteenth Century." *Foucault Studies*, 18 (October 2014): 113–127.

Francis-Devine, Brigid. "Coronavirus: Impact on Household Savings and Debt." Briefing Paper. House of Commons Library, 13 January 2021.

Franklin, Neil. "Working from Home Surveillance Drives Rise of Digital Presenteeism." *Workplace Insight*, 8 April 2021.

Fraser, Douglas. "Scotland to Trial a Four-Day Week." *BBC News*, 1 September 2021.

Fraser, Nancy. "Contradictions of Capital and Care." *New Left Review*, 100 (July–August 2016): 99–117.

Gall, Gregor. "Britain's Coronavirus Wildcat Strikes." *Tribune*, 1 May 2020.

Gayle, Damien. "Toppled Edward Colston Statue Goes on Display in Bristol." *The Guardian*, 4 June 2021.

Gewirtz, Sharon, Meg Maguire, Eszter Neumann and Emma Towers. "What's Wrong with 'Deliverology'? Performance Measurement, Accountability and Quality Improvement in English Secondary Education." *Journal of Education Policy*, 36:4 (2021): 504–529.

Giles, Chris. "UK Government Almost Ran out of Funds, Says BoE Governor." *Financial Times*, 22 June 2020.

Gill, Nick. "Governmental Mobility: The Power Effects of the Movement of Detained Asylum Seekers Around Britain's Detention Estate." *Political Geography*, 28:9 (2009): 186–196.

Gilmore, Ruth Wilson. "Organized Abandonment and Organized Violence: Devolution and the Police." Vimeo, 2015, https://vimeo.com/146450686 (accessed 1 October 2021).

Glaser, Eliane. "Homeschooling Has Revealed the Absurdity of England's National Curriculum." *Prospect*, 28 February 2021.

Good Law Project. "Firm Founded by Tory Donor Provided Substandard Laptops for Vulnerable Children", 24 January 2021, https://goodlawproject.org/update/computacenter-laptops/ (accessed 28 August 2021).

Goodfellow, Maya. *Hostile Environment: How Immigrants Became Scapegoats*. London: Verso, 2020.

Graeber, David. *Debt: The First 5,000 Years*. New York: Melville House, 2011.

Grayson, John. "G4S Promises (Again) to Repaint Asylum Seeker Red Doors and Relocate Families at Risk." *openDemocracy*, 25 May 2016.

Grayson, John. "Behave or Get Deported, Says G4S." *openDemocracy*, 24 April 2017.

Grayson, John. "Beyond English Borders: Asylum Hostels and Asylum Hotels in a Time of Covid-19." Institute of Race Relations, 6 May 2020.

Green, Andy. *The Crisis for Young People: Generational Inequalities in Education, Work, Housing and Welfare.* Basingstoke: Palgrave Macmillan, 2017.

Green, Jeremy, and Scott Lavery. "The Regressive Recovery: Distribution, Inequality and State Power in Britain's Post-Crisis Political Economy." *New Political Economy*, 20:6 (2015): 894–923.

Guild, Elspeth. "Covid-19 Using Border Controls to Fight a Pandemic? Reflections from the European Union." *Frontiers in Human Dynamics*, 2 (2020): 1–13.

Gustafsson, Maja, Kathleen Henehan, Fahmida Rahman and Daniel Tomlinson. *After Shocks: Financial Resilience Before and During the Covid-19 Crisis.* London: Resolution Foundation, April 2021.

Hall, Rachel. "UK University Students Wasted £1bn in a Year on Empty Accommodation." *The Guardian*, 17 February 2021.

Halliday, Josh. "England's Covid Test and Trace Relying on Inexperienced and Poorly Trained Staff." *The Guardian*, 14 December 2020.

Hamilton, Mary, Bryan Maddox and Camilla Addey. *Literacy as Numbers: Researching the Politics and Practices of International Literary Assessment.* Cambridge: Cambridge University Press, 2015.

Hammond, George, and Alice Hancock. "Unpaid Rent: The £6.4bn Dispute That Will Shape the UK High Street." *Financial Times*, 12 August 2021.

Hancock, Alice, and Tim Bradshaw. "Can Food Delivery Services Save UK Restaurants?" *Financial Times*, 28 November 2020.

Hanushek, Eric, and Ludgar Woessman. *The Economic Impacts of Learning Loss.* Paris: OECD, September 2020.

Harari, Daniel, Matthew Keep and Phillip Brien. "Coronavirus: Economic Impact." Research Briefing. House of Commons Library, 2020.

Henley, Andrew. "The Rise of Self-Employment in the UK: Entrepreneurial Transmission or Declining Job Quality?" *Cambridge Journal of Economics*, 45:3 (2021): 457–486.

Henshall, Angela. "Can the 'Right to Disconnect' Exist in a Remote-Work World?" *BBC*, 21 May 2021.

HEPI (Higher Education Policy Institute). "Student's Views on the Impact of Coronavirus on Their Higher Education Experience in 2021", 1 April 2021, www.hepi.ac.uk/2021/04/01/students-views-on-the-impact-of-coronavirus-on-their-higher-education-experience-in-2021/ (accessed 27 September 2021).

Hern, Alex. "Microsoft Productivity Score Feature Criticised as Workplace Surveillance." *The Guardian*, 26 November 2020.

Himmelweit, Susan. "The Prospects for Caring: Economic Theory and Policy Analysis." *Cambridge Journal of Economics*, 31:4 (2007): 581–599.

HM Treasury. "Chancellor Extends Furlough Scheme until October." GOV.UK, 12 May 2020.

HM Treasury. *Build Back Better: Our Plan for Growth*, 3 March 2021.

HM Treasury. *The Mortgage Guarantee Scheme*. Policy Paper, 3 March 2021.

Home Affairs Committee. *Asylum Accommodation Twelfth Report of Session 2016–17*. House of Commons, 31 January 2017.

Home Affairs Committee. "Home Office Preparedness for COVID-19 (Coronavirus): Institutional Accommodation", 28 July 2020, https://publications.parliament.uk/pa/cm5801/cmselect/cmhaff/562/56202.htm(accessed 20 September 2021).

Home Office. *Fairer, Faster and Firmer – A Modern Approach to Immigration and Asylum*, 27 July 1998.

Home Office. "New Asylum Accommodation Contracts Awarded", 8 January 2019, www.gov.uk/government/news/new-asylum-accommodation-contracts-awarded (accessed 20 September 2021).

Home Office. "Police, Crime, Sentencing and Courts Bill 2021: Protest Powers Factsheet", 7 July 2021, www.gov.uk/government/publications/police-crime-sentencing-and-courts-bill-2021-factsheets/police-crime-sentencing-and-courts-bill-2021-protest-powers-factsheet (accessed 20 September 2021).

Home Office. "Coronavirus (COVID-19): Jobs That Qualify for Travel Exemptions", 2021, www.gov.uk/government/publications/coronavirus-covid-19-travellers-exempt-from-uk-border-rules/coronavirus-covid-19-travellers-exempt-from-uk-border-rules (accessed 20 September 2021).

Honig, Bonnie. *Public Things: Democracy in Disrepair*. New York: Fordham University Press, 2017.

Hood, Christopher. *The Blame Game: Spin, Bureaucracy, and Self-Preservation in Government*. Oxford: Princeton University Press, 2011.

Hopkin, Jonathan. "When Polanyi Met Farage: Market Fundamentalism, Economic Nationalism, and Britain's Exit from the European Union." *The British Journal of Politics and International Relations*, 19:3 (2017): 465–478.

Horton, Amy. "Financialization and Non-Disposable Women: Real Estate, Debt and Labour in UK Care Homes." *Environment and Planning A: Economy and Space* (July 2019), doi:10.1177/0308518X19862580.

Hoskyns, Catherine, and Shirin Rai. "Recasting the Global Political Economy: Counting Women's Unpaid Work." *New Political Economy*, 12:3 (2007): 297–317.

Hospitality & Catering News. "Study Shows Mass Exodus of Migrant Workers Due to Covid and Brexit." *Hospitality & Catering News* (blog), 6 April 2021.

House of Commons Public Accounts Committee. "Covid-19: Test, Track and Trace (Part 1)." Forty-Seventh Report of Session 2019–21, House of Commons, 10 March 2021.

House of Lords EAC. *Universal Credit Isn't Working: Proposals for Reform*. London: House of Lords Economic Affairs Committee, July 2020.

Hurley, James, Sudipto Karmakar, Elena Markoska, Eryk Walczak and Danny Walker. *Impacts of the Covid-19 Crisis: Evidence from 2 Million UK SMEs*. Bank of England Working Papers, Bank of England, 11 June 2021.

Huws, Ursula. *Reinventing the Welfare State: Digital Platforms and Public Policies*. London: Pluto Press, 2020.

Huws, Ursula, Neil H. Spencer and Dag S. Syrdal. "Online, on Call: The Spread of Digitally Organised Just-in-Time Working and Its Implications for Standard Employment Models." *New Technology, Work and Employment*, 33:2 (2018): 113–129.

Ideland, Malin. "Google and the End of the Teacher? How a Figuration of the Teacher Is Produced Through an Ed-Tech Discourse." *Learning, Media & Technology*, 46:1 (January 2021): 33–46.

IER (Institute of Employment Rights). "New Bill Will Abolish Insecure Work." Institute of Employment Rights, 26 May 2021, www.ier.org.uk/press-releases/new-bill-will-abolish-insecure-work/ (accessed 1 October 2021).

ILO (International Labour Organization). "ILO Monitor: COVID-19 and the World of Work. 2nd Edition", 7 April 2020, www.ilo.org/global/topics/coronavirus/impacts-and-responses/WCMS_740877/lang--en/index.htm (accessed 1 October 2021).

IMF Blog. "Toward an Integrated Policy Framework for Open Economies." *IMF Blog*, 13 July 2020.

IPPR (Institute for Public Policy Research). "Commit to New Deal for Healthcare Workers or Risk 'Deadly Exodus', IPPR Warns Government." Press Release, 30 March 2021.

Ireland, Ben. "Covid Tests 'Cost Travellers £1.1bn This Summer.'" *Travel Weekly*, 10 September 2021.

Ireson, Judith, and Katie Rushforth. "Private Tutoring at Transition Points in the English Education System: Its Nature, Extent and Purpose." *Research Papers in Education*, 26:1 (2011): 1–19.

Jackson, Tim. *Prosperity without Growth*, 2nd edition. London: Routledge, 2016.

James, Malcolm, and Sivamohan Valluvan. "Coronavirus Conjuncture: Nationalism and Pandemic States." *Sociology*, 54:6 (2020): 1238–1250.

Jameson, Hannah. "The Beecroft Report: Pandering to Popular Perceptions of Over-Regulation." *The Political Quarterly*, 83:4 (2012): 838–843.

Jensen, Tracey. "Welfare Commonsense, Poverty Porn and Doxosophy." *Sociological Research Online* 19:3 (2014): 277–283.

Jerrim, John. *Extra Time: Private Tuition and Out-of-school Study, New International Evidence*. London: Sutton Trust, 2017.

Jolly, Jasper. "Number of Billionaires in UK Reached New Record During Covid Crisis." *The Guardian*, 21 May 2021.

Johnson, Paul, Robert Joyce and Lucinda Platt. *The IFS Deaton Review of Inequalities: A New Year's Message*. Institute for Fiscal Studies, January 2021.

Johnston, Anna. *Lessons Learned: Where Women Stand at the Start of 2021*. London: Women's Budget Group, 2021.

Jones, Katy. "Active Labour Market Policy in a Post-Covid UK: Moving Beyond a 'Work First' Approach." In Philip McCann and Tim Vorley (Eds.), *Productivity and the Pandemic: Challenges and Insights from Covid-19*. Cheltenham: Edward Elgar, 2021.

Jones, Ken. *Education in Britain: 1944 to the Present*. London: Polity, 2016.

Jones, Lee, and Shahar Hameiri. "COVID-19 and the Failure of the Neoliberal Regulatory State." *Review of International Political Economy* (1 March 2021): 1–25, doi:10.1080/09692290.2021.1892798.

Judge, Lindsay, and Daniel Tomlinson. *Home Improvements: Action to Address the Housing Challenges Faced by Young People*. London: Resolution Foundation, April 2018.

Kale, Sirin. "'I Feel She Was Abandoned': The Life and Terrible Death of Belly Mujinga." *The Guardian*, 25 August 2020.

Katsomitros, Alex. "The Emerging University Bonds Market." *World Finance*, 20 April 2018, www.worldfinance.com/markets/the-emerging-university-bonds-market (accessed 5 October 2021).

KCL (King's College London). "COVID-19 Pandemic Significantly Increased Anxiety and Depression in the UK." Press Release, King's College London, 16 September 2020.

Kelton, Stephanie. *The Deficit Myth*. London: John Murray, 2020.

Klein, Naomi. *The Shock Doctrine: The Rise of Disaster Capitalism*. London: Penguin, 2014.

Kleinman, Zoe. "Confusion Over Use of NHS App as Covid Passport." *BBC News*, 29 April 2021.

Knox, Jeremy, Ben Williamson and Sîan Bayne. "Machine Behaviourism: Future Visions of 'Learnification' and 'Datafication' across Humans and Digital Technologies." *Learning, Media & Technology*, 45:1 (January 2020): 31–45.

Kolioulis, Alessio, and Rahel Suss. "Why Does Finance Care So Much About Students?" *Greater Manchester Housing Action* (blog), 28 September 2020, www.gmhousingaction.com/finance-students/ (accessed 28 August 2021).

Kolkman, Daan. "'F**k the Algorithm'? What the World Can Learn from the UK's A-level Grading Fiasco", *LSE Blog*, 26 August 2020, https://blogs. lse.ac.uk/impactofsocialsciences/2020/08/26/fk-the-algorithm-what-the-world-can-learn-from-the-uks-a-level-grading-fiasco/ (accessed 29 August 2021).

Krippner, Greta. *Capitalizing on Crisis: The Political Origins of the Rise of Finance.* Cambridge, MA: Harvard University Press, 2012.

Lambert, Peter, and John Van Reenen. *A Major Wave of UK Business Closures by April 2021? The Scale of the Problem and What Can Be Done.* Covid-19 Analysis Series. London: Centre for Economic Performance, January 2021.

Langley, Paul, and Andrew Leyshon. "Platform Capitalism: The Intermediation and Capitalisation of Digital Economic Circulation." *Finance and Society*, 3:1 (2017): 11–31.

Lavery, Scott. *British Capitalism After the Crisis.* Basingstoke: Palgrave Macmillan, 2019.

Lawrence, Mathew, Adrienne Buller, Joseph Baines and Sandy Hager. *Commoning the Company.* London: Common Wealth, April 2020.

Leaker, Debra. "Painting the Full Picture: What Our Statistics Tell Us about the Labour Market." *National Statistical – ONS* (blog), 29 January 2021.

Lefebvre, Henri, *The Production of Space.* Translated by Donald Nicholson-Smith. Oxford: Blackwell, 1991.

Lepanjuuri, Katriina, Robert Wishart and Peter Cornick. *The Characteristics of Those in the Gig Economy.* London: Department for Business, Energy & Industrial Strategy, February 2018.

Leslie, Jack, and Krishnan Shah. *(Wealth) Gap Year: The Impact of the Coronavirus Crisis on UK Household Wealth.* London: Resolution Foundation, 2021.

Lewis, Paul, David Conn and David Pegg. "UK Government Using Confidential Patient Data in Coronavirus Response." *The Guardian*, 12 April 2020.

Lewis, Sarah, Alasdair Munro, George Davey Smith and Allyson Pollock. "Closing Schools is Not Evidence Based and Harms Children." *BMJ*, 372: 521 (February 2021).

Liberty. "Challenge Hostile Environment Data Sharing." 25 August 2021, www.libertyhumanrights.org.uk/campaign/challenge-hostile-environment-data-sharing/ (accessed 20 September 2021).

Link Asset Services. *UK plc Debt Monitor*. No. 2. (August 2019).

Littler, Jo. *Against Meritocracy: Culture, Power and Myths of Mobility.* London: Routledge, 2018.

Liverpool, Layal. "Why Coronavirus Hit People from BAME Communities So Hard." *Wired*, 25 August 2020, www.wired.co.uk/article/bame-communities-coronavirus-uk (accessed 20 September 2021).

Lowe, Tom. "Construction Sites to Stay Open as PM Orders England into Strictest Lockdown since March." *Building*, 4 January 2021.

Mairs, Nicholas. "Boost for Theresa May as Number of People in Work Hits New All-Time High." *Politics Home*, 19 March 2019.

Makortoff, Kalyeena. "UK House Prices 'Likely to Keep Rising Despite Hitting Record High.'" *The Guardian*, 7 June 2021.

Mandler, Peter. *The Crisis of the Meritocracy: Britain's Transition to Mass Education Since the Second World War.* Oxford: Oxford University Press, 2020.

Marmot, Michael, Jessica Allen, Peter Goldblatt, Eleanor Herd and Joana Morrison. *Build Back Fairer: The Covid-19 Marmot Review.* London: The Health Foundation/Institute of Health Equity, 2020.

Mathy, Gabriel. "The First Services Recession." *Phenomenal World*, 25 March 2020, https://phenomenalworld.org/analysis/the-first-services-recession (accessed 1 October 2021).

McGettigan, Andrew. *The Great University Gamble: Money, Markets and the Future of Higher Education.* London: Pluto, 2015.

McNeil, Clare, Henry Parkes, Kayleigh Garthwaite and Ruth Patrick. *No Longer "Managing": The Rise of Working Poverty and Fixing Britain's Broken Social Settlement.* London: IPPR, 26 May 2021.

Mehrling, Perry G. "First Liquidity, Then Solvency." Institute for New Economic Thinking, 6 October 2011.

Mezzadra, Sandro, and Brett Neilson. *Border as Method, or, the Multiplication of Labor.* Durham: Duke University Press, 2013.

Milanovic, Branko. "The First Global Event in the History of Humankind." *Social Europe,* 7 December 2020.

Milburn, Keir. *Generation Left.* Cambridge: Polity, 2019.

Miliband, Ed. "How Labour Would Invest in Jobs through Our Green Economic Recovery." The Labour Party, Speech, 25 March 2021, https://labour.org.uk/press/full-text-of-ed-milibands-speech-on-how-labour-would-invest-in-jobs-through-our-green-economic-recovery/ (accessed 23 September 2021).

Mitchell, Timothy. "Fixing the Economy." *Cultural Studies,* 12:1 (1998): 82–101.

Mitchell, Timothy. "No Business of Yours: How the Large Corporation Swallowed the Future." Lecture given at Kings College London, 17 January 2019.

Montgomerie, Johnna, and Mirjam Büdenbender. "Round the Houses: Homeownership and Failures of Asset-Based Welfare in the United Kingdom." *New Political Economy,* 20:3 (2015): 386–405.

Montgomerie, Johnna, and Daniela Tepe-Belfrage. "Caring for Debts: How the Household Economy Exposes the Limits of Financialisation." *Critical Sociology,* 43:4–5 (2017): 653–668.

Morris, Marley, and Amreen Qureshi. *Locked Out of a Livelihood: The Case for Reforming 'No Recourse to Public Funds'.* London: IPPR, 2021.

Moss, Gemma, Rebecca Allen, Alice Bradbury, Sam Duncan, Sinead Harmey and Rachael Levy. *Primary Teachers' Experience of the Covid-19 Lockdown – Eight Key Messages for Policymakers Going Forward.* London: UCL Institute of Education, June 2020.

Moss, Gemma, Rob Webster, Sinéad Harmey and Alice Bradbury. *Unsung Heroes: The Role of Teaching Assistants and Classroom Assistants in Keeping Schools Functioning During Lockdown.* London: UCL Institute of Education, March 2021.

NAO (National Audit Office). "Covid-19 Cost Data." COVID-19 Cost Tracker, https://nao-mesh.shinyapps.io/Covid_cost_tracker/ (accessed 4 May 2021).

NAO (National Audit Office). *Implementing Employment Support Schemes in Response to the COVID-19 Pandemic.* London: National Audit Office, 23 October 2020.

NAO (National Audit Office). *The UK Border: Preparedness for the End of the Transition Period*. London: National Audit Office, 6 November 2020.

NAO (National Audit Office). *Support for Children's Education During the Early Stages of the Covid-19 Pandemic*. London: National Audit Office, March 2021.

NAO (National Audit Office). *Investigation into Government Procurement During the COVID-19 Pandemic*. London: National Audit Office, 26 November 2021.

NAO (National Audit Office). *Investigation into the Free School Meals Voucher Scheme*. London: National Audit Office, 2021.

Narwan, Gurpret. "G4S Made £14m from Scandal-hit Immigration Centre." *The Times*, 22 July 2019.

Neilson, Daniel H. *Minsky*. Cambridge: Polity, 2019.

Neville, Sarah, and Gill Plimmer, "NHS and Private Sector Forge New Partnerships to Clear Patient Backlog." *Financial Times*, 25 April 2021.

NHS Digital. "Survey Conducted in July 2020 Shows One in Six Children Having a Probable Mental Disorder." 22 October 2020.

Non una di Meno, "La vita oltre la pandemia." *Dinamopress*, 2020, www.dinamopress.it/news/la-vita-oltre-la-pandemia/ (accessed 20 September 2021).

O'Connor, Michael, and Jonathan Portes. "Estimating the UK Population During the Pandemic." *ESCoE* (blog), 14 January 2021.

O'Dwyer, Michael. "Consultants Awarded over £600m of UK Covid Contracts." *Financial Times*, 4 May 2021.

OBR (Office for Budget Responsibility). *Coronavirus Reference Scenario*. London: Office for Budget Responsibility, 14 April 2020.

OBR (Office for Budget Responsibility). *Welfare Trends Report*. London: Office for Budget Responsibility, March 2021.

OBR (Office for Budget Responsibility). *Fiscal Risks Report*. London: Office for Budget Responsibility, July 2021.

OECD (Organisation for Economic Co-operation and Development). *OECD Economic Surveys: United Kingdom 2015*. Paris: OECD, 2015.

OECD (Organisation for Economic Co-operation and Development). "COVID-19 and Global Capital Flows." Paris: OECD, 3 July 2020.

OECD (Organisation for Economic Co-operation and Development). *The State of School Education: One year into the Covid Pandemic.* Paris: OECD, March 2021.

Ofsted. "COVID-19 Series: Briefing on Early Years, November 2020", 15 December 2020, www.gov.uk/government/publications/covid-19-series-briefing-on-early-years-november-2020 (accessed 5 October 2021).

Olivarius, Kathryn. "The Dangerous History of Immunoprivilege." *New York Times*, 12 April 2020.

Oliver, Kelly. *Carceral Humanitarianism: Logics of Refugee Detention.* Minneapolis: University of Minnesota Press, 2017.

ONS (Office for National Statistics). "Trends in the UK Economy – Office for National Statistics", 27 February 2015.

ONS (Office for National Statistics). "Women Shoulder the Responsibility of 'Unpaid' Work", 10 November 2016.

ONS (Office for National Statistics). "Household Debt in Great Britain: April 2016 to March 2018", 5 December 2019.

ONS (Office for National Statistics). "Coronavirus and the Economic Impacts on the UK – 23 April 2020", 23 April 2020.

ONS (Office for National Statistics). "Coronavirus and Key Workers in the UK", 15 May 2020.

ONS (Office for National Statistics). "Coronavirus and Homeworking in the UK – April 2020", 8 July 2020.

ONS (Office for National Statistics). "GDP Monthly Estimate, UK: June 2020", 12 August 2020.

ONS (Office for National Statistics). "The Impact of the Coronavirus So Far: The Industries That Struggled or Recovered", 9 September 2020.

ONS (Office for National Statistics). "Public Sector Finances, UK: August 2020", 25 September 2020.

ONS (Office for National Statistics). "UK National Accounts, The Blue Book Time Series", 30 October 2020.

ONS (Office for National Statistics). "Business Insights and Impact on the UK Economy", 7 January 2021.

ONS (Office for National Statistics). "Coronavirus (COVID-19) Related Deaths by Occupation, England and Wales", 25 January 2021.

ONS (Office for National Statistics). "Coronavirus and Redundancies in the UK Labour Market", 19 February 2021.

ONS (Office for National Statistics). "Comparison of Furloughed Jobs Data, UK", 5 March 2021.

ONS (Office for National Statistics). "Homeworking Hours, Rewards and Opportunities in the UK: 2011 to 2020", 19 April 2021.

ONS (Office for National Statistics). "Earnings and Employment from Pay As You Earn Real Time Information, UK", 20 April 2021.

ONS (Office for National Statistics). "UK House Price Index: February 2021", 21 April 2021.

ONS (Office for National Statistics). "Public Sector Finances Tables 1 to 10: Appendix A", 23 April 2021.

ONS (Office for National Statistics). "How Has Lockdown Changed Our Relationship with Nature?" 26 April 2021.

ONS (Office for National Statistics). "X07: Labour Force Survey Weekly Estimates", July 2021.

ONS (Office for National Statistics). "Overseas Travel and Tourism, Provisional: January to March 2021", 23 July 2021.

ONS (Office for National Statistics). "Gross Domestic Product: Year on Year Growth: CVM SA %", www.ons.gov.uk/economy/grossdomesticproductgdp/timeseries/ihyp/pn2 (accessed 12 August 2021).

ONS (Office for National Statistics). "EMP17: People in Employment on Zero Hours Contracts", 17 August 2021.

ONS (Office for National Statistics). "UK House Price Index: June 2021", 18 August 2021.

ONS (Office for National Statistics). "Internet Sales as a Percentage of Total Retail Sales (Ratio) (%)", 17 September 2021.

OSSS (Office of the Secretary of State for Scotland), Defra (Department for Environment, Food and Rural Affairs), George Eustice and Alister Jack. "Up to 30,000 Workers to Help Reap 2021 Harvest." GOV.UK, 22 December 2020. www.gov.uk/government/news/up-to-30000-workers-to-help-reap-2021-harvest--2 (accessed 7 August 2021).

Palantir, "Responding to Covid-19", www.palantir.com/covid19/ (accessed 20 September 2021).

Pana, Tiberiu, Sohinee Bhattacharya, David Gamble, Zahra Pasdar, Weronika Szlachetka, Jesus Perdomo-Lampignano, Kai Ewers, David McLernon and Phyo Myint. "Country-level Determinants of the Severity of the First Global Wave of the COVID-19 Pandemic: An Ecological Study." *BMJ Open*, 11:2 (2021): 1–10.

Partridge, Joanna. "Serco Expects 50% Jump in Profits on Back of Covid Contracts." *The Guardian*, 30 June 2021.

Parveen, Nazia. "England's Travel Traffic-light System Replaced and Testing Requirements to Change." *The Guardian*, 4 October 2021.

Patrick, Ruth, and Tom Lee. *Advance to Debt: Paying Back Benefit Debt – What Happens When Deductions Are Made to Benefit Payments?* York: Covid Realities, January 2021.

Pearson, Ruth, and Diane Elson. "Transcending the Impact of the Financial Crisis in the United Kingdom: Towards Plan F—a Feminist Economic Strategy." *Feminist Review*, 109:1 (2015): 8–30.

Peck, Jamie, and Rachel Phillips. "The Platform Conjuncture." *Sociologica*, 14:3 (2020): 73–99.

Pezzani, Lorenzo. "Hostile Environments." *E-flux*, 2020, www.e-flux.com/architecture/at-the-border/325761/hostile-environments/ (accessed 18 September 2021).

Piketty, Thomas. *Capital in the Twenty-First Century*. Cambridge, MA: Harvard University Press, 2014.

Pistor, Katharina. *The Code of Capital: How the Law Creates Wealth and Inequality*. Oxford: Princeton University Press, 2019.

Pollin, Robert. "De-Growth vs a Green New Deal." *New Left Review*, 112 (2018): 5–25.

Pollock, Allyson. "Multinational Care Companies Are the Real Winners from Johnson's New Tax." *The Guardian*, 14 September 2021.

Power, Anne, and Ellie Benton. "Where Next for Britain's 4,300 Mutual Aid Groups?" *LSE COVID-19 blog*, 6 May 2021.

Poynter, Gavin. *The Political Economy of State Intervention: Conserving Capital over the West's Long Depression*. London: Routledge, 2020.

Preciado, Paul. "Learning from the Virus." *Artforum*, May/June 2020.

Provan, Sarah. "Majority of Covid Test Providers Unaccredited, Says UK Assessor." *Financial Times*, 4 August 2021.

PwC. *Covid Recovery and Improvement: Locking in the Benefits and Overcoming the Challenges*, January 2021.

Quinn, Ben "UK Government Spends More Than £163,000 on Union Flags in Two Years." *The Guardian*, 6 August 2021.

Qureshi, Amreen, Marley Morris and Lucy Mort. *Beyond the Hostile Environment*. London: IPPR, 2021.

Rae, Charlie. "What Does the Supreme Court Decision in the Uber Case Mean for Employers?" *Shoosmiths*, 3 March 2021.

Rahman, K. Sabeel, and Kathleen Thelen. "The Rise of the Platform Business Model and the Transformation of Twenty-First-Century Capitalism." *Politics & Society*, 47:2 (2019): 177–204.

Rai, Shirin, Catherine Hoskyns and Dania Thomas. "Depletion: The Cost of Social Reproduction." *International Feminist Journal of Politics*, 16:1 (2014): 86–105.

Rao, Rahul. "On the Statues." *The Disorder of Things*, 2 April 2016, https://thedisorderofthings.com/2016/04/02/on-statues/ (accessed 19 September 2021).

Raval, Anjli. "Inside the 'Covid Triangle': A Catastrophe Years in the Making." *Financial Times*, 5 March 2021.

Razieh, Cameron, Francesco Zaccardi, Nazrul Islam, Clare L. Gillies, Yogini V. Chudasama, Alex Rowlands, David E Kloecker, Melanie J. Davies, Kamlesh Khunti and Thomas Yates. "Ethnic Minorities and COVID-19: Examining Whether Excess Risk Is Mediated through Deprivation." *European Journal of Public Health*, 31:3 (2021): 630–634.

Reed, Howard, and Jonathan Portes. *Cumulative Impact Assessment: A Research Report by Landman Economics and the National Institute of Economic and Social Research for the Equality and Human Rights Commission.* Manchester: EHRC, 2014.

Reich, Justin. *Failure to Disrupt: Why Technology Alone Can't Transform Education.* Cambridge, MA: Harvard University Press, 2020.

Reuschke, Darja. "The Surge in Homeworking and New Key Issues for Regional Studies." *Regions*, 2020, doi:10.1080/13673882.2021.00001081.

Reuters, "Thousands Join Black Lives Matter Protest outside US Embassy in London", 7 June 2020, www.voanews.com/a/europe_thousands-join-black-lives-matter-protest-outside-us-embassy-london/6190683.html (accessed 20 September 2021).

Rhodes, Chris, and Georgina Hutton. "Retail Sector in the UK." Research Briefing. House of Commons Library, 21 June 2021.

Rhodes, Rod. "The Hollowing Out of the State: The Changing Nature of the Public Service in Britain." *The Political Quarterly*, 65:2 (1994): 138–151.

Rhodes, Rod. "The New Governance: Governing without Government." *Political Studies*, 44:4 (1996): 652–667.

Rosen, Michael. "Dear Gavin Williamson, Could You Tell Parents What a Fronted Adverbial Is?" *The Guardian*, 23 January 2021.

Rubery, Jill, Arjan Keizer and Damian Grimshaw. "Flexibility Bites Back: The Multiple and Hidden Costs of Flexible Employment Policies." *Human Resource Management Journal*, 26:3 (2016): 235–251.

Sadowski, Jathan. "Cyberspace and Cityscapes: On the Emergence of Platform Urbanism." *Urban Geography*, 41:3 (2020): 448–452.

Sadowski, Jathan. "The Internet of Landlords: Digital Platforms and New Mechanisms of Rentier Capitalism." *Antipode*, 52:2 (2020): 562–580.

Samson, Adam, and Philip Stafford. "UK Sells Negative-yielding Government Bonds for First Time." *Financial Times*, 20 May 2020.

Şandor, Alina. "What the First COVID-19 Lockdown Meant for People in Insecure, Poor-Quality Work." Briefing. London: Joseph Rowntree Foundation, 29 March 2021.

Sasse, Tom, Sarah Nickson, Colm Britchfield and Nick Davies. *Government Outsourcing: When and How to Bring Public Services Back into Government Hands*. London: Institute for Government, June 2020.

Scott, Peter, and Steve Williams. "The Coalition Government and Employment Relations: Accelerated Neo-Liberalism and the Rise of Employer-Dominated Voluntarism." *Observatoire de La Société Britannique*, 15 (2014): 145–164.

Scott-Smith, Tom, and Mark Breeze (Eds.). *Structures of Protection? Rethinking Refugee Shelter*. New York: Berghahn Books, 2020.

Selwyn, Neil. "'The Human Labour of School Data: Exploring the Production of Digital Data in Schools." *Oxford Review of Education*, 47:3 (May 2021): 353–368.

Shubber, Kadhim, Jim Pickard and Max Harlow. "Property Donors Provide One-Quarter of Funds Given to Tory Party." *Financial Times*, 29 July 2021.

Sibieta, Luke. "School Spending in England: Trends Over Time and Future Outlook." Briefing Note. Institute for Fiscal Studies, 2 September 2021.

Sibieta, Luke. "The Growing Gap Between State School and Private School Spending." Observation. Institute for Fiscal Studies, 8 October 2021.

Sibieta, Luke, and Ben Zaranko. "HM Treasury: Stingy and Short-sighted, or Prudent and Practical?", *IFS Blog*, 4 June 2021, https://ifs.org.uk/publications/15472 (accessed 28 August 2021).

Simpson, Mollie. "Britain's Historic Wave of Student Rent Strikes." *Tribune*, 21 January 2021.

Singer, Lauren, and Patricia Alexander. "Reading on Paper and Digitally: What the Past Decades of Empirical Research Reveal." *Review of Educational Research*, 87:6 (December 2017): 1007–1041.

Singer, Natasha. "How Google Took Over the Classroom." *New York Times*, 13 May 2017.

Skills for Care. *The State of the Adult Social Care Sector and Workforce 2020*. Leeds: Skills for Care, 2020.

Skills for Care. *Workforce Nationality Figures*. Leeds: Skills for Care, 2020, www.skillsforcare.org.uk/adult-social-care-workforce-data/Workforce-intelligence/publications/Topics/Workforce-nationality.aspx (accessed 7 August 2021).

Slobodian, Quinn. "Hayek's Bastards: The Populist Right's Neoliberal Roots." *Tribune*, 15 June 2021.

Soper, Kate. *Post-Growth Living: For an Alternative Hedonism.* London: Verso, 2020.

Srnicek, Nick. *Platform Capitalism.* London: Wiley, 2017.

Stanley, Isaac, Adrienne Buller and Mathew Lawrence. *Caring for the Earth, Caring for Each Other: An Industrial Strategy for Adult Social Care.* London: Common Wealth, 2021.

Stevano, Sara, Alessandra Mezzadri, Lorena Lombardozzi and Hannah Bargawi. "Hidden Abodes in Plain Sight: The Social Reproduction of Households and Labor in the COVID-19 Pandemic." *Feminist Economics*, 27:1–2 (2021): 271–287.

Stronge Will, and Aidan Harper (Eds.). *The Shorter Working Week: A Radical and Pragmatic Proposal.* London: Autonomy, January 2019.

Stubbington, Tommy, and Chris Giles. "Investors Sceptical over Bank of England's QE Programme." *Financial Times*, 5 January 2021.

Sunak, Rishi. "Budget Speech 2020." GOV.UK, 11 March 2020.

Sutton Trust. *Remote Learning: The Digital Divide*, 11 January 2021, www.suttontrust.com/wp-content/uploads/2021/01/Remote-Learning-The-Digital-Divide-Final.pdf (accessed 27 September 2021).

Taylor, Diane. "Immigration Detainee Allegedly Choked by G4S Guard Demands Public Inquiry." *The Guardian*, 25 September 2017.

Taylor, Diane. "Inspectors Condemn Covid Safety of Barracks Used to House Asylum Seekers." *The Guardian*, 8 March 2021.

Taylor, Diane. "More than 50 Died in Home Office Asylum Seeker Accommodation in Past Five Years." *The Guardian*, 25 July 2021.

Taylor, Diane. "Controversial Napier Barracks in Line to House Asylum Seekers Until 2025." *The Guardian*, 27 August 2021.

Taylor, Matthew. *Good Work: The Taylor Review of Modern Working Practices.* London: Department for Business, Energy & Industrial Strategy, 2017.

Taylor, Nick. "A Job, Any Job: The UK Benefits System and Employment Services in an Age of Austerity." *Observatoire de La Société Britannique*, 19 (2017): 267–285.

Tazzioli, Martina, and Maurice Stierl. "Europe's Unsafe Environment: Migrant Confinement under Covid-19." *Critical Studies on Security*, 9:1 (2021): 76–80.

TBIJ (The Bureau of Investigative Journalism). "Deliveroo Riders Can Earn as Little as £2 an Hour During Shifts, as Boss Stands to Make £500m." *The Bureau of Investigative Journalism*, 25 March 2021.

TES Reporter. "Teachers Feed and Clothe Pupils Hit by Covid Pandemic." *TES*, 7 April 2021, www.tes.com/news/child-poverty-teachers-feed-and-clothe-pupils-hit-covid-pandemic (accessed 27 August 2021).

Thomas, Daniel, Delphine Strauss and Jim Pickard. "UK Businesses Push for Return of Office Workers." *Financial Times*, 6 July 2020.

Thomas, Tobi. "Referrals to UK Gaming Addiction Clinic Triple in Year of Lockdowns." *The Guardian*, 20 June 2021.

Thorley, Craig, and Will Cook. *Flexibility For Who? Millennials and Mental Health in the Modern Labour Market*. London: IPPR, 27 July 2017.

Timmins, Nicholas. *Schools and Coronavirus: The Government's Handling of Education During the Pandemic*. London: Institute for Government, August 2021.

Tinson, Adam, and Amy Clair. "Better Housing is Crucial for Our Health and the COVID-19 Recovery." *The Health Foundation* (blog), 28 December 2020.

Tomlinson, Daniel. "The Government Is Not Paying Nine Million People's Wages." Resolution Foundation, 1 August 2020, www.resolutionfoundation.org/publications/the-government-is-not-paying-nine-million-peoples-wages/ (accessed 1 October 2021).

Tooze, Adam. *Shutdown: How Covid Shook the World's Economy*. London: Allen Lane, 2021.

Transparency International. "Concern Over Corruption Red Flags in 20% of UK's PPE Procurement." Press Release, 21 April 2021.

Treasury Committee. "Oral Evidence: Economic Impact of Coronavirus." House of Commons, HC 306, 7 June 2021. https://committees.parliament.uk/oralevidence/2319/html/ (accessed 1 October 2021).

Trussell Trust. "The Trussell Trust – End of Year Stats." The Trussell Trust (blog),   www.trusselltrust.org/news-and-blog/latest-stats/end-year-stats/ (accessed 8 June 2021).

TUC (Trades Union Congress). "TUC Poll: 7 in 10 Requests for Furlough Turned Down for Working Mums." London: TUC, 14 January 2021.

TUC (Trades Union Congress). ""Fire and Rehire" Tactics Have Become Widespread during Pandemic – Warns TUC." London: TUC, 25 January 2021.

TUC (Trades Union Congress). "Jobs and Recovery Monitor – Update on Young Workers." London: TUC, 27 March 2021.

TUC (Trades Union Congress). *Covid-19 and Insecure Work*. London: TUC, April 2021.

TUC (Trades Union Congress). *The Future of Flexible Work*. London: TUC, June 2021.

TUC (Trades Union Congress). "Beyond Furlough: Why the UK Needs a Permanent Short-time Work Scheme." London: TUC, August 2021.

Tussell Database. "Latest Updates on UK Government COVID-19 Contracts and Spending", www.tussell.com/insights/covid (accessed 2 June 2021, 6 October 2021).

UCL Institute of Education. "Break Time Cuts Could Be Harming Children's Development", 10 May 2019, www.ucl.ac.uk/ioe/news/2019/may/break-time-cuts-could-be-harming-childrens-development (accessed 27 August 2021).

UK Debt Management Office. "Quarterly Review for Apr–Jun 2021." UK DMO, 17 August 2021.

Understanding Society. "Covid-19 Survey Briefing Note: Home Schooling." University of Essex and ISER, 2020.

USDAW (Union of Shop, Distributive and Allied Workers). "How Many Retail Job Losses Does It Take for the Government to Act?" Union of Shop, Distributive and Allied Workers, 11 February 2021, www.usdaw.org.uk/About-Us/News/2021/Feb/How-many-retail-job-losses-does-it-take-for-the-Go (accessed 20 August 2021).

van Dijck, Jose, Thomas Poell and Martijn de Waal. *The Platform Society: Public Values in a Connective World*. Oxford: Oxford University Press, 2018.

Vezyridis, Paraskevas and Stephen Timmons. "E-Infrastructures and the Divergent Assetization of Public Health Data: Expectations, Uncertainties, and Asymmetries." *Social Studies of Science*, 51:4 (2021): 606–627.

Vogl, Joseph. *The Ascendency of Finance*. London: John Wiley & Sons, 2017.

Wall, Tom. "HSE Refuses to Classify Covid as a 'Serious' Workplace Risk." *The Observer*, 14 February 2021.

Wallace-Wells, David. "How the West Lost COVID: How Did So Many Rich Countries Get It So Wrong? How Did Others Get It So Right?" *New York Magazine*, 15 March 2021.

Walsh, David, Gerry McCartney, Jon Minton, Jane Parkinson, Deborah Shipton and Bruce Whyte. "Changing Mortality Trends in Countries and Cities of the UK: A Population-Based Trend Analysis." *BMJ Open*, 10:11 (2020).

Walters, William, and Barbara Lüthi. "The Politics of Cramped Space: Dilemmas of Action, Containment and Mobility." *International Journal of Politics, Culture, and Society*, 29:4 (2016): 359–366.

Waring, Marilyn. *If Women Counted: A New Feminist Economics*. London: Macmillan, 1989.

Warren, Tracey, and Clare Lyonette. "Carrying the Work Burden of the Covid-19 Pandemic: Working Class Women in the UK, Briefing Note 1: Employment and Mental Health." Version 6-11-20. Nottingham: Nottingham University Business School, November 2020.

Warren, Tracey, and Clare Lyonette. "Carrying the Work Burden of the Covid-19 Pandemic: Working Class Women in the UK, Briefing Note 2: Housework and Childcare." Nottingham: Nottingham University Business School, December 2020.

WASD (Welfare at a Social Distance). *Work and Pensions Select Committee Inquiry: The DWP's Response to the Coronavirus Outbreak*. Salford: Welfare at a Social Distance, December 2020.

Waters, Richard. "Microsoft Looks to Make 2021 the Year of Teams." *Financial Times*, 5 January 2021.

Watson, Matthew. "The Contradictory Political Economy of Higher Education in the United Kingdom." *The Political Quarterly*, 82:1 (2011): 16–25.

Watson, Matthew. "Michael Gove's War on Professional Historical Expertise: Conservative Curriculum Reform, Extreme Whig History and the Place of Imperial Heroes in Modern Multicultural Britain." *British Politics*, 15:3 (2020): 271–290.

Weale, Sally. "UK Tutoring Scheme Uses Under-18s in Sri Lanka Paid as Little as £1.57 an Hour." *The Guardian*, 19 March 2021.

Wearmouth, Rachel. "Exclusive: 27 Academy Trusts Given Just ONE Free Laptop Each from Government." *Huffington Post,* 18 August 2020, www.huffingtonpost.co.uk/entry/exclusive-27-academy-trusts-handed-just-1-free-laptop-despite-gavin-williamson-pledge-to-help-disadvantaged_uk_5f3ba21bc5b61100c3ac316d?ncid (accessed 27 August 2021).

Webber, Ashleigh. "PwC Facial Recognition Tool Criticised for Home Working Privacy Invasion." *Personnel Today* (blog), 16 June 2020.

Weir, Lorna, and Eric Mykhalovskiy. "The Geopolitics of Global Public Health Surveillance in the Twenty-first Century." In Alison Bashford (Ed.), *Medicine at the Border.* London: Palgrave Macmillan, 2006.

Westwater, Hannah. "How Priti Patel's New Policing Bill Threatens Your Right to Protest." *The Big Issue,* 13 September 2021.

Whitehead, Christine, and Martina Rotolo. "Everyone In: The Numbers." *LSE Blog,* 10 May 2021, https://blogs.lse.ac.uk/lselondon/everyone-in-the-numbers/ (accessed 13 September 2021).

Williams, Martin. "'Spy Tech' Firm Palantir Made £22m Profit After NHS Data Deal." *openDemocracy,* 23 August 2021.

Williamson, Ben. "New Pandemic EdTech Power Networks." *Code Acts in Education,* 1 April 2020, https://codeactsineducation.wordpress.com/2020/04/01/new-pandemic-edtech-power-networks/ (accessed 26 August 2021).

Williamson, Ben. "Decoding ClassDojo: Psycho-policy, Social-emotional Learning and Persuasive Educational Technologies." *Learning, Media & Technology,* 42:4 (October 2017): 440–453.

Williamson, Ben. "Education Technology Seizes a Pandemic Opening." *Current History,* 120:822 (2021): 15–20.

Williamson, Ben, and Anna Hogan. *Commercialisation and Privatisation in/of Education in the Context of Covid-19.* Brussels: Education International Research, July 2020.

Williamson, Ben, Rebecca Eynon and John Potter. "Pandemic Politics, Pedagogies and Practices: Digital Technologies and Distance Education During the Coronavirus Emergency." *Learning, Media & Technology,* 45:2 (April 2020): 107–114.

Williamson, Ben, Felicitas Macgilchrist and John Potter. "Covid-19 Controversies and Critical Research in Digital Education." *Learning, Media & Technology,* 46:2 (April 2021).

Women's Budget Group and Runnymede Trust. *Intersecting Inequalities: The Impact of Austerity on Black and Minority Ethnic Women in the UK*. London: Women's Budget Group, 2017.

Women's Budget Group. *Creating a Caring Economy: A Call to Action*. London: Women's Budget Group, 2020.

Wood, Alex J. *Despotism on Demand: How Power Operates in the Flexible Workplace*. Illustrated edition. Ithaca: Cornell University Press, 2020.

Wood, Zoe. "UK Food Firms Beg Ministers to Let Them Use Prisoners to Ease Labour Shortages." *The Guardian*, 23 August 2021.

World Bank. *Global Economic Prospects, January 2021*. Washington, DC: The World Bank, 2021.

Yandell, John. "Learning under Lockdown: English Teaching in the Time of Covid-19." *Changing English*, 27:3 (July 2020): 262–269.

Yandell, John, Brenton Doecke and Zamzam Abdi. "Who Me? Hailing Individuals as Subjects: Standardised Literacy Testing as an Instrument of Neo-Liberal Ideology." In Seyyed-Abdolhamid Mirhosseini and Peter De Costa (Eds.), *The Sociopolitics of English Language Testing*. London: Bloomsbury, 2020.

Yanow, Dvora. *How Does a Policy Mean? Interpreting Policy and Organisational Actions*. Washington, DC: Georgetown University Press, 1996.

Zoellner, Danielle. "'Pay Them More': Biden Uses Stage Whisper to Tell Business How to Fix Staff Shortages." *The Independent*, 24 June 2021.

Acknowledgements

The authors wish to thank all those who reviewed and commented on chapter drafts, at various stages of completion: Mark Carrigan, Jeremy Green, Mathew Lawrence, Friederike Metternich, Matthew Watson and Ben Williamson. We are also grateful to others who offered support and advice over the course of this project: Jack Cregan, Carla Ibled, Ken Jones, Nils Peters, Carys Roberts, Alice Rudge, Tom Shakhli, Hannah Trippier, and all our colleagues in the Department of Politics and International Relations and Political Economy Research Centre at Goldsmiths. We would also like to acknowledge the support of the ESRC Centre for Understanding Sustainable Prosperity (ESRC Grant No: ES/M010163/1), Tim Jackson and all the participants in CUSP, who have been much-valued colleagues to William Davies and Nick Taylor over recent years.

Finally, thanks to Sarah Kember, Susan Kelly and everyone at Goldsmiths Press for supporting our vision for this book.

Index